Paulo Freire

Also available from Bloomsbury

Education for Critical Consciousness, Paulo Freire
Pedagogy in Process, Paulo Freire
Pedagogy of Hope, Paulo Freire
Pedagogy of the Heart, Paulo Freire
Pedagogy of the Oppressed, Paulo Freire
Reinventing Pedagogy of the Oppressed, edited by James D. Kirylo
The Student Guide to Freire's 'Pedagogy of the Oppressed', Antonia Darder

Paulo Freire

A Philosophical Biography

Walter Omar Kohan

Translated by
Jason Wozniak and Samuel D. Rocha

BLOOMSBURY ACADEMIC
LONDON • NEW YORK • OXFORD • NEW DELHI • SYDNEY

BLOOMSBURY ACADEMIC
Bloomsbury Publishing Plc
50 Bedford Square, London, WC1B 3DP, UK
1385 Broadway, New York, NY 10018, USA
29 Earlsfort Terrace, Dublin 2, Ireland

BLOOMSBURY, BLOOMSBURY ACADEMIC and the Diana logo are trademarks
of Bloomsbury Publishing Plc

Originally published in Portuguese by Editora Vestígio, an imprint of Grupo Autêntica,
under the title Paulo Freire mais do que nunca: uma biografia filosófica (2019).

First published in Great Britain 2021

A catalogue record for this book is available from the British Library.

A catalog record for this book is available from the Library of Congress.

ISBN: PB: 978-1-3501-9598-1
HB: 978-1-3501-9599-8
ePDF: 978-1-3501-9600-1
eBook: 978-1-3501-9601-8

Typeset by Deanta Global Publishing Services, Chennai, India

To find out more about our authors and books visit www.bloomsbury.com
and sign up for our newsletters.

To Paulo Freire,
To his life of equality, love, errantry, and childhood;
And to the ragged, torn, and threadbare lives who, in it,
Encounter joy and hope.

Contents

Foreword   viii

Acknowledgments   xiii

A Note on the English Translation   xv

Introduction: Beginnings and Senses of a Reading   1

1   Life   17

2   Equality   43

3   Love   67

4   Errantry   93

5   Childhood   113

Epilogue   151

Appendices   175

References   257

Index   269

Foreword

I hope at least the following will endure: my trust in the people, and my faith in men and women, and in the creation of a world in which it will be easier to love.

Paulo Freire[1]

We find ourselves in the midst of an authoritarian climate of neoliberal fascism,[2] where progressive educators around the world are facing tremendous difficulties in keeping alive Paulo Freire's dreams for a more just and loving world. It is in this very contentious political moment that Walter Omar Kohan's biography of Freire is published with a clear and deliberate significance: Freire is needed *more than ever*. The book arrives at a historical moment—*strange times*, according to Kohan—when in Freire's own beloved Brazil, a right-wing reactionary government seeks to disavow the impact of his educational philosophy, renounce his socialist legacy, and erase his intellectual contribution to an education for freedom and equality. Yet, in the face of the political arrogance and neoliberal logic of greed and profit that inform this outlandish disregard for liberatory knowledge, we are graced with the intellectual force of this lovely tribute to Paulo Freire's life and works.

As might be expected from a Brazilian critical education philosopher, Kohan openly unpacks the dialectical tensions that undergird any volume that emerges from translation. He correctly reminds us that the question of translation was a meaningful one to Freire's own intellectual biography. It is quite easy for those who are monolingual English-speakers to miss or dismiss the significance of this issue. In light of this,

---

[1] See: Freire, P. (2005). *Pedagogy of the Oppressed* (thirtieth anniversary edition). New York: Continuum (40).

[2] See: https://camri.ac.uk/blog/Articles/henry-a-giroux-and-the-culture-of-neoliberal-fascism/.

Kohan's candid discussion reminds us of the hegemonic struggles tied to language that were so important to Freire's work as a sociolinguist and scholar of literacy. Hence, as Kohan speaks to the struggle he faced with the translation of the title of this book, I am reminded of the epistemological differences that persist between the North and the South in how we conceptualize and express, through the medium of our languages, our diverse readings of the world. A language that permits us to say, for example, *Paulo Freire Mais do que Nunca* (*Paulo Freire, More than Ever/Never*) without sense of contradiction or tension also points to differences in cultural sensibilities about our human nature, our relationship with time and space, and our interrelationships within the world, expressed through the cultural rhythms, tones, sounds, and arrangement of words.

As may be correctly surmised, the struggle of translation Kohan raises early in the text is a profoundly political question—a question that persists, given the linguistic tensions that have existed historically between the colonized and the colonizer. As it is with this book, the question of translation is evident in Freire's *Under the Shade of the Mango Tree*, whose English translation is *Pedagogy of the Heart*. Lost is an understanding of the mango tree as both an organic and a cultural metaphor from which Freire could ponder and unveil reflections on a variety of themes. For those of us whose epistemological sensibilities are more deeply anchored in the South, something powerful is lost in translation, a different cultural essence, sensibility, and way of knowing the world—one that valiantly speaks to the pain and suffering that robs from the oppressed their rightful time, space, and place to be truly free.

It is impressive to see how Kohan courageously leaps across typical approaches to reading Freire, by diving deeply into a sea of consciousness that takes us on a rich intellectual journey into Freire's life. Rather than simply remaining on the surface of Freirean thought, Kohan reinvigorates Freire's ideas through enacting curiosity, imagination, and playfulness, in his critical pedagogical process of entering into dynamic conversation with Paulo Freire's writings and lectures, as well as interviews with family and comrades. Through his dialogue with Freire's life, Kohan offers us an excellent reinvention of Freire's *pedagogy of the question*, inviting us to bravely enter into new beginnings (or re-beginnings) in how we understand the theory and practice of liberatory education today. More importantly, the expressed purpose and intention of his contribution is twofold. First, to provide readers with a better understanding of the political challenges educators face within the current political climate; and second, to reengage Paulo Frere's life in a way that can (re)inspire liberatory educational struggles in these difficult times.

Drawing philosophical insights from his careful exploration into Freire's diverse intellectual and lived history, Kohan asserts five critical principles or *engines of thinking* as a way to think about and with Freire. The five philosophical principles—life, equality, love, errantry, and childhood—are meant to provoke educators to ask new questions about the world as it is, as well as to ask new questions about the world as it could be. The pedagogical principle of *life* speaks to the importance of an educational philosophy and practice that opens us to questioning the self, our relationships with others, and new ways of living. Through this affirming principle of life, educators not only remain attentive to the meanings we give life but to the possibilities of bringing a new force of life to our teaching, through our adventurous encounters with those disquieting questions that so often remain silenced, to the detriment of our humanity.

The principle of *equality*, as an epistemological concept, politically attributes equal value to all life. This principle is indispensable to a Freirean pedagogy in that it promotes self-affirmation, while simultaneously encouraging dialogical interactions that support emancipatory schooling. *Love*, the third principle, refers to a vital political force of encounter that inspires solidarity and collective sensibilities among learners. Moreover, this creative energy is recognized as an essential ingredient to the labor of liberatory educators. Inspired by the notion of Freire as *wanderer traveling all his life to many places*, the fourth principle of *errantry* is one of the most innovative in Kohan's theory. A philosophical and practical place is conceived where learners can freely wander in the process of their intellectual formation. Moreover, this principle also opens the space to err, where making mistakes is understood as necessary to emancipatory educational experiences. Freire's notion of unfinishedness is also echoed here, in that the pedagogical space created for reinvention makes another world possible. This is particularly so for those whose humanity has been systematically negated by the ravages of advanced capitalism.

Finally, Kohan's last and very unexpected principle is that of *childhood*. However, as Kohan describes it, the principle of childhood points to the human place of beginnings and, as such, points to a new transformational politics of education. This sense of childhood inscribes a sense of hope and possibility in our lives and our practice. Here, Freire's long-standing concern with epistemological curiosity is highlighted in a way that reminds us of the manner in which new beginnings are indelibly marked by both disquieting uncertainties and attentive presence, which leads us to both ask questions and to renew our expectations of what can be. Cultivating this childlike dimension in our educational practice is especially salient, in that Freire was not timid about beginning anew. He considered it essential for educators and activists committed to the struggle for liberation to cultivate this quality, in that youthful hopefulness is what allows us to embrace the present moment, remain open and curious about the world, exist with humility, and be touched and changed in our political and pedagogical relationships. More importantly, it is precisely this sense of childlike presence that is a formidable antidote against cynicism, despair, and powerlessness.

There is no question that Kohan's biography of Paulo Freire clearly provides us a fresh intellectual lens, by which we can both understand and practice the beauty of Freire's life and the power of his intellectual contributions to the world. The book offers educators, who are forced to wander and labor within the oppressive pedagogical and curricular constraints of neoliberalism, a grounded sense of hope and possibility, so we might better rethink and reinvent our current practices, as well as discover new pedagogical approaches to enliven our revolutionary dreams for a more just world. True to Freire's philosophy, the book ends at the beginning. Kohan reminds us here that, despite the difficulties and struggles we face at this historical moment, it is a time when we can embrace the extraordinary presence Freire's life and passion of his pedagogy of love to propel ourselves toward new liberatory beginnings, where we can create together *a world in which it will be easier to love.*

Antonia Darder
Endowed Chair of Ethics and Moral Leadership,
Loyola Marymount University, USA
Distinguished Visiting Professor of Education,
University of Johannesburg, South Africa

Acknowledgments

Several people read preliminary versions of this manuscript and made observations that not only allowed me to improve it but also allowed me to see what, prior to those readings, I had not perceived. Carla Silvia accompanied the writing of the chapter on childhood, making sharp and significant contributions. At various points in the writing, Ivan Rubens Dário Jr., always with his usual patience and generosity, revised the Portuguese and provided precise references. Laura Agratti read and followed several preliminary versions sensitively and critically. Edna Olímpia da Cunha did a first revision of the Portuguese, corrected many mistakes, and made me smile with her loving, enthusiastic, and poetic reading. Maximiliano Durán helped me see how much the inventor, schoolmaster, and other figures, including myself, cross these lines and also allowed me to get even closer to Paulo Freire's wandering spirit, which flies like a bird. Fabiana Martins made some corrections and also several comments that allowed me to think about different issues throughout the book. Marcos Lorieri pointed out many Hispanisms and helped me, thus, to strengthen the original Portuguese style. Inés Fernández Mouján read the manuscript with passion and made connections with various Freirean interlocutors. Mauricio Langón not only encouraged me to write this book but also made succulent comments on its presentation. Alejandro Cerletti pointed out various tensions in the text and asked some disturbing questions that helped me to clarify certain ideas and to present others differently. Jorge Larrosa renewed my spirits when he told me that his reading of the manuscript had inspired him to put himself in a "good position" just when he was reading Freire with his students. Carlos Skliar read the text lovingly and helped me rethink the very structure and organization of the book, as well as some voices that ended up welcomed here. Facundo Giuliano presented me with his critical view of Freire. Alessandra Oliveira dos Santos made me read Alain Badiou's precious text on love. Barbara

Weber took me to Roberto Juarroz and received me in Vancouver, along with Ariadne, Elias, and Kirk, with hospitality and sensitivity. Karyne Dias Coutinho did a reading that only a very "beautifully wise" girl can do, full of wisdom and beauty. Esther Grossi, with her extraordinary energy and vitality, helped me see what I was not seeing. Angela Biz Antunes and Moacir Gadotti opened the doors of the Paulo Freire Institute for me and endowed me with precious editions of some of their books in his honor. They also read a preliminary version of this book and provided me with invaluable observations and comments. Lutgardes Costa Freire received me with the generosity, attention, and the kindness of a Freire. Federico Brugaletta, the translator of the Spanish version, was an extraordinary traveling companion to rethink what was written. Colleagues from the Department of Childhood Studies (DEDI) and the Postgraduate Program in Education (PRODEd) of the State University of Rio de Janeiro (UERJ) gave me the time to study and write this book. The colleagues of the Nucleus of Studies of Philosophies and Childhoods (NEFI) of the UERJ are a permanent source of inspiration. The National Council of Scientific and Technologic Development (CNPq) and the Foundation of Support of Research of the State of Rio de Janeiro (FAPERJ) supported the investigation that resulted in this writing. Mark Richardson, from Bloomsbury, welcomed the English edition with enthusiasm and commitment. I am also grateful to blind reviewers who offer precious insights. In Jason Wozniak's careful hands, I feel that my words not only pass to the English language but more deeply into the English spirit. Sam Rocha took up the review work with commitment and passion. I am deeply grateful to both of you. Magda Costa Carvalho helped me with the revision of the English proofs. Finally, to my daughters, for being who they are and helping me to be who I am, I thank you. They are very present in this writing, in the inspiration, in the joy, in the creative energy that they breathe and emanate. Of the three, Giulietta was the one who accompanied me on various reading and writing moments in Vancouver. Likewise, Milena and Valeska, each in their own way, leave their mark here, as in everything else that I do.

A Note on the English Translation

This edition in English has given us the opportunity to take a learning journey in the midst of the Covid-19 pandemic that took over the world in 2020, especially affecting countries where governments have had a senseless, insensitive, and criminal response. The United States and Brazil are the worst examples, and are leaders in the ranking of infected and deaths. In this context, bringing these words inspired by Paulo Freire has been a sobering reason to renew our hope.

Like any text, this translation has a history. Some chapters were originally translated separately; chapter 2, "Equality," was translated from Portuguese by Bryan Pitts, and chapter 5, "Childhood," by Sam Rocha together with Mateus Hernandez. Jason Wozniak translated the other three chapters thereafter, along with the epilogue and the interview with Lutgardes Costa Freire. Jason and Walter also produced the interview that serves as one of the Appendixes to the book. Walter wrote the piece on Freire and Philosophy for Children with the English help of Susan Gardner. Finally, Sam Rocha translated the Introduction, the interview with Esther Pilar Grossi, revised and unified the English throughout the entire book, working from the Portuguese and Spanish editions, and provided, with Walter, the English references of Freire's quotations.

Putting this book together has been an intense and rich experience. We consulted two previous editions, the original in Portuguese and the Spanish translation, which is Walter and Sam's mother tongue. As Lutgardes Costa Freire reminds us in the interview, the main condition for Freire is to do all things with love, and we have taken care to do that as best we can. This book had to be translated lovingly, taking stock and care of every word, savoring new inspirations, enjoying the opportunity to be writing and rewriting Paulo Freire in a new language, in the one that is most read in the whole world, rather than in his native Portuguese.

We had the extraordinary possibility of making this trip accompanied by friends, colleagues, students, Freire scholars in so many countries, teachers, as well as social activists whom we had in mind when we came to impossible words or other forms of thinking, writing, and living education. When traveling in a good and loving company, the end of the road finds us smiling, feeling privileged to bring this book on the thought and life of Freire to life in another language.

This book arises from a conversation with more than twenty books, interviews, and lectures by Freire made at different times in his life throughout his significant intellectual contributions. This is to extract quotes, integrate them with Freire's ideas, and spread them throughout the book in order to offer what Freire wanted from his readers: a reinvention, another Freire, many Freires; each different, with the extraordinary richness of his thought and his life. When those references are published in English, we make use of the translation of an already published edition. When those translations are not available or absent in the published works, the translation is by Sam Rocha.

On the other hand, it is worth noting that the question of translation has been very important in Freire's own intellectual biography. Let's consider *Pedagogy of the Oppressed*: Freire wrote it between 1967 and 1968 in Santiago, Chile. A translation of the original manuscript in Portuguese was published for the first time in Spanish by the Uruguayan publisher, Tierra Nueva, a Protestant Christian publishing house in Montevideo in 1970. That same year another Protestant Christian publisher, Herder and Herder, in New York, published it in English in a translation by a Brazilian student Freire met at Harvard in 1969, Myra Bergman Ramos, which is still the only translation in use today. We smile when we realize that this is the same writing path for this book: Portuguese, Spanish, and English, although circumstances made it possible for us not to delay the publication of the original in Portuguese so long.

Pedagogy of the Oppressed began to circulate rapidly on a global scale. And it continues to do so to this day. Why did Freire spread so rapidly around the world? Perhaps because there was a great need for his words, because Freire is, since the 1970s, a symbol (not only in Latin America but throughout the world) of the search for a transformative, liberating, utopian education. To this very day when "more than ever" it is necessary to read Freire.

It is time to clarify the title of this book. The original in Portuguese (which the Spanish translates literally) is: *Paulo Freire mais do que nunca: Uma biografia filosófica*. Deciding upon a title in English was difficult. Some reviewers praised a literal translation: Paulo Freire more than ever: A philosophical biography. A literal translation was attractive to us, too, because of the temporal dimension in the reading that we offer in this English edition of the book. However, in the end, we chose to follow those who saw that expression somewhat confusing or ambiguous and opted for a drier title, but also one that is more direct, strong, and without hesitation: *Paulo Freire: A Philosophical Biography*. In the epilogue, readers will find more substantive reasons to understand the scope of what is at stake in these titles. In fact, we have revised the epilogue from the previous Portuguese and Spanish editions, rewriting parts of it with English-language readers in mind.

Two chapters and one appendix of this book were previously published in English. "Equality" was published as "Paulo Freire and the Value of Equality in Education" *Educação e Pesquisa*, São Paulo, v. 45, e201600, 2019. "Childhood" was published as "Paulo Freire: Other Childhoods for Childhood," *Educação em Revista*. Belo Horizonte, v.34, e199059, 2018. The Appendix "Paulo Freire and Philosophy for Children" was published as "Paulo Freire and Philosophy for Children: A Critical Dialogue" *Stud Philos Educ*. 37, p. 615–629, 2018.

These are very strange times in Brazil for a government to choose an educator as its main enemy; in many respects this government resembles others where the English language is spoken, notably the United States, the United Kingdom, and Australia. Of course, the differences are also notable, but understanding why the creator of a pedagogy of the question is considered a public enemy can help us understand the political challenges of those who work in education in those political contexts and climates. That is what authoritarian governments hate and fear, even if they have been elected in "democratic" elections: a people who ask and wonder. That is also why we find it moving and exciting to be offering this edition of *Paulo Freire: A Philosophical Biography* to English readers: it is like offering a question, the power of a question, the world that a question opens to us when we dare to think about the world we live in and the other worlds that we could think and live in.

Jason Wozniak, Sam Rocha, and Walter Omar Kohan
Between Philadelphia, Vancouver, and Rio de Janeiro, July 2020,
In times where, more than ever and everywhere, Black Lives Matter.

Introduction

Beginnings and Senses of a Reading[1]

I always say that the only way anyone has of applying in their situation any of the propositions I have made is precisely by redoing what I have done, that is, by not following me. In order to follow me it is essential not to follow me!

(Freire in Freire and Faundez, 1989, p. 30)

I don't mind repeating here that the idea that the aesthetic dimension of language should concern only artists, not scientists, is false. It is the duty of all those who write to write beautifully.

(Freire, 1996, p. 80)

Paulo Reglus Neves Freire, or rather Paulo Freire, is an extraordinary figure not only for Brazilian education but also for Latin American and global education.[2] His contributions are not limited to his written work, much less to a method or even a theoretical paradigm, but also refer to a practice and, more generally, to a life dedicated to education, a life made into a school, that is, a way of occupying the space of educator that took him on a lifelong trip around the world "making school," educating in many countries of Latin America, Europe, Asia, and Oceania, in the United States, and in Portuguese-speaking parts of Africa.

---

[1]   We have adapted this presentation to English-language readers to remove specific issues from the Brazilian context.

[2]   In a discussion with Sérgio Guimarães, Freire clarifies that his second name, "Reglus," comes from a civil registry error: he was supposed to be named Paulo "Regulus." Anyhow, the name did not survive and from then on he recalls being called Paulo Freire (Freire and Guimarães, 2010 [1987], p. 21).

This opening appreciation is a more or less obvious observation for anyone who works in education and circulates in the academic field in Brazil or, even more, outside it. Recent research by the Paulo Freire Chair of the PUC-SP shows that between 1991 and 2012, in Brazil alone, no less than 1,852 postgraduate works (1,428 academic master's theses, 39 professional master's theses and 385 doctoral theses) make reference to the thought of Freire (Saul, 2016, p. 17).

One can discuss his way of understanding education, some of his practical experiences, his political bets and bargains, and much can be disputed about him, but there is no denying that Freire dedicated his life to education in an inspiring way, and that is why he is recognized throughout the educational world. Just look at the bibliographies of books or academic works published in the field of philosophy of education (or, even more, the programs related to that discipline in institutions of higher education located in countries on all continents) and it will be difficult to find the name of another Latin American and, far less, one with the frequency with which the most outstanding Brazilian educator is found. *Pedagogy of the Oppressed* is among the first most consulted books in The Open Syllabus Project database, which includes more than a million English-language university programs from the last ten years.

And although the bibliographic references focus almost exclusively on *Pedagogy of the Oppressed*, we believe that work would not be so widely read and studied if it were not for the peculiar movement of the author's life that accompanies it before, during, and after its publication. Recent research in Google Scholar by Elliot Green shows that *Pedagogy of the Oppressed* is the third most cited work in the world in the field of social sciences (Green, w.d.). The numbers and the data are impressive: cited more than seventy-two thousand times, the book is the first in the world in the area of education. Considering the whole of the social sciences, it appears just behind *The Structure of Scientific Revolutions* by Thomas Kuhn (philosophy), and, only by very little, of *Diffusion of Innovations* by Rogers (sociology). Here is a curious fact: the Spanish edition of the book have more citations than the Portuguese edition. Nobody is an "absolute" prophet in their own land.

And it is not only in the specific field of the philosophy of education and popular or youth and adult education that the figure of Freire and that particular book appear, but also in very diverse areas such as anthropology, the sciences of religion and theology, theatre, psychology, communication, nursing, social service, cultural studies, letters, journalism, and so on.

Paulo Freire's life involves a pilgrimage throughout the third world, although he resides, for some part of that journey, in the first world: after the 1964 coup and after a rapid passage through Bolivia, he lived for several years in Chile, then he lived for almost a year in the United States, and, finally, he went to Switzerland for around a decade, where, as coordinator of the Education Sector of the World Council of Churches, in Geneva, he carried out literacy campaigns in countries such as Nicaragua, Guinea-Bissau, Santo Tomé and Príncipe, Cape Verde, and Tanzania. He received dozens of honorary doctorates and many awards, including the UNESCO Peace Prize in 1986. His main works have been translated into more than twenty languages. His relevance to the world of education is highlighted by leading academics from various countries. By way of example, let us hear from some testimonials about his figure: "Paulo Freire is the exemplary organic intellectual of our time" (West, 1993, p. Xiii); "The name of Paulo Freire was received in almost iconic proportions in the United States, in Latin America, and even in many parts of the world" (Aronowitz, 1993, p. 8); "The catalyst, if not the main animator of innovation and pedagogical change in the second half of the century" (Torres, 1990, p. 12); "The most important educator in the world in the last fifty years" (Macedo cited in Wilson, Park and Colón-Muñiz, 2010, p. xv); "The life and work of Freire are inscribed in the pedagogical imaginary of the twentieth century, constituting a mandatory reference for several generations of educators" (Nóvoa, 1998, p. 185). The list could fill many and many pages. Freire even achieved some symbolic feats in Brazil, such as disproving popular sayings (i.e., he is a prophet in his land) and inspiring miracles. In Brasilia, a city without corners, the Universidade Católica (UCB) created a corner called "untested feasibility" one of the concepts of Paulo Freire.

In this way, for better or for worse, to the pleasure or displeasure of Freire himself, he ends up becoming an icon, a myth, a global symbol. I will give a small, personal example, just to illustrate that presence. In 2013, I was invited to participate in some academic activities in Japan, at the universities of Osaka and Sophia (in Tokyo). At the airport, three students from Osaka University were waiting for me: one of them had a sign with my name on it, another had a plaque with the expression "P4C" ("philosophy for children"), and the third wore a t-shirt (a very pretty t-shirt, by the way) with the expression "filosofia como libertação" (like this, in Portuguese) and a very expressive and well-done cartoon-drawing of Freire's face. I was not going to do anything related to Freire on that visit, nor was there anything significant about his work in my academic curriculum with them, but it was enough that I came from Brazil, from the field of philosophy and education so that, as I found out later, they made a special t-shirt with Freire's face to receive me.

This significant symbolic place of Freire is not only the product or result of academic work but also of a continuously militant commitment throughout his life. Without trying to carry out a strict periodization, we could point out three stages or highlights in the life of Freire.[3] The first is the one that begins with his birth and culminates when the National Adult Literacy Plan, recently started under his coordination, is suspended by the dictatorship established in Brazil in 1964. Freire is imprisoned and is first forced to go into exile in Bolivia and then Chile, and then later still in the United States and Switzerland. The second moment occurs precisely during this exile. In Chile, he advises the Ministry of Education and the Institute for Training and Research for Agrarian Reform; in the United States, he teaches at Harvard University and is in contact with various organizations and social movements; in Switzerland, he is a special consultant for education of the World

---

[3] With the help of Moacir Gadotti, Lidia Rodríguez (2015) shows the limits of this periodization and defends his preference for a reading that, before periods, demonstrates a return to a spiraling development of certain themes that remain in the texts of Freire. We hold here the reference to stages because we privilege, as we will see, a reading of his life more than his works.

Council of Churches in Geneva, from which he launches various literacy campaigns, already mentioned. The third stage began in 1980, with his return to Brazil, where he participated in the founding of the Workers' Party (PT). He is secretary of education for the city of São Paulo in the management of Luiza Erundina (a position he resigned from before he finished his term), leads several popular education organizations and is a professor at some São Paulo universities (UNICAMP, PUC-SP) until his death on May 2, 1997.

As a consequence of this significant symbolic place, the result of his militant commitment to the oppressed and excluded classes, and of having made his own life a cause in favor of his convictions and ideas, the image of Freire is not indifferent to anyone and has generated deep love and heartbreak, happy and sad passions, animosities and resentments, all together and often mixed and confused. And, above all, *exaggerated.*

In the context of the current political situation in Brazil, things appear more pronounced and hyperbolic. At least since the street demonstrations of 2013, he is placed, by groups such as the Movimento Brasil Livre (MBL) and Revoltados Online (RO), as the person in charge of an alleged "Marxist indoctrination" in schools and the root of almost all problems of education in Brazil, although the actual reality of Brazilian education has very little to do with the teachings of the Pernambucan educator. In the educational program of the current president of Brazil, Jair Bolsonaro, the need to change the method of management and of modernizing the content (which includes literacy) entails "purging Paulo Freire's ideology from Brazilian education" (Bolsonaro, 2018, p. 46).[4]

In April 2012, Freire was appointed by federal law (#16,612) as the patron of Brazilian education. The practical effects of this law in schools are not very evident, although some programs from the Lula and Dilma

---

[4] I have addressed some of the critiques against Freire in Appendix IV "A few critiques of Paulo Freire," see p. 203.

Rousseff government are said to be inspired by Paulo Freire. It is, more than anything else, the value of symbols, words, and gestures. It is a law much more striking for its symbolic content than for the tangible practical effects.

Dictionaries say that a patron is a "protector, defender, godfather, lawyer." All those words fit very well with Freire, who was a lawyer by training and managed to exercise all those other roles by vocation. However, if a large part of the educators in Brazil, especially those who work with the most excluded sectors, consider this measure a simple act of justice, many sectors opposed to the Workers' Party tried to overthrow the tribute as soon as they found a more favorable political situation. The truth is that, although the attacks reveal a great deal of ignorance of Freire's work and have failed so far, they do not diminish their ferocity and show a hatred and contempt that in this book we will try to think about.

In this scenario, it is not easy to write a book about or based on Freire, mainly because of the position in which he has been placed. Because he is a committed figure, with a clearly defined political position, he has generated both admiration and rejection, and even some contempt in academic and political circles. In that sense, the dazzling and passionate rejection similarly provoked by his figure converge in an uncritical position (be it reverential or defamatory), equally uninteresting to think more freely from the tensions present in the work and in the life of the educator of Pernambuco.

Thus, the first move, necessary but difficult, is to get Freire out of the political confrontation in which he is involved: the policy made by the parties and, more precisely, the policy made by the PT and those who attack the PT, the anti-PT. For this reason, in this book I do not understand "politics" as what is done within the logic of the representative democratic system, but, in a broader sense, the exercise of power based on the relationships established with others in a community, social context, and, more specifically, the ways of exercising power in teaching and learning. Accordingly, far from being inspired by Freire to attack or defend partisan politics or a specific ideology, I do it to openly think about the political meanings that are affirmed when inhabiting an educational space.

To that end, I try to understand the educational and philosophical value of the thought and life of that man who provokes so much in the field of education. How is it possible that, around the world, the editions of his books are read by millions, while in his own land people intend to purge him from national education? How ought we to appreciate the value of this figure outside the logic of political parties? How ought we to consider his contributions from a non-partisan perspective, to think more broadly about the "politicality" of education?

In other words, there are at least two senses of politics at work here: a more restricted and specific one (in the case of Brazil, the institutional system, the three powers, the elections, the political parties); and a broader one, derived from the Greek word "*polis*," which means "the way in which power is exercised in a community." Education is political not because it is partisan, but because it requires ways of exercising power, of organizing a collective, of building a community: there is always an implicit political way in the ways of teaching, educating, making school, whether inside or outside of educational institutions, within formal or informal education, with children and adults, in urban or rural contexts, with students of the most diverse ethnicities, genders, and social classes. It is this political dimension that I propose to consider in this book: an exercise in thought, inspired by the ideas and life of Freire, which rescues his contributions to think about the "political nature" of education outside of partisan blindness.

The problem is so complex and can be thought of in so many ways that we will try another way of posing it. Some contemporary authors (e.g., Biesta [2006; 2014], Masschelein and Simons, [2013]) argue that politics has taken over education and education has lost its freedom to be educational. That education needs the autonomy and freedom to lead a life outside of any other means or ends that tend to want to command and control it. In this sense, there is no real difference between whether education follows an oppressive or an educational political aim defined from the outside. Could we still, inspired by Freire, defend education as political and not subordinate or condition it to an external political end? This is the question this book aims to consider.

Freire is read copiously, and writing about him is also copious, with many apologias and as many condemnations. Even within the Freirean world there are wildly dissimilar readings. For example, Ana Maria Araújo Freire ("Nita"), the "official" widow who continues his legacy, affirms that there is only one Freire, the one from *Pedagogy of the Oppressed*, that "gives true unity to all his work, in coherence and communion with his whole life" (Ana Maria Freire, 2001, p. 31). Rosa María Torres, also a Freirean, in a work entitled "The multiple Paulo Freire," sees the infinity of readings by the Pernambucean educator as a symptom of the impossibility and even the futility of trying to answer the question "What did Paulo Freire really say?" (Torres, 1999).

The infinity of Freires is more a symptom of the richness of his thought than a problem to be solved. We are not interested in any way to elucidate "the real Paulo Freire," much less the only one or the most authentic one. Instead, I propose to seek, in his life and in his thinking, forces and inspirations from which we can think of education as politics and face some of the current challenges and problems of education. For this reason, the difficulties do not diminish: in the face of so many works on the Pernambuco educator, how can we not repeat what has already been written? How can we not abuse what has already been thought? And does one recreate his thought in our present time without reproducing what has already been produced? Here's another challenge in this book.

I think that Freire, despite being a red-hot iron in Brazil today, or precisely *because* of that, is an extraordinary and precious figure to think about for at least three reasons: (a) because that relationship between education and politics is one of the fundamental intersections that structures his thought, one of the main world references in the field of educational philosophy; (b) because he not only thinks about this relationship but also tries to put it into practice in different ways and in different contexts; and (c) because his life and thought are inextricably linked to a reality that is still ours. In other words, he is someone who, even during exile, lives for and thinks obsessively about contributing to Brazilian education, with the problems and demands that still permeate her, more than twenty years after his death. The study of his life and work can also help us understand more clearly a controversy that far exceeds him.

When defining a structure for this book, I had many doubts. I hesitated and hesitated. I considered various alternatives. I opted for one route, not without objections and uncertainties, in light of the sense already expressed: to think philosophically with Freire on the specificity of the political value of the task of educating. Thus, I ended up delimiting five principles that configure that space in a way that Freire would call emancipatory, liberating, and democratic, and here we will name in different words and think differently. They are powerful, joyous, and fair beginnings of a political education. (The English reader should also be aware of a play on the word "princípio" that is nested inside the idea of the English word "principle": a beginning, a start. So take these principles as beginnings and starting points.)

Some will think that these principles do not do justice to the thought of Freire. Others will say that he affirms principles contrary to those I propose here. Both may be right. That shouldn't scare us or distract our attention too much. Freire himself would explain it by the dialectical and lively nature of his thought, or by the different interests that move different readings. I do not embark on a disinterested reading. I will be highlighting some aspects not always observed, leaving aside others that are often exalted.

I affirm a certain image of what it means to "think and write philosophically, educationally, politically." It is certainly not the only one, just one among many possible ones. I hope, with the help of readers, that this text is a contribution to problematize a significant issue for anyone who enters a classroom or who intends to define a policy for education, and, more specifically, a way of practicing any educational task, it doesn't matter at what level or context.

One of the challenges of this book is to write with the generosity and openness necessary for justice to be done to a life like Freire's, which seems larger than any pretense to write about it and to justify the already countless readings of his work, the countless pedagogical experiences inspired by it. The tensions revealed here are simply that they are tensions derived from an inspiring, dynamic, and sensitive thinker, like few others, in a world also in motion. For this reason, these tensions should not be read as traumatic inconsistencies: they are, on the contrary, a sign of Freire's vitality, of his sensitivity to come and go along the path of thought and life in education, in Brazil, and not only in Brazil.

So, I structured this text based on principles that I learned in reading the Pernambucan educator, in his books ("spoken and written"), interviews, conferences, letters, and essays of various kinds. I read and re-read his books. I heard his voice in Portuguese, Spanish, and English in different contexts, places, and times. I asked myself: how could I present the thought and life of Freire in a more appropriate way? I considered various alternatives, for example, presenting a study of his works, in particular his pedagogies. Or, to write in the explicit form of a biography. I also needed to find a way to present his life and work that would do justice to the importance of dialogue for Paulo Freire. In that sense, I considered writing fictional educational conversations with him, made-up dialogues, a dream book, utopian.

However, I ended up thinking that the dialogic nature of a writing does not depend so much on its form, but on the readings it can express or provoke; more important than the structure of writing is that it is dialogic as a "necessary posture" (Shor and Freire, 1987, p. 98) of the person who writes as a way of critical relationship with their reality. And that she be able to recreate Freire in a proper way, as he insisted so many times. I hope that this is the case and that this exercise of thought also provokes dialogic readings that meet other readings, readers who also dare to attempt other exercises of thought, to other writings.

In the book spoken between Paulo Freire and Ira Shor (Shor and Freire, 1987), the former emphasizes the importance of "dialogue-books" due to the creative and recreational effect that dialogue has for authors and readers. And it defines in an unusual way the meaning of dialogic writing and what a book "with rigor" would be in relation to its readers, one ready "to challenge the readers and not just give answers to them. If we are able to make our readers uneasy, fill them with some uncertainty, then the book will be important. If we can do that, then the book will have rigor. We will be rigorous" (Shor and Freire, 1987, p. 4). In his response, on this same page, Ira Shor adds another sense of a book with rigor: "Maybe rigor is also a communication which challenges the other to take part, or includes the other in an active search."

They are very inspiring words about the sentiment and sense of this writing. I would only add that, thus characterized, dialogue (which enables the creation and recreation of authors and readers) and rigor (which provokes the other to participate, to question themselves, to leave the certainties) can inhabit books beyond the number of authors and the form of writing. There may be dialogical and rigorous books by a single author and non-dialogical and non-rigorous books written by two or more authors, exchanging opinions. I hope, therefore, that this book affirms deep dialogue and rigor. In other words, that it leads its readers to become actively involved in reading and to question their certainties. Writing itself is doing that job with me. I hope that your reading will also do that work with whoever reads it. If you succeed, this writing will have been worth it.

The result presented here may not convince the worshipers or the slanderers of Freire. My hope is placed on those who want to think together, even, or above all, on those who think differently. I hope to generate unsuspected dialogues. Who knows if I will be contributing to enhance the meaning of an immense work such as that of the most recognized Brazilian educator, and also the readings that are really interested in his potentiality to think, and not in deifying or condemning him? Beyond the work and life of Freire, and I hope I am not being too ambitious and immodest, I wish to contribute to thinking about a relevant problem for a philosophical education: how to understand that education is political, or, more precisely, that the act of educating is a political act.

The beginning principles highlighted here for thinking about this problem are inspired and presented in various ways in the work and life of the great Pernambucan educator. I will present each of these principles and put them in dialogue with other traditions, some more or less related, others more unexpected. I do not seek to consecrate this or that current, origin, or school. What interests me is the potentiality of other works and other lives to think about a problem common to any educational life: that of a policy for education that deserves that name. In other words, it is the problem of how to think philosophically, which means theoretically but also vitally, as we shall see, an educational life; still in other words, the issue is what makes an educator a politically consistent figure, that is, a figure who offers powerful political meanings to understand and practice the act to educate here and now.

As I mentioned, there are five principles. They could be more or less. The number is arbitrary, and so is the order and the way I present them. As I noted parenthetically, "principles" here do not mean fixed points, axioms, or substantialities. "Principles" mean "births": beginnings, ways of being born in the world, of beginning to think and to live philosophically, a life attentive to what a policy of educating means. They are forms from which a political path can be born to walk in a philosophically educating life. I suspect that, at least in the fields of thought and life, it is never too late to start. Or, better yet, it is always time to start.

To put this in other words, I will offer five ways in which a way of thinking and living philosophically about the relations between politics and education unfolds, centered on the act of educating and on the figure of educators. Simpler still: five philosophical gestures to inspire someone who educates and thus affirm a politically interesting educational practice and life. Or simplest: five gestures to inspire the political, educational, and philosophical form of any life.

Those five principles could also be presented in other ways, with other words. For example, they could be presented as ways of answering a question: What does a teacher need to know in order to teach what they teach in a (politically) appropriate way? Or as ways of paying attention to another question: Where does teaching knowledge begin in a practice that, due to the political meanings that it opens, we are interested in affirming? Or even: What is it that anyone needs to know if they want to pay attention to the philosophical, educational, and political forms of their life?

And what does it mean to know? There are many types of knowledge that can contribute to the task of teaching and that are generally emphasized to answer the question at hand: knowledge related to a number of aspects that are part of the acts of teaching and learning. For example, beyond the more obvious ones, relative to the programmatic "content" to be transmitted when teaching is guided by subjects, disciplines, or even attitudes or behaviors, there is knowledge related to the socio-historical and political context in which the work takes place. This is inserted into the questions of the most appropriate teaching techniques for the groups with which we work, to the game of affections that populate pedagogical relationships and their inhabitants, and to how we think what we think (in particular, when we teach and learn), and even into the fields of cultural activities of the various actors involved in the pedagogical relationship, and so on.

The list of knowledge could be extended almost to infinity and thus cover the wide spectrum of the different "educational sciences." Even so, a good part of Freire's work could be read as an effort to describe what it is that is necessary to know in order to educate according to a logic of freedom, emancipation, and autonomy. In fact, it seems that he tried to do this in the last of his books published while he was alive, *Pedagogy of Freedom*, which has precisely the subtitle *Knowledge necessary for educational practice*.[5]

However, without disqualifying or detracting from that path and the framework of knowledge of the teaching task that he would allow

---

[5] In the English edition the subtitle is *Ethics, Democracy and Civic Courage*. In Portuguese, the complete title is *Pedagogia da Autonomia. Saberes necessários à prática educativa*. A literal translation would be *Pedagogy of Autonomy. Knowledge needed for educational practice*.

to unravel, here I will affirm five principles that, instead of positing knowledge that should be known, are opportunities to question that very space of knowledge and the pedagogical relationships that are fostered from it, in its most diverse fields: formal and informal education; urban and rural; levels of education, too: initial, primary, secondary, higher; technical and professional education; teacher training; the organization of pedagogical work, and so on.

The five beginnings are intended to become principles for thinking about "another" education, politically musical, vibrant, for "any" educator. They are triggers to question the meaning and value of what we do politically when we educate. They do not indicate "how one should be educated" versus "how one educates," but rather how another way of inhabiting the educational space could be initiated by questioning the way in which that same space is inhabited in relation to five words that can promote its reboot. They are, thus, an invitation for a pedagogy of wondering, of putting ourselves in question, hopeful in the political senses that such a beginning can provide to our educational lives.

I have made an effort to get closer to the ideas of Freire, to incorporate what I feel about them that can help us to think about an educational politics. In that sense, this writing has transported me to other places; it has made me add some words, leave others, and reformulate some questions. I have made an effort to read Freire carefully and openly, to be sensitive to his problems, his spirit, his ideas, and his life. Thus, I have practiced something quite close to (at least) one of the meanings that, as we have just seen, Freire gives to the word "dialogue." This is the greatest tribute that a writing can bring to the guardian of the most diverse pedagogical utopias: to celebrate it not by praise or easy agreement, but by the living and vital exercise of the essentially dialogical nature of his thought.

The five principles could be summed up in five words: life, equality, love, errantry, and childhood (or infancy). In other words, I affirm the "politicality" of education inspired by Freire, trusting the presence and power of those five words: a form, a place, a time, a rhythm, a disposition for education to begin starting from life, equality, love, errantry, and childhood (infancy). Each of the chapters of this book begins with a paragraph that synthesizes it, and then presents one of the principles and places it into dialogue with the life and thought of the Pernambucan educator and other thinkers. An epilogue that takes up the main problematic follows these chapters.

As an appendix, the book includes three interviews: one with Freire's youngest son, Lutgardes Costa Freire; another interview with Jason Wozniak that took place after he had done a first translation draft of the book, and another with the well-known Brazilian educator Esther Pillar Grossi, a colleague and friend of Paulo Freire. Also, as another appendix, the book includes a piece on a few academic critiques of Paulo Freire and another on the relationship between Freire and philosophy for children (P4C), focusing on the educator's political role.

In this way, among so many apologias and detractions, I intend to draw a philosophical appreciation of Freire's life that is sensitive to his teachings, that resists the double temptation of reverence or defamation, and that moves his figure toward other relationships, beyond worship and hatred. What is the philosophical value of thinking about the "politicality" of education? As I wrote this text, I told some friends about my writing project. One of them, Mauricio Langón, noted something that, I feel, is quite close to the meaning of this writing: "I find it particularly delicious that you are getting your teeth into Freire. The constant references to him dull and spend him. I am sure that the effect of your work will be the opposite." Hopefully my friend Mauricio is right, and this writing contributes to renewing and recreating the readings inspired by the life and thought of Paulo Freire.

Walter Omar Kohan
Rio de Janeiro, July 2020

1

Life

Let us begin with this first principle: *a political education is a philosophical education*. In this principle, life and philosophy, education, school, and thinking are all intertwined. Life is not left to one side. Philosophy is affirmed as a dimension of education and as a form of life. As such, a philosophical education, one which Freire might call "emancipatory," "liberating," or "transformative," has a distinctly political touch and affect upon one's life; it increases one's potency for life and living. Those who exercise a political education call into question the very sense of life itself with others and themselves. To be clear, I repeat: *a political education is a philosophical education*.

> Paulo Freire is a thinker committed to life: he does not think *ideas*; he thinks *existence*. He is also an educator: his thought exists within a pedagogy in which the totalizing effort of human praxis seeks, from its interiority, to retotal itself as a 'practice of freedom.'[1] (Fiori in Freire, 1974, p. 1)

> We need an education in which teachers are no longer merely transmitters of knowledge that other people created and about whose origins the teachers know nothing—reinforcing a way of teaching where teachers transfer this knowledge, without any kind of historical curiosity, to the students, who also receive the knowledge in this manner. To change this, education needs to embrace philosophy; we need not only—exclusively—technology and science but also philosophy of science, philosophy of technology, philosophy of

---

[1] The foreword by Fiori is not included in the English translation of *Pedagogy of the Oppressed*.

knowledge. We must seriously question how we think and how we know. (Freire in Darder, 2002, p. xii)

Philosopher of Education?

There is a preponderance in academic philosophy that understands philosophy as a group of ideas, doctrines, and theoretical systems on certain themes or problems. In this tradition of thought, there is a subdiscipline commonly referred to as "philosophy of education." Although, for many, Freire may not be, strictly speaking, a philosopher (this is especially true in Brazil as a result of overly strict and technically prejudicial conceptions of philosophy), he is commonly studied within this field, especially when studied outside of Brazil.[2] Many of these studies have highlighted Freire's philosophical sources and, as a result, they inscribe him within certain traditions of thought. In other words, at the very same time that it is debated whether Freire is a philosopher, innumerable studies in Brazil, but above all outside of Brazil, attempt to identify "the philosophy of Paulo Freire." These attempts carry tremendous academic and disciplinary burdens, as we have seen, and result in the use of the philosophical presuppositions of a particular current of thought as the condition which determines Freire's inscription within that very line of thinking.

Freire is generally thought to be influenced by the most venerated thinkers and traditions of what is often called Western philosophy. This certainly raises a polemical question, given that it not only presupposes a certain conception of philosophy and of the European tradition that it is often identified with, but also because it obfuscates the singular, hybrid, and often eclectic form of Freire's thought, his special way of "reading" each author in this tradition according to a problematic that

---

[2] This coincidence should not surprise us, since the philosophy of education is usually considered to be a more educational or pedagogical field than a philosophical one, and is seen with a certain disinterest, condescension, or indifference by academic philosophers.

was his own. In the same way that Freire changed his mind during his life, depending on the particular demands of the work he was doing, so too diverse traditions are at times confronted and at other times unconsidered. More radically, in some cases, the exact same influence is read in different ways, resulting in different forms, according, of course, to the demands of the reading itself.

In any case, the emerging intellectual portrait is complex in the extreme and the result is surprising: there is practically no philosophical current in these European traditions of thought that are not, in some way or to some degree, related to the educator from Pernambuco. To begin to perceive the multidimensional and complex nature of this life and thought, consider a mere sketch that signals a few of these readings, incorporating the most highlighted influences by these studies which include a diverse array of figures from different intellectual camps. From this sketch there emerge many Freires: the Marxist (sometimes firm, sometimes eclectic, at times even lukewarm), the Liberation Theologian, the existentialist, the phenomenologist, the Critical Pedagogue, the progressive educator, the personalist, and more. Edson Passetti interestingly named Freire a "Christian anarchist" (Passetti, 1997, p. 10).

More specifically, J. Irwin (2012), for example, has shown how Freire was influenced by existentialism (in particular, by Erich Fromm's conceptualization of "the fear of freedom"), by Marxian formulations of philosophy, history, and the dialectic, and by Marxism, for example, Franz Fanon's analysis of cultural action for freedom in third world nations. John Elias highlights the five most impactful influences: political and educational progressivism (liberalism), existentialism, phenomenology, Catholic theology, and a revolutionary Marxist humanism (Elias, 1994, pp. 32–46).

Peter Mayo (1999) has emphasized the proximity to and importance of Gramsci's work for Freire's perspectives on adult education. Dermeval Saviani (1987) highlights Mounier's personalism as well as the existentialism of Marcel and Jaspers as the most meaningful marks on Freire, and characterizes Freire's philosophy as dialectical and idealist. Jose Luiz Zanella (2007) suggests that the most recognizable philosophical influence on Freire is existential phenomenology, in particular Husserl and Jaspers, while also noting the influence of Dewey's pragmatism. At any rate, for Zanella, Freire's resistance to accepting "scientific laws and dialectics of the real" impedes his comprehension of reality as a dialectic totality and, hence, leaves him imprisoned within an idealistic framework that makes it impossible to consider Freire's philosophy as Marxist (Zanella, 2007, p. 114).

Oliveira and Ghiggi (2004) highlight the influence of authors like Buber, Jaspers, and Dewey for the concept of dialogue, which they consider to be the central element in Freire's philosophy. Freire's relation to pragmatism, in particular with Dewey, is frequently studied in the United States by scholars such as Feinberg and Torres (2002) and Abdi (2001), and in Brazil by Maocir Godotti (2001), and, more recently, among others, by Guilherme (2017). Morrow and Torres (2002) trace a parallel between Freire and Habermas from a common conception of the subject, pedagogical practice, the human sciences, and the crisis of modern science with an emphasis on the interface between Freire and German philosophy.

J. Simoes Jorge (1975) marks the unclassifiable character of Freire's philosophy and highlights the following as relevant philosophical influences and concepts: Trastão de Athayde, the Brazilian Catholic humanist who developed a concept of human value, the personalism of Mounier on the dignity of the person, the existentialism of Kierkegaard and his notion of the concrete human being, Gabriel Marcel's being-with, Heidegger's conceptualization of man as one that questions the world as horizon, Jaspers' emphasis on the value of dialogue and communication, Fromm's critique of mass production, alienation, and oppression, and finally, Marx's dialectic, his notion of utopia, and the importance of praxis in his critique of capitalist society.

Bauduino Andreola takes this wide tent and widens it even further. He includes those already mentioned and adds to them an ample group of twentieth-century personalities: Gandhi, Martin Luther King Jr., João XXIII, Teillard de Chardin, Lebret, Don Hélder Câmara, Nelson

Mandela, Simone Weil, Teovedjre, Che Guevara, Mother Teresa of Calcutta, Ivan Illich, the Dalai Lama, Garaudy, Fritjof Capra, Betinho, Pierre Weil, and Leonardo Boff (Andreola, 2001).

As one can see, Freire's repertoire is vast, and here we have only completed a tiny synthesis of existing literature. One could extend this analysis by including Freire's own testimonies on those who influenced him. For instance, toward the end of his life he displayed a distaste for fatalistic and neoliberal postmodernism, while expressing an affinity for what he termed a "progressive postmodern" view (Freire, 1994, p. 166) to the point of defining himself on those terms. This picture could easily be made even more complex. Without a doubt Freire was an obstinate and dedicated reader interested in, and open to, distinct traditions of thought which helped him think through the problems of his time. It is also important to remember his steadfast confessional Christian faith, which he never abandoned and which he reconciled with various philosophical currents, although some of them, like Marxism, were in tension with it. In the end, the winding road of his library and of the philosophical influences he received on this road were arduous, long, and complex.[3]

---

[3] A recent epistolary dialogue by Inés Fernández Mouján, written after visiting Freire's library, makes a relation between the books that he read between the 1950s and the end of the 1970s. The list is expressive: Jaspers' *Origin and Method of History*; Husserl's *Ideas*; Marx and Engels' *Holy Family* and *Selected Works*; Lenin's *What to Do?*; Rosa Luxemburg's *Reform or Revolution*; Lukács' *Ontology*; Jean-Paul Sartre's *Being and Nothingness, On Man and Things, The Transcendence of the Ego, Questions of Method, Colonialism and Neocolonialism*; Simone de Beauvoir's *The Political Thought of the Right*; James Cone's *Black Theology and Black Power* and *Black Liberation Theology* (Freire wrote the prologue to this book); Bachelard's *Dialectic*; Marcuse's *An Essay on Liberation, Reason and Liberation* and *Eros and Civilization*; Goldmann's *Epistemology and Political Philosophy*, Hegel's *Phenomenology of Spirit*; Horkheimer's *Traditional and Critical Theory*; Heidegger's *The Question Concerning the Thing*; Gramsci's *The Modern Prince and Other Writings, The Prison Notebooks, Notes on Machiavelli, Modern Politics and the State*; Mao Tsé-Tung's *Little Red Book*; Memmi's *Colonized Portrait* and *The Liberation of the Jew*; Fanon *The Wretched of the Earth, Sociology of a Revolution, Black Skins, White Masks*; Erich Fromm's *The Fear of Freedom, The Heart of Man*; Amílcar Cabral's *Revolutionary Practice, The Arm of Theory, Unity and Battle, Revolution in Guinea*; Davidson's *The Liberation of Guinea*; Malcolm X's *Autobiography of Malcolm X*; Mendel's *The Decolonialization of the Child* and *Sociopsychoanalysis of Authority*; Althusser's *Marx's Revolutionary Theory*; Merleau-Ponty's *Phenomenology of Perception*; Furter's *Education and Life*; Vieira Pinto's *National Conscience and Reality*; Foucault's *The Order*

Other Traditions: Marx and the
Demand of Transformation

I am not going to take the approach, outlined above in brief, which seeks to situate and understand an author by connecting them to other authors or traditions of thought. I will walk a different path, inspired by the very same history. Two traditions have a special character which allows us to consider the relation between Freire and philosophy. What those traditions share in common, as we will see, is that they both understand philosophy more through its effects in relation to what is outside of them than with a specific content or theory. In other words, I will not try to contextualize this or that aspect of the thought of Freire in order to try and identify this or that influence in this or that book. The two traditions I have chosen here both indicate an approach that, in some form, dissolves this method of approximating an author through a philosophical highlight report. As I noted, these two traditions both point to something that is outside of philosophy: politics, education, and life.

The first of the traditions comes from Karl Marx in a particular way. I am referring here to the late Marx, the critic of speculative philosophy. Perhaps the best evidence for this is the famous Thesis 11 on Feuerbach, "Up until now the philosophers have only interpreted the world, but the point is to transform it" (Marx and Engels, 1970). Numerous commentators on Freire have noted the influence of the late Marx on Freire. For example, C. West (1993, p. xiii) has demonstrated how Freire, the educator of Pernambuco, is highly sensitive to Marx's critique of traditional speculative philosophy and how he bets on the force of a problematizing and philosophical education capable of changing not only the ways or modes of thought, but, above all, the prevailing forms

---

of Things; Spinoza's *Theo-political Treatise*. There were also others: Darcy Ribeiro, Juan D. Perón, Hernández Arregui, Fernando Henrique Cardoso, Enzo Faletto, Fernández Castro, Laclau, Che Guevara, Fidel Castro and Getúlio Vargas.

of life. Seen in this way, the Marxist notion of praxis is particularly important in Freire's work.

To repeat: Freire inscribes himself within these traditions which consider philosophy to be explicitly committed to the transformation of the status quo. For example, in a 1973 interview with the Institute of Cultural Action in Geneva, Freire (1976a) critiques the diverse forms of dualist visions of subjectivism and objectivism and proposes instead that we understand philosophy as praxis: action and reflection, dialectical unity of subject-object, theory and practice.

As we have seen, for Freire, philosophy contains a dimension of reflection and another of action, and both dimensions are necessarily world-transforming when they lead to conscious, profound, and "scientific" readings. As such, reading the world is a transformative praxis. In *Cultural Action for Liberation*, Freire affirms that, contrary to what he proposes, the idea of a philosophy having the mere role of "explication of the world and instrument for its acceptance" is proper to a political analphabet (91).

In this way, philosophy for Freire is much more than just a tool to understand reality or our position of being human in the world, as almost all the aforementioned philosophical traditions affirm; paradoxically, these traditions are also signaled as strongly present in his work. It is true that, especially in the first period of his thought, the idea of "conscientization," densely influenced by the phenomenological tradition, has a singular importance for Freire.[4] But his notion of conscientization cannot be separated from its transformative effects upon the conditions of life of the oppressed. Philosophy as a dimension of a problematizing education which permits the conscientization of the conditions of oppression is a way to reunite theory and practice, abstraction and concreteness, reflection and action, thought and life. Moreover, if a philosophical education only allows the oppressed a

---

[4] Fernández Mouján shows that the Marxist influence in Freire gains weight in the idea of conscientization, especially through the life of Fanon, in the notion of double or dual consciousness (Fernández Mouján, 2016).

theoretical take of their condition and doesn't lead to transformations in their material conditions of life, then such an education cannot be considered liberating. For Freire, life is, in a certain way, inseparable from thought.

Thus, when one compares Freire's work with these traditions that certainly influenced him, as he himself readily admits, we can see certain tensions emerge. Freire himself criticized "very good Marxists" who had never set foot in a favela or in the house of a worker (Shor and Freire, 1987, p. 136). They could have an extensive knowledge of Marxist theory, and have a deep understanding of Marx's ideas, but, nevertheless, for Freire this would not qualify someone as a true or plentiful Marxist, because for them Marx is simply a group of texts to study. For these "very good Marxists," Marx is reduced to concepts and theory without life.

In a similar vein, we could ask: "What would Paulo Freire say about the phenomenologists that do not give life to phenomenology? Or the existentialists that do not give life to existentialism? Or anyone who does not give life to their ideas?"

In any case, Freire is clearly a Marxist in the sense that he affirms a philosophy that not only contemplates or understands the problems of education but also seeks to transform educational practices. In this way, Freire never abandoned his original bet on the transformative power of an education which was politically orientated toward the liberation of the oppressed. In this sense, and especially after the 1964 Brazilian coup, he perceived more clearly the limits to the transformative effects of education and began to defend a more prudent posture, a critical optimism, something between a disingenuous and naïve optimism (i.e., thinking that education can be direct lever of social transformation) and a terrible pessimism (i.e., thinking that education only reproduces the dominant ideology) (Shor and Freire, 1987, p. 136).

In his texts written in 1992, after overcoming the difficult test as the Secretary of Education of São Paulo, Freire nonetheless maintained his belief in the positive role of education, "even if it can't do everything, education still plays a fundamental role in the reinvention of the world"

(Freire, 2001b, p. 10). This refrain repeated in many interventions that Freire made during this period. For instance, at a conference in Jamaica, he affirms that "if it is right that education cannot do everything, it can still do something" (Freire, 2001b, p. 42). In one of the letters that are included in his 1993 book *Professor Yes, Auntie No* (translated as *Teachers as Cultural Workers*), a line appears that almost becomes a motto for Freire in his final years: "It is true that education is not the ultimate lever for social transformation, but without it transformation cannot occur" (Freire, 2005b, p. 69). In his final works, Freire believes that "changing the world is as hard as it is possible" (Freire, 2004, p. 14).

Freire never stopped believing that the transformative power of a theory or idea resides in its ability to incite ways of living that seek a greater comprehension of life. This is definitive. For this reason, he would accept the Marxist critique of all traditions of thought, including those that marked his own thinking, which remained purely at the speculative level.

Another Tradition: Foucault and Life as a Philosophical Problem

Inscribing Freire into the second wave of European thought is more controversial and less explored in the literature.[5] It is deeply related to the first when we look to Michel Foucault, as we will see, who was a careful and capable reader and who also found quarrels with philosophy, including the praxical philosophy of Marx. At the same time, Foucault

---

[5] In Brazil, a few connections between Freire and Foucault like I intend to make here have been produced. For example, see the works of Mafra (2008), Berino (2008), Maciel (2017), and Oliveira (2017). Berino sees the "aesthetics of experience" as a bridge because of a curious letter sent to Freire by a "masked reader," which recalls an interview where Foucault referred to himself as "the masked philosopher." Berino reproduces the letter and adds commentary approximating the shared preoccupations of Foucault and Freire (Berino, 2008, p. 35). I have offered a more detailed reading of the last course of Foucault in Kohan, 2015b.

(1996) critiqued the Marxist tradition in a way that Freire himself, especially the late Freire, would have agreed with. Mindful of this, I inscribe Freire into this latter tradition realizing that I am introducing a certain inner tension with my own interpretation. To read a Christian humanist through the lens of an anti-humanist atheist has its risks. Let us see what comes of it.

At the same time, my inscription of Freire into this second wave will allow me to relate him to more remote figures, apparently distant from our time and place. What is most important to me is the potential for an encounter between Freire and interlocutors who are less explored, which almost seems to be a joke if we believe in the more orthodox readings of the educator from Pernambuco.[6]

In his final course at the Collège de France, on the notion of *parrhesia* (frank speech), titled *The Courage of Truth*, Foucault proposed a philosophy of the history of philosophy that, to a certain degree, recreates Marx's critique of speculative philosophy in a different way, following other lines of thought. This means that, well beyond the intellectualist and speculative traditions of doctrines, abstract problems, and concepts noted by Marx, Foucault discovers a new one: "a history of the philosophical life as a philosophical problem, but also as a mode of being and as a form both of ethics and heroism" (Foucault, 2011, p. 210). This new discovery was not considered by Marx (nor, surely, by many others).

In this final course, then, Foucault sets out to investigate the history of ethico-philosophical heroes, not because of the supposed brilliance of doctrines or ideas, but instead because of the heroic and ethical character of their ways of life. That is to say, not because of what they

---

[6] After reading a preliminary version of the present chapter, Facundo Giuliano expressed his dissatisfaction over email for my reading of Freire from the "metanarratives of modernity/coloniality" (e.g., Marx and Foucault) which Freire critiqued (see Giuliano, 2018). The question, I think, is much more complex. I prefer to think that before we consider authors who are colonial or not colonial, there are colonizing or decolonizing readings of authors of diverse traditions. More than a thought, it is the use and sense given to a thought that has a colonizing or decolonizing value.

thought or wrote, but rather because of the explosive, militant, and revolutionary power of their paths and styles of life; because of the strength that they had to add themselves, critically and devastatingly, into the tradition of how a philosophical life ought to be lived, including what, in the name of philosophy, one should do in one's life.

For a Frenchman like Foucault, Socrates and the Cynics of classical antiquity are the first heroes of a European tradition of a philosophical life that can be traced all the way to our time. It is a minor tradition, silenced in Europe proper, but no less philosophical than the more dominant discourses. In this very work under discussion, Foucault believes that the history of philosophical lives can be reconstructed in modernity through figures like Montaigne and Spinoza. In other words, Foucault does not pretend to be inaugurating this tradition in the way Marx's aspiration seems to indicate ("Until now the philosophers . . ."). To the contrary, the tradition is ancient. The issue is only that this tradition has been erased, forgotten, ignored by the history of triumphalist philosophy. Marx's philosophy of the history of philosophy pretends to interrupt an entire tradition and generate a new beginning. Again, to the contrary, Foucault's philosophy of the history of philosophy seeks to help us to perceive something that already has existed but was not perceived.

Consider the case of Socrates. In him, speculative philosophy, philosophy as theory or understanding, is also present. In truth, if we attend carefully to Plato's *Dialogues*, with all of their hermeneutical difficulties, the two conceptions of philosophy contrasting earlier are reunited: philosophy as understanding or intellectual activity, what Foucault designates as a "metaphysics of the soul," and philosophy as the form or wisdom of life, what he designates as "the aesthetics of existence" (Foucault, 2011, p. 157). Plato, the author, shows how the relations between each sense of philosophy are complex, flexible, and variable. If we take *Alcibiades I*, where Socrates, in dialogue with Alcibiades, understands philosophy from the point of view of knowing one's self, we have an example of philosophy understood as the metaphysics of the soul. Here Socrates attempts to evaluate the real conditions under which Alcibiades might dedicate himself to politics; he argues that, for this, he will have to be educated to take care of others and that one can only take care of others when they know how to care for their own self. And what is required to take care of the self? Something that only the philosopher seems to be in the condition for doing in the *polis*: to know one's self and, within this self, to understand its most important aspect, the soul. In this way, in this dialogue, Socrates seems to affirm a vision of philosophy that is associated with a certain understanding or intellectual activity.

In the same course, Foucault juxtaposes the above to the vision offered in *Laques*, where Nicias, one of Socrates' interlocutors, notes that conversations with him can begin on any topic but they will all equally and fatalistically return toward the interlocutor themselves, who must supply reasons for their way of life, that is, for the way in which they live. In other words, what is philosophical in this dialogue is not the intellectual activity but, instead, the form of life. This is philosophy as a style and aesthetic of existence. It is worth noting that in both dialogues the principal question, operating in the background of the conversations between Socrates and his interlocutors, is how to educate Athenian youth, how to confront what is perceived as an educational crisis in order to give importance to that which is necessary in the education of the new Athenian generations.

In this way, from these two Socratic openings, Foucault highlights philosophy as a problematizer of life. This sense of philosophy can be found more or less suggested in various of the first dialogues of Plato. The other line of philosophy is also born of these dialogues. The two opening lines are born mixed, knotted, inside-out, and, many times, confused. Nonetheless, gradually, they separate. Philosophy as a cognitive activity emerges as, above all else, the intellectual exercise that is generated from the examination of the questions that one seeks to understand. It is the history of philosophy as intellectual understanding, as a system of thought, of questions and answers, that Plato reinforces in his mature dialogues and Aristotle projects in an even more organized and systematic way. This is the philosophy that emerges, let us say, victorious in the academic world, with particular emphasis from what Foucault calls the "Cartesian moment," European modernity. It is this tradition that is critiqued by Marx, that marks philosophers according to their doctrines as existentialists, pragmatists, personalists, Marxists, phenomenologists, postmodernists, and more.

These two lines of philosophy are certainly not disconnected. There are many ways to relate them and to relate one's self to them. By rescuing that tradition erased by the more dominant philosophy, Foucault highlights in Socrates what most interests him, the philosophical problem that anguishes him in his moments of life: how to justify, before the proximity of death, a life that has been worth the pain of being lived and how to situate this life into a tradition of thought that gives significance and reason to Foucault's own style of life. In other words, what interests Foucault, at this height of living, is how to inscribe his manner of doing philosophy, his life lived in accord with philosophy, within a European tradition of thought understood as Western philosophy. He does not feel comfortable in this intellectualist tradition of philosophy and finds, in the life and death of Socrates, a beginning of a tradition for his own philosophical life.

To be sure, Foucault does not find inspiration for this in Socrates alone. The next step in this tradition takes us to the philosophical school of the Cynics, who continue to take flesh in this way of living and dying to such a degree that their lives become a scandal. In Antiquity, the Cynic's school of philosophy has been characterized much more for representing a way of life than for having developed theories or systems of thought. There is no proper "Cynic doctrine" because it is a very limited grouping of precepts that constitute themselves as a prolegomenon toward a style of existence more than a grouping of knowledge or systematic theories. Moreover, the Cynics teach no theory whatsoever, they transmit no knowledge, they demonstrate with their very lives the absurdities of those lives lived effectively in the *polis* so that other lives can be lived. They are like bridges: they do not offer lives to be imitated, but, instead, they show the artificiality of the lives that dominate the city so that, in this way, other lives can emerge.

Diogenes of Sinope, the founder of the school most emblematic of the Cynic philosophers, took without problem or protest the nickname of "Dog." From this nickname the name "Cynic" emerges as the translated Greek adjective *"kynikos."* "Life of a dog" is a good translation of Cynicism: life without modesty, shame, or respect, life without intimacy or secrets, an impudent and indifferent life that requires nothing, life that is absolutely visible and natural, that fights against and barks at its enemies. At last, life that cares and salves the life of the beloved and also the life of beloved Nature. Life without nothing but life itself. In this way, the cynicism of the ancients appears as a deepening of Socratic life, a continuation, projection, and deepening of a true life, that the tradition constructed from Platonism did not doubt or cease praising, but by isolating itself more and more in texts and distancing itself from the concrete life of philosophers. This is the affirmation of another life so that an existence that is effectively philosophical can spring. Here we see their singular educational value.

For this reason, in a certain way, ethics and heroism become intensified in the flesh of the ancient Cynics, since in them there is still less theory, doctrine, and body of thought than in Socrates. For the Cynics, a philosophical life is the right and proper body of philosophy; it expresses life in a direct, profound, coherent, and radical way with its philosophy. The philosophy of the Cynic is a life made flesh, expressed in a heroic and ethical way in the public space of the *polis.*

In this way, in Foucault's lectures (2011), Cynicism deepens the relation that Socrates himself establishes between truth and life, as he presents it before his accusers in the *Apology of Socrates* of Plato. Various Cynics, in fact, were judged and condemned for their irreligiosity, in the same way as Socrates was condemned for his impieties. This life of a Cynic requires courage, and has no room for embarrassment or fear, in order to affirm a true saying without limits, which is intolerable and insolent to the *polis.*

But what is it that the Cynics understand to be a true life? Diogenes, the most notable Cynic, as we have seen, is said, like Socrates, to have received a mandate from the Oracle at Delphi which he also took as his mission: "change, alter, the value of currency" (Foucault, 2011, p. 226). Working from the etymological proximity between "coin" (*nomisma*) and "norm," "law" (*nomos*), Foucault interprets this mission as a task to respond philosophically and politically to the present order so as to transform it. The true life of the Cynic would then be a life that denounces the life of the *polis* as the opposite of a true life. Unlike the true life, the life of the *polis* is hidden, pure, right, and inalterable. Cynicism, for Foucault in his final course, is an extrapolation, an inversion so radical that it is impossible for the dominant philosophy of the present epoch to not accept some part of Cynicism and, at the same time, impossible to not mistreat it and even to pretend to expel it from the world of philosophy as a precious caricature, as a "scandal of a true life" (Foucault, 2011, p. 353).

In this way, the Socrates and Cynics of Foucault are, perhaps, limit situations, mythic exemplars of thinkers who can be found almost exclusively on the side of life. The first, Socrates, for his characteristic way of affirming a philosophical life from the point of view of its relation to knowing, intersected by not knowing, and for his refusal to place his thought into writing. The second, the Cynics, go even further, owing to their way of understanding philosophy as precisely the gestures of the body in life without adding anything beyond these gestures. They both share the absence of registered direct writing, an absence and void that augments the possibility of inspiring renewed feelings when one attends to the testimonies of their lives.

Another important aspect of this form of affirming the philosophy that Foucault brings to life with Socrates, and which the Cynics project, is constituted by the fact that a philosophical life is, at the same time, an educational life. The hero of philosophy educates by example with their life. We could say that the ethical value of this kind of life reveals itself as an educational value. This is not about an accessory or decoration; it is essential: without this educational revelation this philosophical life is nothing, it loses all of its significance. Life is lived in such a way as to inspire other lives. Moreover, life can only be lived if it inspires other lives.

It is terribly difficult to differentiate up to what point and in what sense an ethical life is a philosophical life or an educational life. Socrates is, again, a good example since all the accusations against him were religious ("he does not believe in the Athenian gods," "he introduces new gods") and educational ("he corrupts the youth"). His manner of defending himself is to identify these accusations as accusations against "all who philosophize" (Plato, *Apology*, 23d). In other words, he is accused of the educational effects of his philosophical life and he responds that the accusation is symbolic but that, in truth, it is directed against a certain way of living which he calls "philosophical." This is an accusation against himself, but also against "all who philosophize." He responds in the same way to the second accusation as well. By living in this way, by questioning and philosophizing with the citizens of Athens, he is realizing a mission determined by the most sacred god of the Athenians: Apollo. He goes on to state that, even if the judges were to pardon him on the condition that he would abandon this form of living, he would not accept the terms, since the unexamined life is a life not worth living (*Apology*, 38a). If we unite these two responses, we could say, then, that the philosophical life, with its educational mission, is an inevitable and sacred task for someone chosen by a god, a hero.

Let us try and take up this exercise that this heroic life proposes and return to the questions about this type of intervention, this kind of politics, of the hero in the *polis*. By responding in this way to his accusers, is Socrates philosophizing? Is he educating? Who is this Socrates before the court of Athens? A philosopher? A professor of philosophy? An educator who philosophizes? Or is he merely a politician looking to dress up his philosophy and his education in sacred garb in order to affirm a political questioning of political institutions?

We could propose the same questions about the heroic life of the Cynics, the value of their public interventions and even the value of the corpus of their own thought. Are they philosophical, educative, or political expressions? Are they a bit of each? Can we see expressions of lives that educate politically through the exercise of philosophy, or that philosophize and enact politics through education, or that inscribe a politics of confrontation into the order of things in the name of an education in philosophy?

Here we find a third dimension of this tradition of philosophical life that Foucault conceives as being born in Socrates and the Cynics: it is necessarily political. Let us recall the etymology of the word "politics." It is derived from the Greek noun *"polis,"* which refers to the form of life organized in common. The philosophical and educational life cannot not be political because, outside of the *polis*, life lacks significance. For example, this is what Socrates argues to Crito, in the dialogue by the same name as his interlocutor, when Crito wants to convince Socrates to escape from prison. Not only would it be unjust to escape, because it would undermine the norms of life in the *polis*, it would also, above all, make no sense, because outside of the *polis* life would be empty. That the educational life of the philosophy of Socrates and the Cynics is political does not mean that it requires membership or adherence to a party; this would have been absurd to the Greeks since their democracy was direct, without representation. Nor does this political dimension entail a specific form of the exercise of power or a political program of common life. That this ethical and heroic life is also political only means the impossibility of imagining life, education, and philosophy without those who share the public space of that life, that public life.

As Foucault argues in his last course at the Collège de France, the relations between the two dimensions of philosophy as an intellectual form of understanding and as a way of life are complex, they oscillate, and they are varied. In one sense, the intensity of the questions that life in common presents us with is more important than their answers and, in a certain way, these questions outlive and survive whatever answers are offered. In a different sense, a philosophical life feeds itself from the answers that its philosophy seeks to offer. Whatever the case may be, in the camp of life, philosophy, education, and politics are not easily separated nor are they fixed in a body of knowledge or a metaphysics of the soul, as Foucault would say in his final lecture, and despite what the dominant philosophers since Plato have tried to demonstrate and reveal. The strength of lives that ethically and heroically ask questions in the way of Socrates or the Cynics prevails in front of the attempts to understand those lives in a systematic unity and totality of thought.

Paulo Freire and the History of Life as a Philosophical Problem

We might say that Freire is inscribed into this tradition of a philosophically educational life, political, ethical, and heroic whose beginnings and continuations are identified, respectively, as we have seen, by Foucault in Socrates and the Cynics, on one side, and in the Christian ascetics in our time, on the other side. Since Freire was a confessed Christian, it may be interesting to pay attention to this Foucaultian recuperation of the ascetics of Christ since, for Foucault (2011), Christianity is an example of a metaphysics of the soul that is relatively stable during the centuries that, at the same time, gave a special place to an aesthetic of existence and varied forms of life. In this tradition, the Christian ascetics are inspired by the Cynics to establish a type of spiritual combat against the impurities of the world. Among the diverse and even divergent forms that the Christian ascetics can take, one seems particularly interesting to the inscription of this line of thought of the guardian of pedagogical dreams: the militant figure who critiques real life and the actions of the human beings entering into a battle that ought to bring about the transformation of the world.

Nonetheless, it is also the case that there seem to be at least two aspects of Christian asceticism that seem to confront Freire's thought, both quite opposed to his ideas: on the one hand, the importance that the Christian ascetics have for another world, a world beyond the present world, a world much more significant than the task of making this world into another world; on the other hand, the principle of obedience (to the Lord, to the law, to God) which, for the ascetics, is foundational to their way of life. These two aspects are in tension with a way of thinking and a life such as the life and thought of Freire, who sought to unite doctrines of, to put it in Foucault's terms, the metaphysics of the soul, even those as dissonant as Marxism and Christianity, and sought the transformation of this world into another through education which would be born from the existing, immanent world. Nonetheless, for someone who remained steadfast to the end of his life in his commitment to the transformation of the world and, at the same time, the value of dialogue, neither of those two principles of the Christian ascetics seem to have validity for Freire.

In this sense, the analogy between Socrates and the Cynics gains still even more strength when we recall the way in which the great educator from Pernambuco describes his life. Friere's autodepiction of his life is, as we will see, very close to the Athenians and the Cynics, especially in the sense of one's life being a sacred mission. Let us look now at some of these evident similarities between Socrates and Freire.

There are some works that study this relation. The majority of them center their focus on the notion of dialogue. Among the ones from Brazil, Mario Sergio Cortella (2018) passes through this relation quickly and separates the two more than anything. Marcelo Maia (2008) has dedicated a thesis to study the relation between Socrates and Freire and he only finds a few discordances (such as the Socratic emphasis on the individual versus the Freirean focus on the collective, the knowledge of the teacher which, for Socrates, does not exist or must be troubled, and their different methods) and many more points in common, including the role of dialogue. Among the shared points we find education as a path toward overcoming social problems, a conception of human life as inconclusive and as a vocational project for the human being (i.e., the humanization of life, to be realized as person through education), the role of knowledge and understanding, especially in its ethical dimension as a condition for a free existence, the affirmative role of irony, dialogue practiced among pairs as a path toward a liberating education.

Let us consider more closely this relation between Socrates and Freire. They are both seen as heroes, prophets on a pastoral mission. They both say this explicitly, for example, in their final declarations: Socrates, when he relates the well-known anecdote about the Oracle at Delphi in his defense (*Apology*, 20e ff); Freire (1997) in his last interview, recalling his beginnings in the literacy campaigns for youth and adults in the poor zones of Pernambuco. Let us look, now, at the details.

Socrates interprets the saying of the priestess at the Oracle in this way to his friend Querofont, who asks whether there is anyone wiser than Socrates in Athens. "There is no one wiser than Socrates" does not indicate a site of knowledge but, instead, a mission that Socrates gives to himself and which he remains faithful to throughout his entire life, including when it is at risk. This mission is to show everyone that they do not know what they think they know. This mission aims to exhort those to whom this truth is shown to desire to truly know and put them on the path toward the search of true knowledge. The impact of this teaching in the life of the Athenians is direct in the sense that it permits them to attend to precisely what they failed to attend to, to care for what they did not care for. In this way, Socrates founds a philosophy and the position in which he lives it out as a philosophico-educational mission that seeks to convert everyone into a philosopher, to convert all lives into philosophical lives. Socrates wants everyone to live his philosophical life. Not his in the sense of the life he possesses as himself, but, more radically, the philosophical nature of that life.

Freire also perceives himself to be a pastor, a prophet on an educational mission. He understands the prophet as someone who is firmly anchored in the earth, in the present, and, at the same time, as someone who can foresee the future peacefully, with tranquility, someone with an "imagination at this level is side by side with dreams" (Shor and Freire, 1987, p. 186). He describes his mission in a way that is very similar to Socratic terms we have seen. He conceives of the human being as an unfinished being and understands that his mission is to awaken desire through a pedagogy of the question, a desire for searching and demanding in those who do not recognize themselves in this way (Freire and Faundez, 1989). Here we see the value of his "untried viability," of the epistemological and ontological vocation of human beings to "be more." We can affirm, based on these reasons, that

Freire is very close to the conception of Socratic philosophy, in which philosophy is not a noun, a theory, but, instead, a verb, a certain relation with wisdom that must be exercised. In this sense, in the Socratic and Freirean perspectives there is an anthropology, epistemology, and ontology with strong overlaps and commonalities: a form of being, understanding, and dwelling in the world based upon the question, in curiosity in incompleteness, and in the desire that life becomes a way to accept and, at the same time, confront this condition as "critique." The Socratic dictum of the *Apology*, "the unexamined life is not worth living" (Apology, 38a), would have made make a great deal of sense for Freire's life had he lived in Athens centuries before Christ; he would have probably been one of "those who philosophize," who Socrates identifies as the true target of the accusations against him.

Of course, when we try to specify the most concrete ways and forms in which Socrates and Freire perceive their common mission, we find that there do exist obvious and notable differences proper to their markedly different historical, social, political, and cultural contexts. Let us survey a few of them. Freire perceives and presents himself as a pastor in the name of the Christ of the poor and excluded. We could say, inspired by Foucault, that in elitist and slave-owning Athens, Socrates calls to the other citizens to care for what they are caring for, without any other basis but radical trust in the power of questioning and submitting life to examination without preoccupation by the situation of those who are literally outside of this minority of Athenian-born adult men, then, likewise, Freire, in a peripheral region of a peripheral nation like Brazil, seeks to care for the oppressed who very few appear to care about, with his religious Christian and scientific Marxist faith in the form of thinking through social and political relations. Socratic questioning is political and directs itself to those who dedicate themselves to politics in Athens. Freire's questioning is also political, but in a sense that is still more radical: he questions the basis of the social order that sustains the very condition of oppression which he confronts.

In the relation with the modes of conceiving philosophy, there are also clear differences. While Socrates does not present any theory whatsoever that sustains his philosophical life, Freire supports himself with dialectical materialism in order to sustain his educational life, which longs to realize Christian ideals on earth. In other words, Freire the pastor trusts a Marxist conception of class struggle and dialectical history in order to infuse Christian values and the class consciousness of the oppressed within the capitalist system through a practice of revolutionary education. These are values that transform the lives of the habitants of a "developing" nation like Brazil in the 1950s and 1960s and, to be more geopolitically specific, a region so viciously injured like the Northeast of the country, where Freire was born, grew up, and was formed. He describes his work in the favelas and with the working poor of his region at the beginning of his pedagogical journey in this way, in his own words:

> When I was just a boy, a very young boy, I would go to the mangroves of Recife, to the streams and hills of Recife, to the rural parts of Pernambuco to work with the peasants and slum dwellers. With dry eyes I confess that I went there moved by a certain fidelity to Christ who was, more or less, my comrade and friend. But what happened was that, when I would get there, the harsh reality of the favela, the harsh reality of the peasants, the denial of there being as people and the tendency to that adaptation (which we talked about earlier), to that almost inert state before the denial of freedom, that all took me back to Marx. I always say: it was not the peasants who said to me: "Paulo, have you read Marx?" No! They didn't even read the newspaper. It was their reality that brought me back to Marx. And so I went to Marx. And that is where European journalists in the seventies did not understand my statement. The more I read Marx, the more I found a certain, fundamental basis for remaining Christ's comrade. So, my reading of Marx and extended understanding of Marx never suggested to me that I should stop finding Christ on the corners of the slums . . . I stayed with Marx in his worldliness, looking for Christ in his transcendence. (Freire, 1997)

Look at the proximity of the religious foundations of these two stories. Socrates has his wisdom made legitimate by the god Apollo, the supreme divinity of the Athenians. Freire is a comrade and friend of Christ in Christian Brazil. "The more I read Marx, the more I found a certain objective foundation to continue as a comrade of Christ," affirms Freire. Here we see his impressive docility, theoretical malleability, both intellectual and vital. Only someone who is extraordinarily open to tensions and challenges from real antagonisms of a philosophy and a religion could see Marxism as a foundation for realizing the Christian ideal when, in so many ways, these two metaphysics of the soul mutually negate each other.[7] Of course, Freire was not alone in this project; his proximity to theologians of liberation is an obvious indication of his autoinscription into a tradition, a spirit of an age, especially in the field of the interfaces between theology, education, and politics. Nonetheless, Freire seems to have taken the role of education in a scene burdened by tensions and contradictions further than any other.[8]

Be that as it may, in Freire we can see the presence of the tradition of the ancient heroic philosophy sharply imbued into the figures of Christ and Marx (the first in relation to the field of faith, the second in the name of the science of society). Freire seeks to make his existence into an ethical and heroic life, of which philosophy, education, and politics form part of a way that is not simply about disassociation. As an intellectual committed to Christianity, Freire nourishes his mission with the values of a Christian ethic: trust, faith, solidarity, compassion, humility, tolerance, heroism. And at the same time, he uses the social

---

[7] In a difficult and complex work to read, Cintra (1998) offers a reading of this double inspiration from Greek and Jewish categories. Freire would take and combine elements of two matriarchal humanisms of the West: Hellenism (philosophy) and Judaism (communion).

[8] In a date after the publication of the *Pedagogy of the Oppressed*, *A Theology of Liberation* (by Gustavo Gutiérrez, in Lima, 1971) and *A Theology of Human Hope* (by Rubem Alvesin New York, 1969, another book by an exiled person published first in a foreign language—in this case in English—and later in Spanish by Tierra Nueva, in 1970 in Montevideo under the title *Religión: ¿opio o instrumento de liberación?*) were published. In 1973, Freire writes the prologue to the Spanish edition of James Cone's *A Black Theology of Liberation* (*Teología Negra. Teología de la liberación*. Buenos Aires: Lolhe), a product of a seminar taught by Freire with Assmann, E., Bodipo-Malumba, and Cone at the World Council of Churches.

theory of a "critical" dialectical materialism on a "humanist and not doctrinal" slope, as Greene puts it (2001, p. 155). What is more or less interesting is that he never abandons this throughout his entire life, and his thought was nonetheless enriched by other traditions of thought.[9] A Christian Socratic Marxist, a Marxist Christian Socratic, a Socratic Christian Marxist: all these figures, in every combination and emphasis, fit within the life and thought of this utopian hero who championed the liberation of the oppressed.

As we have seen, Freire is a pastoral philosopher and a philosophical pastor with his shepherd's rod guided by Christianity and Marxism. And, as Freire himself has said, pastoral power makes subjects of individuals in two ways: through the control and dependence in relation with others and through the sense of conscience or self-understanding it promotes. In this sense, it is possible to ask to what measure and degree this particular form of exercising pedagogical power can effectively be emancipatory. It is also possible that we can detach from his own words and look behind or beneath the clothing in which he dresses his ideas and read his life as a militant form in favor of a dialogical education that, through a collective and rational construction, points toward the transformation of the world. Far beyond the form in which his ideas are presented and the traditions that cloak them, an immanent nucleus persists and resounds in his life that makes education into a collective and dialogic challenge, seeking a world without oppressors or the oppressed where one can part company from his own faith and beliefs.

In this way, by relativizing the formula that Freire assigns to his heroic-philosophical life, he helps us to imagine the possibilities of philosophy, seeing that it can be a theory or system of thought as much as an affirmation of life with proximate and intimate connections to education and politics. For this reason, it is very difficult to separate one from the other. Freire, then, is a philosopher in this specific sense:

---

[9] Fernández Mouján allows us to see how, for example, his reading of Fanon and Sartre were very important during his exile; in these texts was inspired to put anti-imperialism, antiracism, and anticolonialism together (see Mouján, 2016).

not only for the theories or systems in which he seeks to sustain his practice, nor for the philosophical quality and rigor of his theories or thought, but, instead and above all, because of the way in which he makes his life into a philosophical problem, and, likewise, makes his philosophy an existential question in the search for and journey to a world without oppressors or oppressed.

As Socrates dedicates his life to try and awaken Athenians to what he considers to be an existence without self-examination, so Freire dedicates his life to try and lift the oppressed from that condition and, at the same time, to awaken the oppressors to their condition as oppressors. Freire does not do this with mere theoretical works. No. He does this through his militant life, seeking to favor this cause. His philosophy, then, consists in this: to not separate his life from his thought or in making his way of life a way of expressing his thought. It is this dimension which seems most inspiring for imagining a politics for education. This is neither necessarily nor primarily because of the historical coincidence of his particular life overlapping with the heroic and ethical way of the ancients. Instead, it is for the projection that is offered to our time, a time in which the dominant forms of the school and philosophy seem to be disassociated from the preoccupation for the lives on the outside, on the margins. Freire's life is a philosophical life of an intellectual militant for today and tomorrow, not only yesterday.[10]

This priority of life appears in Freire in many other ways since, far from only being a philosophical problem, it is firstly the source of normal preoccupation and everyday inspiration. It is life that carries theory, not the other way around; it is the ground we walk on that supports the reading of books, not the books that tell us how to read that land and good earth. Diverse stories of Freire mark the preeminence of life. For example, responding to a question from Macedo about what motivates and carries his constant preoccupation for the education of

---

[10] This is how Freire defines himself in a dialogue with Macedo about a book project on Amílcar Cabral, which would be titled "The pedagogue of the revolution": "I am a militant intellectual" (Freire and Macedo, 1987, p. 73).

the oppressed classes, he relates how, since his childhood, he has had contact with working- and peasant-class children and how, as an adult, he has made new contact with workers, peasants, and fishermen: "This new confrontation was much less naïve and *much more than any book*, it led me to understanding my personal need to delve more deeply into pedagogical research" (Freire, 1985, p. 176, emphasis mine).

In this way, for Freire the philosopher, the priority of life is the beginning of not only his conception of philosophy but also of education and, in a more general way, of his intellectual militancy. This makes him adopt a critical posture in relation to educational reality. To say it with Freire, in his own words, in the school and in philosophy there exists a growing disassociation between the reading of words and the reading of the world (Shor and Freire, 1987). The words that are read in school are words that do not speak of the world; they are separated from the lived world from those who are inside the school. The double consequence of this is that we learn to read a world of schooling that is not the one we live in outside of the school, and we do not learn to read the world we live in. What we read in the school does not help us to read the world; with the letters of school we cannot read the world. Who knows, reading Freire's works and life might teach us not only the possibilities of another school and another education but also another way of life.

2

Equality

Second principle: in terms of what a life can be, all lives are equal, all lives have the life potential, not a single life is superior to another life. This is true in and out of a classroom, in and out of any educational space. A political education works from the principle that all lives have the same value and are equally capable of calling individual and social life into question.

> Intellectuals need to discover that their critical capacity is of neither greater nor less worth than the sensitivity of the people. (Freire and Faundez, 1989, p. 29)

> We are all different, and the manner in which living beings reproduce is programmed for what we are to be. This is why the human being eventually has need of fashioning the concept of equality. Were we all identical, like a population of bacteria, the notion of equality would be perfectly useless. (Freire, 1994, p. 97)

From his earliest writings, Paulo Freire argued in favor of the equality of teachers and students, a position that he maintained over the course of his entire life. "Nobody is superior to anyone else" (Freire, 1998, p. 108), he states clearly in the last book he published before his death. He portrays this claim as "one of the few certainties that I am sure of" (Freire, 1998, p. 108). As we will see, the context of this phrase elucidates the importance of educators putting equality into practice through knowing how to listen to their students. The implication of this is that true, attentive listening demands permanent availability to others and a series of

> qualities or virtues, such as a generous loving heart, respect for others, tolerance, humility, a joyful disposition, love of life, openness to what

is new, a disposition to welcome change, perseverance in the struggle, a refusal of determinism, a spirit of hope, and openness to justice. (Freire, 1998, p. 108)

In his support of these conditions, Freire (1998, p. 108) adds that "to accept and respect what is different" is one of the conditions for listening to others. The one who believes that their opinion is the only correct one, who thinks that "standard" grammar is the only acceptable way to speak or write, is not listening on Freire's view. They are disdaining and mistreating the other instead. It is for this reason that, according to Freire, humility is a fundamental virtue for an educator. Humility is based on the negative presupposition that anyone who sees themselves as superior will never listen to others. As a result, the affirmation of humility as a pedagogical virtue is, for Freire, a value that is simultaneously ethical, political, and epistemological. Its absence indicates arrogance: a false sense of superiority that renders an education based on the aforementioned principles impossible. From the equality implicit in the principle, "Nobody is superior to anyone else," it follows that education be emancipatory. But what, exactly, does this requirement mean?

This question is complex. On the one hand, the society that gave sense and meaning to Paulo Freire's life and work promotes a vast array of economic, political, social, cultural, and educational inequalities. Seen under this light, equality is absent, and, thus, it would seem that Freire is not referring to this type of equality. Does this mean that, as has been argued many times, the Brazilian educator dreamed of a form of education that prioritized equality as a goal in the struggle for a less unequal society? Is equality simply the objective of the type of education that Brazil's social inequality requires?

It is certainly intuitive to think of equality as a worthy goal to pursue in the economic, social, and political spheres. But, as we have seen, there are strong indications that Freire argued in favor of equality as a basic principle in other areas as well. One of these planes is ontological. As Carlos Rodrigues Brandão has noted, for Freire, one of education's fundamental postulates is "the ontological equality of all people" (Brandão, 2015, p. 172).

In *The Ignorant Schoolmaster* (1991), Jacques Rancière restores the legendary Joseph Jacotot to his rightful place. In the nineteenth century, Jacotot affirmed human beings' intellectual equality as a basic principle of an emancipatory education of the people. In an interview published a year after the Brazilian version of the work was released, Rancière notes some differences between Jacotot and Freire. The former promotes intellectual and individual emancipation, based precisely on the principle of equality of intelligence, whereas Freire envisions social emancipation. Nonetheless, as Rancière suggests, the difference rests upon a common point:

> There thus exists a distance between Jacotot's project of intellectual emancipation and movements like Freire's. But they also have something in common, for this process of intellectual emancipation is a vector for movements of political emancipation that break with a social and institutional logic. (Vermeren; Cornu and Benvenuto, 2003)

So, we must ask ourselves, does Freire share Jacotot's axiom of equality of intelligence that makes social emancipation possible? The answer to this question appears to be an obvious yes: without this conviction of the equal intellectual capacity of human beings, it would be difficult to envision equality in other areas where social inequality reigns. Along these same lines, Lidia Rodríguez shows that, in Paulo Freire's conception of education, for those whom a banking education dismisses, initial equality is a necessary condition for their ethical and political liberation (Rodríguez et al., 2007; Rodríguez, 2015). In a recent book on Freire, Moacir Gadotti and Martin Carnoy argue, following Muniz Sodré, that intellectual emancipation should be understood as a general principle, one that Freire understands as awareness-raising (Gadotti and Carnoy, 2018, p. 16).

Another scholar of Freire, Alípio Casali (2001), suggests that in the wake of *Pedagogy of the Oppressed*, and in the environment of antiauthoritarian rebellion of the 1970s, a literal understanding of this equality was taken to an extreme, in a reading that he calls romantic-anarchical-egalitarian. He argues, moreover, that problems arose over the pedagogical roles of teachers and learners, since, "if teachers and students are equal from the get-go, what, then, is the purpose of education?" (Casali, 2001, p. 18). He concludes that eventually people realized that Freire was referring to an ethical and civic equality in education, but that this equality did not cancel out the "indispensable epistemological inequality that ultimately legitimates all pedagogy" (Casali, 2001, p. 20). He also argues that there exists a cultural inequality that justifies the pedagogy proposed in *Pedagogy of the Oppressed*. In other words, the act of teaching encounters its justification in cultural inequality and the knowledge that the educator has and the student does not. For these reasons, both are unequal.

It is clear, however, that we need to examine the epistemological dimension of the problem more deeply. While it is true that some human beings know more than others, it is no less true that all possess an equal capacity and vocation to know and that, as a result, a liberating education ought to demonstrate a commitment to restoring this capacity and vocation when they are oppressed.

Thus the issue of equality is a delicate and complex one that requires greater conceptual clarity at its foundation. Equality is an eminently political term. When it is applied to other fields, like the ontological, epistemological, pedagogical, economic, or cultural ones, it can carry a certain political character that needs to be specified on the basis of the field to which it is being applied. However, the issue also requires the greatest possible clarity regarding the political principles it adopts.

What, then, does it mean in concrete terms to say that nobody is superior to anyone else? If this equality did not have some application to the epistemological field, would we not run the risk of perpetuating a political inequality that would reduce the symmetry in the relationship between the one who teaches and the one who learns? Could we instead retain equality as a principle in this field and differentiate levels of knowledge according to other criteria? How should we think about equality in relation to the cognitive and intellectual capacity of educators and students? In the end, what is the real applicability of the idea of equality for education?

These are some of the questions that this chapter will address in several steps. First, it will offer a detailed conceptual examination of the principle "No one is superior to anyone else." It will then consider the implications of that examination for education. Next, it will introduce the ideas of another advocate of equality in education, Jacotot, who we have been introduced to already, and contrast them with those of Freire in more depth. Finally, we will return to the central issues relating to the value of equality that have been raised already.

Senses of the Affirmation of Equality

Let us revisit Freire's claim "Nobody is superior to anyone else," using an exercise in logic. There are three claims that can logically be deduced from this. The first is equally negative: "Nobody is inferior to anyone else." Superior and inferior are semantically dependent, relative terms, for if nobody is superior to anyone else, then it necessarily follows that nobody is inferior to anyone else. If there are no superior people, then there necessarily are no inferior people. This is what Freire seems to say when he points out the negative consequences that would follow if a teacher considered themselves superior to their students. When this happens, others are inferior, and nobody dialogues with an inferior or, for that matter, a superior. Dialogue can only happen between equals. Thus, nobody can feel superior to anyone else.

The second proposition that can be deduced is also negative: "Nobody is unequal to anyone else," which constitutes a combination of sorts with the other two claims. The concept of inequality encompasses both superiority and inferiority; or, rather, superiority and inferiority are both forms of inequality. According to this logic, if neither superior nor inferior people exist, then neither do unequal people.

The third proposition, by contrast, is affirmative. If there are no unequal people, then there can only be equal people. Thus, the third proposition that can be deduced from Freire's "Nobody is superior to anyone else," is "We are all equal." This phrase expresses equality in affirmative terms, just as the other three imply it, denying either superiority, inferiority, or the combination of both, as well as inequality.

It is worth pointing out that equality is not opposed to difference, but rather, more precisely, to inequality. We can therefore all be both equal and different. What we cannot be is equal and unequal, superior and inferior. And this is exactly what Freire appears to be saying. More than that, he establishes difference as a condition of equality, which can be thought of in the following way: if we were not different, there would be no need for equality. Consequently, we can state that the concept of difference is logically a condition of the concept of equality; that is, without difference, equality would be a superfluous concept. And the opposite? Well, we can see that equality is not logically necessary for difference. We can be different and unequal. However, equality is a political condition of difference. Only among equals is a politically desirable affirmation of difference possible. This also seems to be what Freire suggests. Only someone who considers the other an equal can affirm their difference. Freire ties this claim to the difference in the way others are treated; thus, we can consider respect for the other a measure of the value that exists in our consideration of the other as equal.

We can conclude from Freire's proposition, and from the others we have incorporated, the following: if educators and students place themselves above or below each other, there can be no liberating education that is politically fair; a truly democratic politics of education will be impossible. For the educator, there is a political requirement for equality; no one above, no one below. No superior lives, no inferior lives. For when some lives are superior to others, the result is an emphasis on blind obedience, following orders, pleasing, rewards and punishments, rather than on thinking, dialogue, and listening. Freire gives the example of a simplistic educator who caricatures their working-class or rural students by changing the way they speak to "diminish our own speech or limit it to copying theirs" (Shor and Freire, 1987, p. 153). In this example, the educator sees students as possessing lower intellectual capacity and underestimates them even as they overestimate their own capacity. This follows from the false principle that the students are inferior (Shor and Freire, 1987, p. 153). Consequently, there is no politically democratic education here; this educator is transmitting a hierarchy incompatible with an education that liberates. The students learn from their teacher to feel inferior, when they need to be liberated from precisely this feeling.

Equality in Life, In and Out of School

In the previous chapter, I have shown the way in which Freire joins theory and practice, thought and life. In effect, what matters is not just equality as a concept or an idea, but its impact on the lives of educators and students. Seen in this way, it is important not only to think about or postulate equality but, above all, to live it through educational practices.

As we surely know, the affirmation of equality is disavowed by the realities of social life. It is obvious that we are not, in fact, all equal in our societies. Some are on top and others are at the bottom, some can accomplish more than others, at least in social, cultural, and economic terms, all areas in which, under capitalism, there are clearly superior and inferior people. Schools also appear to disavow equality; some students never set foot in them or are soon expelled, while others succeed, from beginning to end, in the proper developmental sequence, with some progressing much more quickly than the others. What, then, does it mean for affirming a politics of education to say that all lives are equal or that no life is unequal? Or, in what sense is equality necessary (and possible) as a principle for a democratic education when our societies and their institutional institutions are wracked by inequality? Would it be nothing more than a romantic, idealistic claim? Can equality actually be educationally practiced and lived in a social reality like ours, laden as it is with such a wide variety of inequalities? In what way and how?

The principle of equality means, on the one hand, that within the pedagogical relationship the inequalities that reign outside are suspended or interrupted (Masschelein and Simons, 2013). The pedagogical relationship can take place within an institutional setting or outside of it, informally, but the suspension of inequalities is a requirement for a democratic politics of education, whatever the institutional setting. This means that if the teacher and the learner do not position themselves as equals while participating in this relationship, the political power of their educational practice will be significantly curtailed. This is what happens, for example, when the pedagogical relationship takes place in an institutional setting that precludes or renders impossible the realization of equality in pedagogy. If the educator fails to disrupt this unequal logic, they will have no choice but to teach what the institution demands of them. They will be forced to assume their place of superiority and their students' place of inferiority. They can teach the most liberating and relevant theories, but the student will learn and live the logic of the relationship that is being imposed, no matter what content is transmitted.

Therefore, the affirmation of equality that we are proposing is relatively simple. It depends only on the educator's decision and the practice that follows. It can exist in the most varied institutional settings, from the most to the least authoritarian, as long as there are cracks, crevices, and pores that enable the disruption of non-egalitarian practices. This is a moment in which an educator's political role acquires a deep salience and meaning, including times when the broader macro-political educational context is more conservative and authoritarian.

On the other hand, this political role is tied to the public nature of the school itself (Masschelein and Simons, 2013; Rodríguez, 2001; 2016). This is not a sense of public as being administered by the State or of not being run by a private organization. No. School is public and for everyone in the sense that it can be inhabited equally by anyone. It is a space where the inequalities between its inhabitants are suspended and disrupted, whenever anyone and everyone takes up residence there. Different from the political nature of education instituted by those who practice it, the public nature of this practice precedes it; it is constitutive of the egalitarian nature of the school system, and, if it is not present, it cannot be instituted by a political decision of the teacher.

Along these lines, the Latin American tradition of the popular school (Rodríguez, 2001; 2016; Durán and Kohan, 2018) offers a radical vision for public schools that can only be simultaneously social, general, and popular (Kohan, 2015a; Rodríguez, 2016). A school is not truly public in this sense when it establishes requirements that renders equals unequal, when it expels instead of welcoming, or when some of its students can accomplish more than others in the pedagogical relations established by the reigning principles of the society in which it exists, principles that wind up reproducing themselves in the educational system.

Although equality is a condition of the institution and of pedagogical relations, this does not mean that educators and students know the same things, or that educators possess no knowledge that students need to learn from (just as students also have knowledge that their teachers need to learn). Of course educators know many things that students do not, and that is why they hold the positions they do, particularly in societies like ours that regulate their institutions according to the knowledge possessed by those who aspire to those positions. But this does not make these people superior. Educators know things that students do not, just as students know things that they do not. Educators know different things and may even know more in terms of information, books, and libraries, but that does not make them superior to their students. The only thing that sets them apart is that the teacher has developed a capacity to learn, think, and know among equals more fully. They are only superior due to an education structured by a hierarchical logic.

Another Advocate of Equality from Another Tradition

Among those who have treated equality as a precondition or political principle for education, perhaps no one has been clearer and more emphatic than the nineteenth-century French pedagogue Jacotot (1770–1840), creator of universal teaching, also called "panecastic philosophy," popularized today by Rancière (1991). Universal teaching consists precisely of affirming the principle of equality of intelligence and in postulating the freedom to teach and learn in any method on behalf of students' intellectual liberation.

According to Jacotot, the principle of equality of intelligence is not a scientifically proven fact, but, instead, a belief that should be verified. This belief is a type of faith, a political belief in the emancipation of the poor, drawn from a militant philosophy of the popular classes (Vermeren, 2017). This belief is based upon Jacotot's reading of authors like Descartes, Locke, and Newton. On this basis, he explains that the obvious intellectual inequalities that we observe in the social sphere, that is, between a rural farmer and a doctor or university professor, are not due to some sort of natural inequality between them, but due instead to the different stimuli that their intellects received over the course of their education.

For Jacotot, then, an education that liberates is only possible on the basis of the equality of intelligence: liberation only exists when all human beings are intellectually equal. The teacher who ignores this principle and places themselves above their students has by necessity stultified the students' intellectual capacity, leading to a morally insignificant interaction with people they see as inferior. Their students necessarily end up intellectually stultified as they learn and internalize this intellectual hierarchy that the teacher assumes and transmits. Conversely, a teacher who liberates transmits the equality of intelligence, which is the only thing needed to liberate someone. This creates confidence in their own intellectual capacity and in that of every human being.

When this universal teaching works, the teacher ignores what they are teaching and does not know what their student is learning. They are simply a companion who walks the path of learning with their students as fellow travelers, only watching over them so that they pay attention, while trying to ensure that their own will never fails to trust in their students' intellectual capacity (Vermeren, 2017; Rancière, 1991). Indeed, according to universal teaching, teachers must be ignorant on two levels: they must ignore what their student is learning, and, above all, they must ignore the inequality of intellect that the educational institution presupposes and is founded upon. This is the deeper meaning of their ignorance; it is a refusal, a non-acceptance.

In universal teaching, there is, in fact, no method for teaching or learning. The method belongs to the ones who teach and learn. The teacher's freedom to teach leads to the student's freedom to learn. And people who learn think and live freely. In an 1828 letter to the Marquis de Lafayette, Jacotot responds to interest in the United States in his way of teaching and practicing education:

> Any man who is taught is no more than half a man. Wherever schools exist, teachers exist. When the intellect is not free, I do not know what else could be free. I warn the Americans: it is possible to be independent without being free; independence is relative, and freedom is absolute. I am independent when I do not have a teacher, but it is still the work of another. I am free when I do not want a teacher, because then it is my own work. For this desire to be firm, stable, and unchangeable, one must feel its strength, all its strength, not only morally, but intellectually. (Jacotot, cited in Vermeren, 2017, p. 221)

Upon reading this passage from Jacotot's letter, it is impossible not to be reminded of "No one teaches anyone else" from Freire's chapter two of the *Pedagogy of the Oppressed* (Freire, 2005a, p. 80). Both proclaim the freedom of those who learn. In this case, Jacotot argues in favor of the absolute value of freedom, emanating from confidence in one's intellectual capacity; that is to say, a free person is one who considers themselves intellectually equal to anyone else. Where there exists the will of superior and inferior people there exists no freedom. The issue is not simply that the teacher should not set themselves up as a superior teacher. Rather, it is that the student must set themselves up as an equal. In a relationship based on oppression, both oppressors and the oppressed are oppressed, because the very relationship that has been established is an oppressive one. A free person does not want a teacher who stultifies them intellectually because their will trusts in their own intellectual capacity to learn. However, in order to not want that kind of teacher, it is necessary to experience one's own intellectual capacity to begin with.

Does this mean that Jacotot believes that we do not need teachers? Of course not. What Jacotot seems to mean is that an emancipated person does not want a teacher who merely explains things to them or who stultifies them intellectually. We do not need teachers who stultify us, we need teachers who emancipate those who have been stultified and facilitate a liberated relationship between liberated people. According to Jacotot's principle of equality of intelligence, then, we need teachers who help all people develop confidence in their own capacity and who accompany, along the course of their education, those who already have this confidence in themselves. Even among the emancipated, teachers remain important to help others maintain their confidence in their own intellectual capacity, to continue feeling their desire of freedom for themselves.

The Equality of Intellects in Brazil

Jacotot's approach was also known in Brazil. The Panecastic Institute of Brazil was created on May 3, 1847; its goal was "to propagate the immortal Jacotot's principles of intellectual emancipation and to substitute the rights of human reason for authority and pedantry" (Sciencia, 1 [3], 1847, p. 15).[1] One of the proponents of Jacotot's ideas in Brazil was the French homeopathic doctor Benoît Jules Mure, who left his attestation to what he called Jacotot's great principle: "God created the human soul capable of instructing itself, without resorting to teachers to explain [things]" and of the maxim that should orient intellectual labor: "The one who wants to is able to" (Sciencia, 2 [16], 1848, p. 194). What does

---

[1] Suzana Lopes de Albuquerque (2019) worked on the sources that verify the circulation of Jacotot's ideas in Brazil: letters from Castilho and the homeopathy newspaper *Sciencia*, digitized and available on the website of the Digital Newspaper Library of the National Library with its twenty-five editions, five being from 1847 and the others from 1848.

this mean? It means that the one who wants to do something is able to, but since not everyone wants to, and society seems to be inclined to do as much as it can to stop some people from wanting to, perhaps this is where there is space for a teacher who is concerned with education as intellectual emancipation. This work, however, would be an attempt to influence the wills of those who were taught by an unequal society to distrust their own capacity.

Mure proposed that the Panecastic Society develop a "University Plan for Brazil," intended to eliminate monarchical and Catholic principles, emancipate intellects, and elevate Brazil to "the highest pinnacle of knowledge and Enlightenment" (Sciencia, 1 [5], 1847, p. 82).[2] *Sciencia* held a dim view of both the plan itself and its prospects for success in Brazil. These studies highlight the virtues of the universal method (which in fact is not a method, because the learning processes are not prescribed, but rather depend on each person's free will) in the following way:

> This method not only offers the advantage of considerably shortening the time of instruction and making it more profitable, but also, of allowing every father to have his children learn what he himself ignores, it establishes a true equality among men. This is what should sear the name of Jacotot upon the heart of every true friend of humanity. Universal teaching is the method of the poor. (Sciencia, 2 (16), 1848, p. 195)

As we can see, the non-methodical method offers pedagogical advantages. It allows a reduction in the time of instruction and lets students desire to learn rather than being obligated to do so, as usually occurs. Ackermann also reveals the political value of Jacotot's teaching: above all, it serves the poor, the education of the common people, because through it an illiterate parent can teach their children to read,

---

[2] We also know that the first director of the Escuela Normal de Niterói, José da Costa Azevedo, was responsible for the development of a reading method based on the ideas of Jacotot (Albuquerque, 2019).

educate them, and emancipate them. It enables the sons and daughters of the poor and illiterate to learn with their parents what their parents never learned. A rich father or mother can pay for a teacher or a school for their children. However, a poor parent themselves, through universal education, can emancipate their own child. For this to happen, the only thing necessary is for the parents to themselves be emancipated.[3] Thus, universal teaching is the method of the poor, because it allows them to overcome the limitations of their own condition and to achieve the power which their intellect is capable of. Jacotot's universal teaching is revolutionary, which undoubtedly explains its lack of success in Brazil.

Jacotot and Freire

Despite the obvious differences between someone who lived in post-revolutionary France in the nineteenth century and someone who lived in Brazil during the Cold War, there are significant similarities between the ways Jacotot and Freire thought and lived education. As I have shown previously, Paulo Freire is part of a tradition of intellectuals who combine philosophy and pedagogy. This is also true of Joseph Jacotot. Upon the restoration of the Bourbon monarchy, he left France to teach in Louvain, in the Low Countries. To be sure, Jacotot was not forced to flee his country, his life does not seem to have been at risk, but, regardless, both Jacotot and Freire shared, as a result of their politically engaged lives, the experience of exile. For both, exile, however forced or unforced, was a political act that contributed decisively to their educational discoveries and practices, their philosophical bets,

---

[3] Jacotot's ideas could be appropriated by conservative discourse as a "way out" or "solution" for the forced removal of the public school: homeschooling would be a way of overcoming the institutional problems of that school, which would be generating unnecessary expenses and a misuse of the public coffers. However, this "exit," which would remove the responsibility for education from the State and delegate it to families or to the evangelical churches of the poorest communities, is in fact incompatible with the principles and meaning of the universal teaching of Jacotot.

and the political effects of these discoveries among the popular classes. Despite his exile, through difficulty and hardship, Freire had an experience that was ultimately positive. He came to value his exile, which he called an anchor, a song that helped him "connect recollections, recognize facts, deeds, and gestures, fuse pieces of knowledge, solder moments, *re*-cognize in order to *cognize*, know, better" (Freire, 1994, p. 18). Freire gave such importance to his own exile that he saw himself as having lived three exiles, not just one: the first in the uterus of his pregnant mother; the second when his family, beset by economic crisis, fled Recife for Jabotão dos Guararapes; and finally, the third exile abroad, in Bolivia, Chile, the United States, and Switzerland, imposed by the military dictatorship after the coup of 1964 (Freire, 2005b, p. 51).

Foreign languages also play a key role for both authors. For Jacotot, language played a decisive part in his discovery of the principle of the equality of intellects, through his exile in Louvain, where he was unable to speak his own language (French) with his Flemish-speaking students. Thus, it was through exile and the experience of being a foreigner that he was able to escape, once and for all, the comfortable role of a teacher who could explain things in his native language. It was the impossibility of using his own language to explain the things he knew from literature that allowed him to discover the secrets of intellectual liberation. This would not have been possible without his forced encounter with the foreign language of his Flemish students.

As we have seen, Paulo Freire was exiled more than once. Without a doubt, the most brutal of these exiles came after Brazil's 1964 military coup. Initially he went into exile in Bolivia, but soon after his arrival, a military coup there forced him to seek refuge in Chile, a move that he welcomed, due to his difficulties adapting to the altitude in La Paz. As a result, Freire's thought on liberation in his seminal work, *Pedagogy of the Oppressed*, would only be published in 1970 in English (New York: Herder and Herder), without the preface by Ernani Maria Fiori, but with an introduction by Richard Schaull and a preface by Freire himself. It was published in Spanish that same year (Montevideo: Tierra Nueva), also without Fiori's preface. Only later that year would it be published in Portuguese (São Paulo: Paz e Terra).[4] It is not that Freire needed to hear a foreign language to stimulate his thinking, or that his ideas can be separated from his pedagogical experience pre-1964. Rather, as a result of his experiences living in other countries, Freire had to translate himself, to express himself and communicate his ideas about emancipation in foreign languages. And according to Freire himself, exile played a decisive role both in helping him rethink Brazilian reality and in developing his pedagogy and his understanding of the political aspect of education (Shor and Freire, 1987, pp. 30–2). Thus, foreign languages and linguistic difference played a key role in the thought, writings, and lives of both Jacotot and Freire.

Another important coincidence is that both are commonly associated with methods: Jacotot with the universal method, and Freire with a method of literacy, teaching reading and writing to youths and adults. However, neither actually has anything like a method. To put this more radically, method is not one of the most important issues, instead it is the political meaning of using this or that method that matters. Although both are known because of their methods, methods are decisive for neither. For Jacotot, the method belongs to the student (Rancière, 1991, p. 14). For Freire, the transformation engendered by an education that liberates is not a question of method, but rather of establishing "a different relationship to knowledge and to society" (Shor and Freire, 1987, p. 35). Or, more specifically and in greater detail:

> We never spent very long studying adult literacy methods and techniques for their own sake, but look at them in relation to and in the service of a specific theory of knowledge applied in practice, which in its turn, must be consonant with a certain political stance. If the

---

[4] See Note on the editions of *Pedagogy of the Oppressed* in the fifty years commemorative edition (Freire, 2018a, pp. 25–6): In this regard, there is a discrepancy observed by the editors (Freire, 2018a, p. 25, n. 16) of this version examined in copies of the first edition with Freire himself in *Pedagogy of Hope* (1994), in which he affirms that the first edition in Portuguese would have been published in Brazil in 1975. The editors add that Paulo Freire must have received this information from the publisher of Paz e Terra and that, as both have already passed away, the issue cannot be resolved. For a more detailed study of the editions of *Pedagogy of the Oppressed*, see Brugaletta (2020).

educator has a revolutionary stance and if his practice is coherent with that stance, then the learner in adult literacy education is one of the Subjects of the act of knowing. It becomes the duty of the educator to search out appropriate paths for the learner to travel and the best assistance that can be offered so that the learner is enabled to exercise the role of Subject in relation to learning during the process of literacy education. The educator must constantly discover and rediscover these paths and make it easier for the learner to see the object to be revealed and, finally, learned as a problem. (Freire, 2016, p. 10)

There is no specific method for the revolutionary educator. Rather, there is a commitment to revolutionary politics that requires a concomitant educational practice dedicated to affirming human beings' equally inventive power, which renders the educator capable of opening up some of the possibilities of an education that liberates.

Following a point already raised by Rancière, another strong commonality between the authors is their political commitment to the liberation of common people. Both counter the positivist motto "Order and Progress" that is inscribed on Brazil's flag; both interrupt and interpellate the supposed harmony between the order of knowledge and the social order (Vermeren; Cornu and Benvenuto, 2003). In other words, both are critical regarding the role that pedagogical order might play in achieving a more just social order for the excluded. Therefore, both are suspicious of any order and progress originating with the traditional and status quo powers in their respective republics. To put it another way, they are skeptical of the pedagogical order imposed by positivist republics and each affirms the need to interrupt the exclusionary effects to produce emancipating, liberating effects in turn.

Regarding the main differences between Jacotot and Freire, we have seen, in part, how Rancière depicts them. For Rancière, nothing is more alien to Jacotot than a method to achieve social "conscientization" (Vermeren; Cornu and Benvenuto, 2003). Differently from Freire, Jacotot asserts that equality can only happen between individuals, but that it is impossible to institutionalize or propagate it as a form of social emancipation. However, as we have also seen, although intellectual emancipation is only possible individually, there is no social emancipation that does not presuppose individual emancipation. Thus, Jacotot's pessimistic anarchism does approach Freire's optimistic progressivism, though, as Rancière suggests, "a process of intellectual emancipation as a vector for movements of political emancipation that break with a social and institutional logic" (Vermeren; Cornu and Benvenuto, 2003, p. 199). Freire himself suggests something similar, even as he implicitly criticizes Jacotot's merely intellectual and individual conception of emancipation. In his book with Ira Shor, he claims not to believe in individual liberation or emancipation and appears reluctant to endorse any individual, rather than social, feeling of freedom. But, like Jacotot, he considers the former a precondition for the latter (Shor and Freire, 1987). In Freire's words:

> While individual empowerment or the empowerment of some students, the feeling of being changed, is not enough concerning the transformation of the whole society, it is *absolutely necessary* for the process of social transformation. Is this clear? The critical development of these students is absolutely fundamental for the radical transformation of society. Their curiosity, their critical perception of reality, is fundamental for social transformation but is not enough by itself. (Shor and Freire, 1987, p. 110)

The point could not be any clearer. Although Jacotot championed individual emancipation and asserted that this was the horizon of what was possible, both his life and the application of his ideas made him ever more pessimistic about their social application. On the other hand, Paulo Freire, although he also encountered enormous difficulties to put his ideas into practice, never stopped believing that the social emancipation of the oppressed was the primary meaning not only of his own life but also of the life of any educator. Without this social application, emancipation would have little value for Freire. Moreover, the emancipation that Freire has in mind is not just intellectual or cognitive, but economic, social, and political, with all the complexities and difficulties that the relationship between education and society entails and encompasses.

At any rate, conscientization is not a simple concept in Freire's thought. Its main point is to know whether the fullest or most critical consciousness belongs to the educator. (And if it ever did, the pedagogical relationship would not be very emancipatory). How far does the educator lead their students, or do they only contribute to a form of consciousness that they can neither anticipate nor control? In this way, if we think that there is such a thing as settled historical knowledge, for example, historical materialism, which in some way exists *a priori* to educators' and students' own knowledge, the political consequences of this logic are not especially promising for the pedagogical relationship. In other words, if the educator already knows what is necessary to achieve the emancipation of those who are being educated, we could question the value of such an emancipation. In a recent book, Freire's foremost disciple, Moacir Gadotti, combines conscientization with the equality of intelligence as a principle that allows every human being to express their own word (Gadotti and Carnoy, 2018).

For his part, Freire seems to have gone back and forth on this question. For example, in his book-length interview with Ira Shor, he states that the role of the educator who liberates is "directing a serious study of some object in which students reflect on the intimacy of how an object exists" (Shor and Freire, 1987, p. 171). Freire calls this position radically democratic, because it simultaneously takes a gamble on freedom, it does not abdicate the teacher's role in guiding their students, but, even so, it does not deny students their freedom, inasmuch as it trusts in their capacity to think. The conscientizing work of the educator is not about transmitting knowledge that liberates, but rather in stimulating students' own thought so they can "unveil the actual manipulation and myths in society" (Shor and Freire, 1987, p. 172). Of course, if the actual manipulation and myths in society are known in advance by the educator and can only be explained in terms of certain categories and theoretical models (which Freire's own terminology appears to assume), we could question just how much they actually do trust in educators' and students' equal capacity.

In Freire's later works the idea of conscientization becomes less prominent, since by this point he seems to be more skeptical regarding the explanatory power of a revolutionary theory and more receptive to a conversation that is open to other forms of knowledge. The certainties in Freire's texts gradually diminish and, by the end of his work, appear closer to a series of relational principles, like equality, and less situated in the explanatory theories of reality he favored earlier.

Finally, we can return to our initial concern and the common points between Jacotot and Freire inasmuch as they both affirm equality as a principle, not only in their thought and writings but also in their lives. Let us examine how this happens. There is a story about Jacotot worth recalling. He received an emissary sent from Paris to Louvain by the Paris Society of Methods to learn about his educational proposals.

> Before speaking about this, I would like to emphasize that I do not see in you anything more than a curiosity seeker, which is why I place you in the fourth line. If a poor person, a person from the countryside, or a father came to me, he would pass in front of you. (Vermeren, 2017, p. 211)

This story shows us that Jacotot lived the very equality that he affirmed and in which he believed. In the same way, Freire describes several situations in which this same vital feeling of equality can be observed. For example, when he refers to the lectures he gave during the time he worked at the Industrial Social Service (Serviço Social da Indústria— SESI), he relates an event that happened in a SESI center in Recife when, after he had spoken about Piaget, a factory worker gave what he called a class lesson, demonstrating how Freire's academic discourse belonged to someone from a different social class and was very distant from the class that was listening to him. Freire states, "This talk was given about thirty-two years ago. I have never forgotten it" (Freire, 1994, p. 26). This demonstrates that his belief in equality, the word he uses in the following quote, in which he comments on the great influence this experience had on his entire subsequent pedagogical trajectory, was always dear to him.

> Nearly always, in academic ceremonies in which I have had an honorary doctorate conferred on me by some university, I acknowledge how much I owe, as well, to persons like the one of whom I am now

speaking, and not only to scholars—other thinkers who have taught me, *too*,[5] and who continue to teach me, teachers without whom it would have been impossible for me to learn, like the laborer who spoke that night. (Freire, 1994, p. 24, emphasis mine)

In many other books (including, among others Freire and Betto, 1985; Freire and Faundez, 1989; Freire and Guimarães, 1982), Freire describes similar situations from around the world. A factory worker is a thinker equal to and perhaps greater than any scientist, inasmuch as, as in the episode just discussed, they teach a knowledge about life that intersects with a political condition that can never be learned in an academic ivory tower. No longer is the teacher the one who society legitimates as the official transmitter of knowledge, but rather the one who knows life's knowledge for having lived it. Factory workers do not teach an institutional knowledge, but rather a knowledge for a shared life. It is a form of knowledge indissolubly tied to a collective existence, which reveals its truth and its secret intellectual capabilities that these very societal institutions routinely attempt to disguise or belittle.

The Value of Equality in Education

Therefore, inspired by Jacotot and Freire, we can proclaim that equality is an important and crosscutting principle for a democratic politics of the pedagogical relationship. This equality is claimed as a principle or starting point, not as a goal or objective, and intersects with several areas: intellectual life and capacity, but also knowledge, thought, affection, and even that which is not known. The issue of knowledge is crucial for Freire, and the equality of knowledge can easily but mistakenly be equated with an emptiness of the pedagogical role. Political equality, however, means that although teachers and students

---

[5] In Portuguese, Paulo Freire uses the word "igualmente," which, translated more literally, is "equally."

occupy different relative positions of power, hierarchy need not follow from this difference. Their knowledge can have distinct epistemological or aesthetic value and meaning, but this has no relation to the people who possess that knowledge. No form of knowledge has more legitimacy than any other as a result of the position of power occupied by the people who employ it in the pedagogical relationship.

In absurdly unequal societies like ours, there may indeed exist unequal political effects outside of the pedagogical relationship, but never within it. Neither teachers nor students, while they occupy these roles, can accomplish more than each other as a result of what they do or do not know. This is what Freire teaches: to teach and learn in dialogue, all forms of knowledge deserve to be heard and treated equally, they are placed within dialogue on the same level. And it is precisely in this dialogue than an educator teaches and learns, reconstructing their own knowledge through the knowledge of their students.[6]

As Freire claims in the passage included as the epigraph to this chapter, the need to postulate equality is born of the confirmation of the differences among all forms of life. If we were not different, equality would be unnecessary. But our societies are made of differences and inequalities. It is inequality, not difference, that is opposed to equality. It is inequality that inhibits a pedagogical relationship based on dialogue, not differences. Differences, when based on equality, nourish dialogue and make it possible.

Freire strongly emphasizes the issue of knowledge for an emancipatory perspective on education. To be clear, I am not arguing that knowledge is not important to Freire. I am simply noting that if we place an emphasis on thought, then, inspired by Jacotot, affirmation of the equality of intelligence for all human beings as a principle of education is strengthened. In this way, an egalitarian understanding of teachers' and students' capacity to think becomes a necessary political

---

[6] In an interview included as an appendix to this book, another advocate of equality as a principle, Esther Pilar Grossi, Freire's friend and a well-known researcher in literacy, expresses her concerns about how Freire's ideas were applied. See p. 196

condition for those who participate in this educational practice to manifest their equally critical capacity in a coherent way and call into question a given state of affairs.

To be sure, all lives are different, or, rather, the life that permeates existence reveals itself in different ways in human beings, animals, and plants. To educate means to listen, to respect, all while remaining attentive to these sacred differences. Without them, life would be less alive. The political principle of the equality of all lives who are part of an educational practice is a requirement for differences to be enriching and not soul-crushing, to lead in a politically democratic direction so that education can help enable these existences to manifest all the life that they are and contain.

3

Love

Our third principle: to educate is an act of love. "The more you love, the more you love" (Freire in Gadotti, 2001, p. 54). The more you educate, the more you love. By loving more, you educate more. Love is a lifeforce: love for the world, for life, and love of the place you inhabit when you educate. Political love is to live a life in order to expand it, and to never limit it.

> Thus a teacher is a teacher whereas a parent (coddling or not) remains a parent. It is possible to be a parent without loving one's children, without even liking being a parent, but it is not possible to be a teacher without loving one's students, even realizing that love alone is not enough. It is not possible to be a teacher without loving teaching. (Freire, 2005b, p. 28)

> I would like to be remembered as a person who deeply loved the world and its people, animals, trees, waters, life. (Freire, 1997)

> Love is always the possibility of being present at the birth of the world. (Badiou and Truong, 2012, p. 26)

Paulo Freire was a passionate and dedicated reader with a deep love and respect for books. Of the numerous authors he studied, perhaps none garnered greater attention from him than Erich Fromm. Freire did not read Fromm in a passive way; he was also deeply inspired by Fromm's ideas. Keeping this affinity for Fromm in mind, we can say that, on the macro-political level of affects, Freire, the patron saint of Brazilian education, embodied the three dimensions of love that, according to Fromm (1963), allow one to say that they are masters in the art of loving. These dimensions are threefold: theoretical knowledge, practice, constant concern. Freire knew the art of love, practiced it, and cared for it because he considered taking care of this art of loving as essential to being a good educator. In what follows, we will examine and justify this affirmation of love.

There are innumerable accounts of loving gestures that accompany the life of Freire, witnessed by students and teachers from all over the world.[1] As we have seen, his life entailed both a theory or system of ideas along with what we will refer to here as "pedagogical eros."[2] Judging by the feelings he inspired wherever he placed himself, he was no doubt an extraordinary figure who emitted great charisma and emotive force. He carried with him a strongly loving pedagogical energy which permeated and fortified his educational theories. Without this force of eros, nothing which Freire wrote would have been read the way it was read, or activated the feelings that it still, to this day, two decades after his death, provokes. This is like no other educator before or after him and inspired his constant study and rethinking of education.

---

[1] The testimonies are collected in various documents. Among them, cf. Biobibliography, edited by Moacir Gadotti and Carlos Alberto Torres (2001), published for the first time in Brazil in 1996. Among the innumerable books abroad, I suggest *Memories of Paulo*, edited by Wilson, Park, and Colón-Muñiz (2010), which gathers testimonies from the 1960s until the death of Freire. In the preface, Macedo states: "Paulo was a special friend, a refined human being, a lovingly militant intellectual, whose death leaves a turbulent void in our hearts. At the same time, his passion and compassion will always guide and define our collective struggle to eradicate hatred, to the extent that we embrace what he always and attentively shared with us: LOVE" (Wilson et al., 2010, p. xiii).

[2] That is the title of an excellent book by Miguel Escobar Guerrero, *La pedagogía erótica: Paulo Freire y el EZLN* (2012). In this book, similarities between Paulo Freire and the Zapatista movement are presented, based on what the author himself calls "political psychoanalysis." It is not only a theoretical study but also a practice of Freirean inspirations at the Pedagogical College of the National Autonomous University of Mexico, from a direct and intense contact with Freire. The concept of autonomy is a common point between Freire and the EZLN; for both, "the fight for autonomy is essential in the individual and collective construction of the human being" (Escobar, 2012, p. 48). Perhaps the following paragraph synthesizes the main intention of the author: "The Erotic Pedagogy proposal, therefore, is a proposal to bring the eroticism of Eros to life, as an invitation to fight against his adversary Thanatos, who, within the model capitalist globalization of war, has opened the way to the most primitive parts of the human being, combined in their political power of destruction: in the eroticism of Thanatos" (Escobar, 2012, p. 159).

The Love of the Stranger

The reactionary project is always the defence of "our values," casting us in the mould of worldwide capitalism as the only possible identity. The impulse driving reaction is Always a crude reference to identity in one form or another. Now, when the logic of identity wins the day, love is under threat.

(Badiou and Truong, 2012, pp. 97–8)

Here, as we have done before, we can again look to Socrates for inspiration. This time to think of the life filled with eros. Socrates, if we abide by the characteristics listed above, was a master of eros. It bears repeating that we are not trying to brush over differences in historical and social context, nor are we suggesting some sort of immaculate Freirean model character. The aim here is to listen to some echoes of the past that help us flesh out what we are trying to think. Quite reasonably, one could ask, "Socrates, a master of love?" Well, love, as it turns out, is the only thing that Socrates claims to know. The person who claims to know nothing, ends up, at the beginning of Plato's *Symposium*, claiming that the only thing they know is love (*ta erotika*, 177 d). In Ancient Greek, "*ta erotika*" expresses in the neuter plural the adjective "*erotikos*," which means "all regarding love."

How is it possible that this never generated a scandal? How can it be that the one who claimed that he "only knows that he knows nothing" also claim in one dialogue to know something? Is it true that Socrates did not know only nothing? How is it that Socrates can so casually claim to know something about love and still defend himself against the accusations of heresy in the *Apology* by arguing that the principle God of Athens, Apollo, affirmed that he is the wisest person in Athens because he knows that he knows nothing? Mind you, this is in the same dialogue where Socrates defends himself against the accusation of corrupting the youth by claiming that he is the master of no one. So how is it possible that the same Socrates now affirms he knows something about love? All of this adds to the enigma of Socrates, his mysteries and paradoxes (Kohan, 2015b). Nonetheless, by thinking through some of the aspects of this paradox, we can perhaps make greater sense of the enigma.

It is worth reviewing some details here. While making his speech, his eulogy to love during the *Symposium*, Socrates claim to knows something about love. Intriguingly, it is Diotima, a foreign priestess of Mantineia, who taught Socrates what he knows of love (*eme ta erotika edídaxen, Symposium* 201, d). The singularity of Socrates is, once again, on full display here. What he knows about love was learned from a foreign woman who taught him about love and loving, through a careful process of interrogation (*Symposium*, 201 e). That he tells this story to a room full of Athenian men is noteworthy. What is also remarkable is the way he tells the story. Through a dialogue thick with eros, Socrates embodies the lesson he learned from Diotima. Thinking with others in this way is a way of cultivating loving relationships with them in itself. The affective form of the retelling of the story contributes to the content that is learned.

Socrates understands that people learn from conversing with him. This happens with and through their passion and his way of loving others, his way of relating to his own thoughts that he questions; that is, the way he problematizes everything that he thinks. In other words, his is a pedagogy of eros that educates through philosophical questions. To be sure, not everyone appreciated this eros, and often it was not received with love, but this too adds to the enigma of Socrates, the enigma of his pedagogical eros.

Socrates' love of thinking with others about the problems of the city is ultimately an example of the philosophical life we have already described. As such, there is no contradiction between declaring to not know anything and claiming to know how to love at the same time. The knowing nothing that Socrates wants to affirm has to do with the knowledge that the Athenians, who are supposedly in the know, want to transmit to others. Socrates does not know, and does not want to know, the content of that which will be taught. He does not want to be in the know. His only desire is to have the knowledge of a relation, which is the only knowledge he cannot live without. This is the passion that exists in a type of encounter with others through dialogue. This is the only knowledge that Socrates knows: the knowledge, or relation to knowledge, that is identical to the knowledge or relation to knowledge that he calls philosophy. This turns out to be one of the characteristics of eros as Socrates presents it. Eros, we come to understand, is a philosopher that exists between wisdom and ignorance.

Somewhat ironically, Socrates learns how to love to think with the privileged men of Athens from a foreign woman. Such is the way of a philosophical life. An impossible figure teaches another impossible character on how to live the impossible life. For Diotima is as impossible as Socrates, both are completely out of place in their time, strangers in their own cities (*Phaedo*, 230 d), these places where everyone wants to teach and have attributed to their names the title of Master. Socrates rejects this place for himself, and is, instead, and before anything else, a "lover of wisdom."

It is in this way, through an invisible, unexpected, and unrealizable pedagogy that philosophy is born in Socrates along with the love that Plato had for his impossible master. Impossible, but necessary and undeniable. Socrates refused the role of "Master," and yet he did nothing less throughout his whole life than to initiate others into philosophy in a loving manner. This philosophical pedagogy was so vital to him that a life without it would not have been worth living, not only for Socrates himself but for others as well (*Apology*, 38 a). So impossible is this philosophical and educational life that it can only be lived in a way that it leads those who want to live it, by teaching philosophy, to be condemned to death.

Both necessary and impossible, the Socratic life of love for educational philosophy is the only life worth living. Let us recall how Socrates, in the Apology, refuses the offer from his accusers to be declared innocent if he would only renounce his philosophical life. Here he affirms that the only life worth living is the same life that cannot be lived in the *polis*. And we know what happens: Socrates is found guilty of living a philosophical life and is condemned to death. This is the paradox that the enigma of Socrates passes on to those who live a life dedicated to a philosophical education: without it, life is not worth living, but living it can only lead to one's death.

The Pedagogical Eros of Paulo Freire

Principally three. First, there is the romantic interpretation that focuses on the ecstasy of the encounter. Secondly . . . the interpretation based on a commercial or legalistic perspective, which argues that love must in the end be a contract. . . . Finally there is the skeptical interpretation that turns loves into an illusion. My own philosophical view is attempting to say that love cannot be reduced to any of these approximations and is a quest for truth. What kind of truth? you will ask. I mean truth in relation to something quite precise: what kind of world does one see when one experiences it from the point of view of two and not one? What is the world like when it is experienced, developed and lived from the point of view of difference and not identity?

(Badiou and Truong, 2012, pp. 21–2)

Paulo Freire recreates the imperceptible, unexpected, and impossible pedagogical eros of Socrates. One of the great lessons we have received from Freire is that eros is as impossible as it is necessary for living a life full of love, which is a life that can never be fully realized, and yet, remains the only life worth living. This lesson is undeniably present in Freire's pedagogy and in his written works performed from *The Pedagogy of the Oppressed* to *The Pedagogy of Autonomy*. This lesson runs throughout his work from the very beginning in an assertive, affirmative, and categorical way. Even in one of his earliest books, *Education, the Practice of Freedom* (Freire, 1976b), eros is already present. There he defines oppression as a violent relation that is both "unloving and an obituary to love" (Freire, 1976b, n. 14, p. 50).[3] Against it he positions a radical form of dialogue that is critical, confident, courageous, humble, and full of faith, but, more than anything, it is loving (Freire, 1973, p. 10), because to educate is an act of love (p. 38). Thiago de Mello perhaps put it best, when he wrote "A Song for Joy," a poem dedicated to Freire while he was exiled in Chile: love is the music of the thought and life of Paulo Freire, who is made of a song of rebellion and joy.[4]

In *Pedagogy of the Oppressed*, love grounds action, and is a condition for truth, for the oppressed and their oppressors. In the case of oppressors, it measures the true solidarity of their actions (Freire, 2018a, p. 56). The rebellion of the oppressed, on the other hand, is full of love and inaugurates an authentic existence of freedom and passage from the love of death, to the love of life. To love life, the world, and the people that inhabit it is positioned as a condition of a dialogue that declares the creation and recreation of the world. Love and dialogue are expressions of courage and commitment to others for Freire in *Pedagogy of the Oppressed*. It is a committed act that is both necessary for the liberation of the oppressed, and which makes loving more possible in turn because love is not possible when oppression is present (p. 3). Citing Che Guevara, Freire reminds us that all true revolutions are born out of love and, therefore, can only be loving acts (p. 189).[5]

It is worth recalling here the final lines of *Pedagogy of the Oppressed*, "If nothing else remains of these pages, something, at the

[3] This expression does not exist in the only available English translation. The closest equivalent is where presumably the same phrase is translated as "things cannot love" (Freire, 1973, p. 11, n. 9). The expression in the original would be read as follows: "unloving and an obituary to love."

[4] The poem by Thiago de Mello is included in the Brazilian edition of *Education as Practice of Freedom* (Freire, 1976b, pp. 27–8), but was not included in the only available English translation (Freire, 1973).

[5] The references to Guevara in relation to love are many. For example, see Freire (2018b, p. 131), where he also relates another revolutionary, Amílcar Cabral, with love. Likewise, he also relates Che Guevara with Cabral in a dialogue with Faundez, in which he shows how they never renounced a communion with the popular masses (Freire and Faundez, 1989, p. 28 ff.).

very least, we hope will endure: our trust in the people. Our faith in people to create a world where it is less difficult to love" (Freire, 2018a, p. 92).[6] Pay close attention: faith is conceived of here as the belief that it is possible to create a world in which it is easier to love. This is the vital and indispensable passion that runs throughout the entire book and, also, the life and work of Freire. His most cherished pedagogical belief, found in his theory, philosophy, and practice, is this: through education it is possible to create a world in which it is less difficult to love. And this is also the most unnegotiable and undeniable political force which enables him to reveal that capitalism is unacceptable for many reasons, one of which is that it makes a true love impossible.

There is practically not a single book, letter, or interview of Freire's in which love is not present. In the letters that make up *Teachers as Cultural Workers: Letters to Those Who Dare Teach* (Freire, 2005b), love is mentioned alongside humility as one of the key conditions of being an educator. Humility here is positioned not only as a moral virtue that measures self-worth but also as an open, flexible, and critical relation to knowledge. In this way, it is a form of Socratic humility. Being humble is a requirement of all educators who respect themselves as well as those whom they educate. It is an acceptance of fallibility, limitation, and epistemological uncertainty. Freirean humility is a condition that opens up possibilities for hearing what anyone has to say, for acknowledging that everyone has knowledge to share and that we have all ignored some things worth attending to. His is a form of humility that makes possible relations among equals, among incomplete beings who desire to know and be more than they are.

---

[6] This final sentence (along with the final five paragraphs of the original Portuguese) of *Pedagogy of the Oppressed* is not included in the only available English translation. On other occasions, Freire refers positively to a world "where it is easier to love." For example, in the preface of a book by the Mexican Miguel Escobar: "The dream of a world in which loving is easier, of a world that is born from a deep and radical 'no' to the neoliberal project" (Freire in Escobar, 2012, p. 50). However, there the refusal appears in rejection of the neoliberal project.

It is because of this type of humility that "Teachers first learn how to teach, but they learn how to teach as they teach something that is relearned as it is being taught" (Freire, 2005b, p. 32). This reveals how, for Freire, the relationship between teaching and learning is complex and multidirectional. The loving teacher learns what she teaches before she teaches it, in order to teach it, but she also learns or relearns what she teaches as she teaches, so that she can relearn it and teach it again. This process is repeated incessantly. Thus, in a certain way, learning has epistemic and pedagogic priority over teaching, and it is necessary to love learning to teach what one teaches. If we do not love to learn it is not possible to teach, because one cannot teach if one is not learning.

As we can see, the relationship between the love of teaching and the love of learning is complex, multifaceted, and intertwined. The love of teaching needs to nurture the love of learning, and the love of learning needs to nurture the love of teaching; both acts are nurtured by love. Those who teach with love not only learn what they teach, they also learn to love to teach by teaching. Pedagogical love is transformative: the one who loves to teach is transformed by teaching and can never teach in the same way again after learning to love how to teach. In teaching, one learns. In learning, one learns to love teaching in a form that opens the teacher to other ways of being a teacher.

The commonsense logic of education is inverted here: the first principle of the educator becomes the last, and the last the first. What is usually the easiest becomes the most difficult and the most difficult becomes the easiest. Every educator needs to love their love of learning and teaching, but the love of learning is the first condition for the proper love of teaching.

In Brazil and elsewhere, public school teachers teach in conditions that regularly threaten their dignity. For example, in the municipality of Duque de Caxias, a mid-sized city outside of Rio de Janeiro, as well as in many other cities in Brazil, teachers are constantly disrespected at the job, violated in a variety of ways, and they often perform unpaid labor when their salaries are delayed.[7] The schools they work in, and the students that attend these schools, are equally neglected and disrespected. One must wonder in admiration how teachers continue to provide a genuine education under such conditions, where they are treated with so little love. How do they continue to love a pedagogical world that has been neglected for decades, that has been left to decay? Given these conditions, how would it be possible to teach without loving what you teach, without loving the place that you teach, the ground you walk on, and the students you work with? Love, for Freire, is the condition that we cannot do without. As we read in the epigraph that began this chapter, education, teaching, and learning are simply impossible without love.

In this sense, love is not just passion or affection for the other. Loving students means loving the position they occupy and the educational relationship. The very posture of the teacher, in this sense, is loving a common world that can be built from this amorous pedagogical relationship. For that it is necessary to breathe under dignified conditions, to feel respected, and, in turn, to respect the profession. Therefore, teaching emerges as a loving act in multiple ways. An educator loves to teach their teaching, yes, but also the teaching of the one who learns, and the world in which they teach. In addition, the teacher also loves to learn their learning, along with the learning of those who learn from them. This teacher loves to rethink themself permanently and loves to help others to rethink themselves, too; they also love to present themselves with openness, availability, curiosity, uncertainty. This properly amorous teacher loves the curiosity of others.

The value of love transcends a passion or affect for the other. To love students, for Freire, means to love the position one inhabits in an educational relation, the unique position of one who teaches, and of

---

[7] In Caxias, the Nucleus of Studies of Philosophies and Childhoods of the State University of Rio de Janeiro has coordinated a project since 2007 of philosophical experimentation in teacher education. We have been in touch with a significant number of teachers and schools from that district since the project's inception.

one who loves a world that can be constructed in common through an amorous pedagogical relation.

To Love Knowing, Knowing to Love

Educating is a way of loving. If education is in crisis, then love as a relationship is also in crisis. They correspond to one another. It is not a question of seeking attractions for students or reflexivity in the teacher to supply sense and meaning to a relationship that is lost and confused. The tale of knowledge, to be the voice of knowledge, is not a reflection upon oneself, or autobiography. Rather, it is a question of becoming reflection, a voice in which the other, the other who learns, is reflected, looking inside as she is looked at by the voice that listens.[8]

(Ferraro, 2010, p. 24)

Inspired by Socratic and Freirean love, what is under discussion is the philosopher-teacher's knowledge of love. This teacher is someone who knows how to love, and they affirm a philosophical pedagogy by living the love they know. According to Giuseppe Ferraro (2010), this is the true meaning of the word philosophy. Traditionally, philosophy is translated as "the love of wisdom" (*philo-sophia*), but it can also be translated as "the wisdom of love." In this translation, which seems a more accurate one, as both Socrates and Freire demonstrate, philosophy means to have knowledge of love, and to know how to love.[9]

---

[8] In the original Italian: "Educare è un modo di amare e se è in crisi l'educazione è in crisi anche la relazione d'amore. Si corrispondono. Non si tratta di cercare attrattive per gli allievi o riflessività nell'insegnante per ridare senso a una relazione che si perde e si confonde. Il racconto del sapere, farsi voce del sapere non è la riflessione su di sé, né l'autobiografia. Si tratta di farsi piuttosto riflessione, voce in cui l'altro, l'altra, che apprende si riflette, guardandosi dentro come è guardata dalla voce che ascolta."

[9] With philosophy thus conceived, many questions arise about their situation at school: how do we know if someone is sentimentally educated? What are the educational conditions for someone to become an educator of feelings? Is it enough to feel like a philosopher to be able to teach philosophy (or with philosophy)?

The Italian philosopher and professor Ferraro helps us to ponder the value of love in Freire. In his book, *A scuola dei sentimenti* (*The School of Feelings*, 2010), Ferraro reveals the differences between passion, emotion, and feeling. The first we possess, the second we give, but both are transient, ephemeral. Different from these two, feelings are made of time. It is precisely for this reason they can be educated, because they endure in time. Moreover, they must be educated because they are created in the time of relationships, in the bonds that make up who we are as people. They are woven into the embodied social relations that we affirm. Any educative practice that aims to affect institutional life must educate in the ways feelings are woven together.

According to Ferraro, those who teach restore an inner time that was once formed alongside others. When they teach, they give others this time while forming a different one. Thus, teaching restores a time that differs from the institutionalized chronological time of schools. This time is suspended as another temporality is attended to, a time that is created through chords struck in loving relations between people, a time that transcends chronology. This is the time that education needs to care for: the time of feelings, the time of love, the time of philosophy, of the love of wisdom, and, more importantly, the wisdom of love.

In previously published work, I have discussed the differences between the three ways time was conceived in ancient Greece (Kohan and Kennedy, 2008; Kohan, 2016). Briefly stated, chronos is the time of watches, the time that marks the movement between a before and after. It is the time that does not stop. Chronos consists of two elements, the past and future. The present is situated as a moment between the two. It is the time of science, of institutions, of history. Kairos, on the other hand, is the time of opportunity, the precise moment that is singular, unique, non-replaceable and fleeting. Finally, aion is the time of infancy, of the present, and the eternal return. It is the time of play, of thought, of art, of philosophy, and of love. We love in the time of aion, the time of the present, of presence, of giving, of art.

Knowing how to love is the primary principle of a radical education. One must know how to encounter, within the institutional time of chronos—a way to suspend the institutionalized time of school in order to inhabit the time that constitutes a school as school (Masschelein and Simons, 2013). If a school does not create the possibilities to feel this liberated time, then a school is not a school. Even if it forms the "best" citizens, those whom society needs and desires, if it does not do what schools have done since the birth of schools, if the school does not suspend socially regulated time so that those in it can access the time they need to ponder the world they live in, then it is not truly a school.

Love as a feeling is so important to education that, as Ferraro affirms, without an education of feelings education is not possible, because love, and all feelings speaking more generally, is the proper way to inhabit the world, to share the world with others. Feelings offer the tone, rhythm, and measure of life. One can learn to read, to write, or any of the disciplines like mathematics, history, geography, but if we do not learn how to inhabit our relationships that we live, with the proper feelings, then what difference does it make, what vital significance does the learned knowledge have? For this reason, to educate in feelings is to aid a person in building a temporality; it enables someone to come to be within a web of relationships and bonds that constitute who we are and what we can be.

Considered in this way, education becomes an artistic, musical, and philosophical work of feeling. It involves the work of listening to another's voice transmitted through words, creating the conditions for all to compose their proper melody so that, together, we can feel the music that genuinely composes who we are. Moreover, philosophy, as we have already affirmed, is a lived experience of a feeling for wisdom and, at the same time, a wisdom of feelings. And it is this wisdom that we learn in school when a school is more than an institution, when it is philosophical in the most proper sense of the word. Philosophy is therefore an irreplaceable possibility of an educational practice that allows education to truly become educational, and in the process, it also allows people to encounter and inhabit who they really are becoming and who they might be.

As we have seen, and as Ferraro emphasizes, philosophy carries within its very name, it's etymology, a feeling: "*philo-sophia*," the feeling of wisdom, and the wisdom of feeling. When one teaches philosophy, one does not know something, they feel wisdom, they feel the proper time to think and know with others. They know in the same way that one knows the flavor of a dish. One knows how to love because one tastes love. As such, an education is only philosophical insofar as it is an education in, and of, feelings. Philosophy, Ferraro maintains, is not something that can be taught in school, one does not teach philosophy, rather when a school is a school (*schole*), one teaches with philosophy. The value resides not in the fact that it is a discipline, but rather in that it is a knowledge of feelings. When conceived of in this way, one can teach any discipline with or without philosophy, including the discipline of philosophy itself.

Ferraro's elaboration of an education of feeling can illuminate and inspire the love that Freire affirmed through his work and life. In this way, his ideas on education can be read as an affirmation of the philosophical education just presented: one who is taught with the knowledge of feelings, and the wisdom of feelings that makes up philosophy. In chapter 1, I argued that Freire belongs to the philosophical tradition in which philosophy is much more than just a theory or system of ideas. The lines traced above reinforce this idea. It was not only his ideas but also the way of life that Freire lived that created a school (*schole*) of feelings. A school which lovingly affirms an education in feeling and a search for time in which everyone and anyone can have their own time to be who they are, rather than have time imposed on them to meet the conditions of social and economic existence. In other words, Freire dedicated his life to those who no one else listened to, so that they could hear their own voices and express their own words with their own voices.

Political Love

The essence of politics can be subsumed in the question: what are individuals capable of when they meet, organize, think and take decisions? In love, it is about two people being able to handle differ-

ence and make it creative. In politics, it is about finding out whether a
number of people, a mass of people in fact, can create equality.
(Badiou and Truong, 2012, pp. 53–4)

Love also has political elements; it is a militant warrior. It requires
struggle, commitment, and boldness. It is worth citing in full the poem
"Song of an Armed Love" (1979) by Thiago de Mello, the Amazonian
poet who served as Brazil's cultural attaché in Chile in 1964, during
the Brazilian military dictatorship, while Freire was in exile in the
country. His poetry inspires a thought and form of living with love that
is indispensable for education.

"A Song of an Armed Love"

Morning came in the summer wind,
and rapidly it happened.
It is better to not tell who it was or how it happened,
because another story comes that will stay.
It was today and it was here, on the homeland floor,
where the ballot hidden like a kiss
at the beginning of love, universal
like the bird's flight—the vote was always
A sacred duty and right.
Suddenly it was no longer sacred,
suddenly it's not a right anymore,
suddenly it's no longer the vote.
It is no longer everything.
It is no longer an encounter and a path,
It is no long a civic duty,
It is no longer passionate and beautiful
It is no longer a weapon—it has become a weapon,
because the ballot is no longer the people's.
It is no longer the people's vote and it is not,
And nothing happened, but nothing?
Suddenly nothing happened.
No one knows the time

when the people must sing.
But they really sing at the end.
Because they have no vote anymore,
That is not why the people
will stop their singing,
nor will they cease to be persons.
They may have lost their vote,
that was their powerful arm.
But they have not lost their duty
nor their right as people,
which is to always have their arms,
Always within the reach of their hand.
The people's song is of peace,
when they have arms that guard
the joy of their bread.
If it is no longer that of the ballot,
that was taken for treason,
another must be, and whatever
it will be, it doesn't cost the people to know,
no one ever knows the time
that the people have to come.
The people know, I don't know.
I just know it is a duty,
I only know it is a right.
Now it is sacred:
each one has their own weapon
for when the time comes
to defend, more than life,
the song within life,
to defend the flame
of lighted freedom
deep in my heart.
Each one has their own,
any weapon, even
something light and innocent
like this poem in which sings

the voice of the people—a simple song
of love.
But of armed love.
Which is the same love. Only now
with no vote, love sings
in any desired tone
whenever in the defence
of your right to love.
The people, they are not why
it will stop singing.

The 1960s were years of utopian revolutions in the South American continent. They were also the years of repression and dictatorship. These were times of resistance and struggle for a world that would be a little less unjust, a bit oppressive, just a bit less atrocious. They were years of politicized love, a committed and militant love. It was a time to fight for a more loving world. In this context, love was indeed armed in defense of the right to love. Love was, and is, a weapon of those who teach in defense of teaching.

In such a context the loving philosophy of an educator is neither disingenuous, romantic, or abstract. It is political, war-like, and situated. The poem cited above speaks to the situation in contemporary Brazil, which is also marked by eviction, coups, dictatorship, and the usurpation of popular power. In the context of the poem (1966), which is so like the contemporary moment, the poet invites one to resist with whatever weapons one has, including the "light and innocent" weapon of a word, a poem, any act of love. One could even resist a question that puts everything into doubt. An armed love leads one to the struggle, to resistance, it is a song for the right to sing and to love and be loved. It leads us to teach and be taught, to learn and be learned from. The poem of Thiago de Mello seems more contemporary than ever in the current moment in which power cynically arms the population with weapons of death and destruction in the name of confronting a violence that is being promulgated by those in power.

Freire thought through the situation of educators in Brazil, those subjected to a series of robberies, injustices, exclusions, the arbitrary injuries inside and outside of the school system, which produced terrible working conditions and salaries, the neglect of public input in public education, constant repression against militancy, and, indeed, any form of resistance. Faced by this, educational realities need a type of love that seems at once impossible and necessary; a philosophical and political love. A love that is a form of struggle, an armed love; a love that contains a non-renounceable commitment by those who honor the work of an educator confronting that which, on a daily basis, seeks to negate the educator themselves. As such, to educate is to love by fighting, questioning, dialoguing, thinking, and learning.

Contemporary Brazil looks much like the Brazil described above. Almost nothing has changed. Conditions are increasingly deteriorating in Brazilian public education at all levels. Repressions against any movement and protest are constant and promote even more inequality. Life and education are increasingly commodified. And perhaps what is most shocking is that within the current political reality, in February of 2019 to be precise, Freire has been blamed for the educational realities in Brazil, even though he so clearly would be against the current situation.

To purge Freire's ideology from Brazilian education, whether it be either inside or outside of schools, is to purge an ideology of love. For it is love that initiates a philosophical life in education, a love of resistance against all that negates, denies, and dilutes an education for everyone. Freire's ideology of love preaches that whenever those in power pursue an anti-educational policy, educators must take up the weapons of love that give students a time to be who they are and who they can be, and at the same time raise the question of resistance against the anti-education forces.

A weaponized love is a love that resembles the love that perturbs, one that the Cuban musician Silvio Rodríguez sings about in *"Por quién merece amor"* (*"For Whomever Deserves Love,"* 1982). This love that perturbs is a love that positions love as the greatest art; it is a love of humanity that can neither be bought nor sold, an art that is a virtue, and an art of peace. As ridiculous as it sounds, there are many who are greatly discomforted by Paulo Freire's love for a world without oppression. Curiously, a discourse of brutal hatred has been generated against him. But, by looking closely at the current political realities, this is not surprising. There is precedence for this kind of hatred. As we have seen in the figures of Socrates and Simón Rodríguez, two loving educators condemned in their own times, two subversive educators who disturbed the order of things, and who undermined socially acceptable "good" educational practices, the risk of being accused of corrupting the youth existed in times past and exists now.

The French philosopher Alain Badiou separates politics from love. He links the former to the state, and the latter to family. On the contrary, Paulo Freire unites politics and love because he believes that both impact all spheres of life. Badiou affirms that the essence of politics is in this question: are individuals, when they come together, and when they organize, capable of thinking of, and making the decision to, create equality? And he believes that the essence of love resides in this question: are individuals able to assume the value of difference itself while turning it into a creative force? For his part, Freire was able to cultivate a politics of love and a love of politics. As such, he dedicated his life to create equality throughout the world while assuming difference as an affirmative force.

Searching for Love, Finding Exile: To March

So now it is urgent to defend love's subversive, heterogeneous relation-ship to the law. At the most minimal level, people in love put their trust in difference rather than being suspicious of it. Reactionaries are always suspicious of difference in the name of identity; that's their general philosophical starting point. If we, on the contrary, want to open ourselves up to difference and its implications, so the collective can become the whole world, then the defense of love becomes one point individuals have to practice. The identity cult of repetition must be challenged by love of what is different, is unique, is unrepeatable, unstable and foreign.

(Badiou and Truong, 2012, p. 98)

I have included, throughout this book, some poems that affirm certain truths in the way that only poetry can express. I recall another, by the Argentine poet Roberto Juarroz (1991, pp. 15–XII):

Find a thing
and always find another one.
So, to show something,
One must look for what is not.
Search for the bird to find the rose,
seek love to bring exile, seek nothing to discover a man, go back to go forward.
The key to the path that goes on
bifurcations,
your suspicious beginning, your doubtful end,
it is in the caustic mood of its double meaning.
Always arrives, but to another other part.
All comes to pass.
But in reverse.

"Looking for love, we encounter exile," says the poet. Looking for love, Freire traveled incessantly and met exiles. Already in the womb, in the first search for love, he encounters exile. Looking again for love during his infancy in Recife, once more he finds exile in Jaboatão dos Guararapes. As a leader of a National Literacy Plan, seeking love in the oppressed, the third exile is found. Freire searched endlessly for love, always encountering exile. We find three retellings of this exile by Freire in his work, but we can also multiply this number. The last of these three is perhaps the cruelest, most violent, and brutal in the way that it threatens and assaults his life. At a first reading, it seems strange, paradoxical, and difficult to understand how someone could respond to so much hatred with so much love. But through a more profound reading, a poetic reading, his response emerges as a logical consequence of his extraordinary capacity to love.[10]

This capacity to love went beyond loving people; Freire loved ideas, projects, social movements. Not coincidently then, different worldwide social movements in dialogue with, and inspired by, Freire's life and ideas have made love the mobilizing force behind their political struggle. For example, the marches of The Landless Movement of Brazil (MST) that occurred during Freire's return from one of his exiles placed an "impetus of a loving desire to change the world" at the center of their struggle. These marches are expressions of an errant love in search of its place to settle.

The marches of the Landless Movement are testimony to an inventive, critical, rebellious, nonconformist love, and at the same time, and in terms of the poem by Thiago de Mello we read earlier, they are a weaponized love. They testify to the need to fight "to obtain a minimum of transformation" (Freire, 1997). Resistance, struggle, and a constant putting into question of an ever-present "reactionary will" that runs throughout Brazilian history and is, sadly, re-emerging today. Freire lovingly traveled with the men and women of the Landless Movement, perhaps, in the words of Thiago de Mello in an exiled collective search to find a place in common.

The love that Freire defended and affirmed is the love felt and impressed on him from his chronological childhood. From an early age, during the moments of being taught how to read and write by his parents in the shade of the family mango tree in Recife, Freire felt the irreplaceable value of a slow, loving educational temporality of the present. It is perhaps this temporality, lived during the years of learning to read and write, above and beyond the words learned, that Freire's parents passed on to him. Words learned in their own time, a loving, musical childhood time. With his father nearby in his hammock and

---

[10] In a handwritten essay from March 2019, Milena Fresquet Kohan says: it is not hatred that is opposed to love ("because they both remind us of the color red"), but indifference.

his mother at his side, both in a rich present, a time of presence, in the temporality of a loving present, Freire was initiated into the reading of the world of letters and the reading of the world itself.

Freire's mother and father were not education professionals,[11] but nonetheless taught him how to read. They did not possess any specific technical wisdom or knowledge of pedagogical techniques. There were loving educators in the most literal sense of the word: amateurs. They loved what they were doing, which was simply creating a present in which Freire could read and write words and thoughts characteristic of childhood. In this way, Freire was lovingly educated by his parents and in the courtyard of his family home which served as his first school, and also by his first teacher Eunice Vasconcellos in his first formal school. In Freire's own recollection, Eunice was a young teen of sixteen or seventeen years of age who instilled in him the love of the complexities of language, in particular Brazilian Portuguese, that he would live all along his entire life. It is worth reading here a particular way Freire would recall Eunice:

> She didn't get married. Maybe that has something to do with self-sacrifice, the love we have for teaching. And maybe she acted a bit like me: by making teaching the middle of my life, I end up transforming teaching at the end of my life. (Freire in Gadotti, 2001, p. 31)

After reading this recollection, one must ask whether it was Eunice who acted like Freire, or Freire who would later act like his teacher Eunice? The response to this question matters less than noting the extremely strong ways that Freire was marked by the educational experience shared with his parents and with his first teacher. These marks would accompany Freire throughout his entire life. They may have even led to his marriages to two teachers, the first, with Elza, with whom were

---

[11] The mother, in *The Baby's Book*, does not say that they were the ones who made Freire literate and shares that he "began to learn to read on July 15, 1925, at the age of 4. His first teacher was D. Amália Costa Lima, who, along with his daughters, pampered him more" (A. M. A. Freire, 2006, p. 51). Not counting that in July 1925 he was three, and not four years old, we prefer to follow the detailed and repeated testimony of Paulo Freire himself.

born all of his five children. Remarking on his time with Elza, Freire would state, "I lived 42 years with Elza, and during this time I learned from her that the more you love, the more you love" (Freire in Gadotti, 2001, p. 54).

The More You Love, the More You Love

I am really interested in the time love endures. Let's be more precise: by "endure" one should not simply understand that love lasts, that love is forever or always. One has to understand that love invents a different way of lasting in life. That everyone's existence, when tested by love, confronts a new way of experiencing love.
(Badiou and Truong, 2012, p. 33)

Again, I repeat: "The more you love, the more you love." Love is an autogenerative force. It multiplies itself. Love; the rest will take care of itself. Freire experienced the power of love early on in his life in childhood. And he did so in an educational context.

In this way, Freire's relation with the world and with the word, with language and writing, with the art of teaching, and with the force of learning, grew and expanded. This first educative experience was profound and essential for Freire's life, and it left a definitive mark on the way that Freire thought of education. It was this love experienced during his entrance into the world of letters that grew with him and became an irreplaceable condition of his thought and educational practice throughout his entire life.

Stated even more strongly, love is perhaps the principle and irreplaceable value that runs throughout the entire life of Freire. We read or hear Freire reinforcing this view in his own words, and own voice, in various ways. For example, when his first love and wife Elza died, it was as if life itself had come to an end for Freire. The loss of his love put him on death's doorstep. The world seemed impossible to live in without the love of his life who had accompanied him for so long, through the most difficult of conditions. This was a committed love, a love of struggle and of solidarity. A love that was singular, deeply personified in Elza, and irreplaceable. The death of a loved one seemed to signify, for Freire, the death of love itself.

But love was eventually born in another person, and Freire himself seemed to be born again with this new and amorous birth. This new love was found in a former student, the daughter of a school friend-protector who had allowed him to attend junior high school in Recife. The new love is, therefore, a friendly love. Through this love it became possible to love again. In the end, we can say that Freire, above and beyond anything else, loved the world. Because of this, it was always possible, and necessary, to live and love again, to continue loving and manifesting love in the world.

This love is captured in the second epigraph that began this chapter. In his final interview, Freire affirms that he would like to be remembered as someone who, more than anything, deeply loved all that he encountered, "the world and people, animals, trees, water, and life." Every form of life encountered during his life, Freire loved. Such a statement is coherent and logical for someone that loved life first and foremost as an expression of a loving presence in the world.

Freire's youngest son felt the same way about the life and legacy of his father. His love appears as the most important message that sustains the life he shared in common with his father. It is his most persistent memory:

> I was always very loved, even in a life of tensions, travels, displacements, even when instead of dedicating myself to education I chose to be a musician and took a route different than what a teacher father might prefer. I told my father, "Father, I want to play drums, I want to be a musician." And his answer was transparent, clear, and precise, "It's all right, my son. You can do what you want. But promise me one thing: that what you're going to do will be done with love." That was his response. (Lutgardes Costa Freire, *infra* Appendix, p. 174)

You can do what you want to do, you can be who you want to be, try what you want, but on one condition: that whatever you do, you do with love. Judging by the testimony of Lutgardes, Paulo Freire was extremely successful in living in this amorous way. In a recent interview (included in this book), when asked what was the most important thing that he learned in his life with his father, Lutgardes responded: "To love life. To love the birds, to love the sun, love nature, and love people." Freire lived a life of love inside and outside of his home. He loved anywhere and everywhere. He breathed love. And he invented and constantly reinvented, in his loving life, a new temporality of love, one that Badiou points to in the epigraph that begins this section: another time, another present, to live in education. A time that was needed for some and was unbearable for others. In this love of another time, Freire lived and died. For this love, and for this time, he will be remembered both by those who love him, and those who hate him.

4

Errantry

Fourth principle: an educator is someone who walks, wanders, displaces themselves. Without a final destination, they create the conditions to encounter those who are outside—in the present, with presence. The educator wanders the world to show it that it can always be different than it is. The teacher walks the world wandering on the path of a political education that is inspired by the belief that the world can be otherwise, and so that the world becomes so. The world is open, and the wandering educator creates a place for a world that we cannot anticipate.

> Not only have we been unfinished, but we have made ourselves capable of knowing ourselves as such. Here, an opportunity is open for us to become immersed in a permanent search. One of the roots of education, which makes it specifically human, lies in the radicalness of an inconclusion that is perceived as such. The permanence of education also lies in the constant character of the search, perceived as necessary. (Freire, 2000, p. 93)

> Basically our vision initially is to create a society in which a minority does not exploit the majority; to create a society where, for example asking questions would be a common, daily, activity. (Freire and Faundez, 1989, pp. 61–2)

> Thus, I keep insisting, ever since *Pedagogy of the Oppressed*: there is no authentic utopia apart from the tension between the denunciation of a present becoming more and more intolerable, and the "annunciation," announcement, of a future to be created, built—politically, esthetically, and ethically—by us women and men. (Freire, 1994, p. 114)

The Wanderer

No title has been as accurate as *The Wanderer of Utopia*, a radio program produced in 1998 by Radio Nederland with the help of USP and the Paulo Freire Institute.[1] Listening to the opening of this program, one notices how the radio media is a mode of communication similar to the modes that the author of *Pedagogy of the Oppressed* used to fulfill his vocation to make school available to everyone, especially those historically excluded. Radio presents a pure raw word, and is perhaps the means of communication closest to spoken word. Even today, it is still possible to walk or wander with a radio in hand.

The Aurelio dictionary tells us that a wanderer (andarilho) is a species of bird that has the ability to voyage across great distances. It occupies the uninhabited lands of central and southern Brazil. One might point out my weak analogy here, because, in truth, Freire was very fond of people and wandered where people lived. However, in a certain sense we could say that he wandered in the places where people were most dehumanized by capitalism, and in this sense he and the andarilho[2] both passed through lands lacking in humanity. At any rate, the affinities between Freire and the andarilho are strong and not limited to a passion for wandering. Like the teacher from Pernambuco, the andarilho is an endangered species due the devastation of the land it inhabits.

In the entry "andarilhagem" (wanderer) in *Paulo Freire Dictionary* (Brandão in Streck; Redin; Zitkoski, 2008), Carlos Rodrigues Brandão has noted two aspects of Freire that make him a wanderer. Freire traveled a lot, especially while in exile, during which time he engaged in several literacy campaigns in Africa, Asia, Oceania, and Latin America, but he also traveled upon his return to Brazil. Indeed, he continued to

---

[1] The radio program is available at the Paulo Freire Reference Center: < www.acervo.paul oFreire.org:8080/jspui/handle/7891/3279>.

[2] We keep the name of the bird in Portuguese.

travel even while his health was obviously deteriorating. Right up until the moment of his death in 1997, he was planning trips to Cuba, Spain, Portugal, and the United States. These trips ultimately never occurred, due to Freire's passing, but they demonstrate his unceasing desire for travel.

In written correspondence with Faundez, Freire, referencing the moment in which he was in Chile and had received an invitation from Harvard University and The World Council of Churches, explains the principle reason behind his traveling:

> I was by then absolutely convinced how useful and fundamental it would me for me to travel the world, be exposed to various environments, learn of other people's experiences and to take a fresh look at myself through the cultural differences. (Freire and Faundez, 1989, p. 12)

For a wanderer, travel is not only fruitful but necessary. How can one think of a worldly education without traveling around the world, without exposing oneself to its diversity and difference? Thus, one travels to learn and leaves their place in order to understand, with their whole body. For only by traveling and exposing ourselves to the unfamiliar can we learn to see what we are not able to see when we stay within our familiar bounds. But one travels to not only understand others but also to better understand oneself:

> It was by travelling all over the world, it was by travelling through Africa, it was travelling through Asia, through Australia and New Zealand, and through the Island of the South Pacific; it was through travelling through the whole Latin America, the Caribbean, North America and Europe—it was by passing through all these different parts of the world as an exile that I came to understand my own country better. (Freire and Faundez, 1989, p. 13)

Through travel we enter into the world and the world expands; we also bring this large world into our small one. Freire brought a part of Brazil to the world, while bringing the world to Brazil, to better understand both differently and more.

Exiles and Travels

Let's go back in time a bit. Travel and errantry were a part of Freire's life since birth. As we have seen, Freire believed himself to have passed through three exiles, not one. The first when he was in the womb of his mother. The second was when his family moved from Recife to Jaboatão. And finally, the third and most well-known exile was when he spent time outside of Brazil during the dictatorship of 1964 (Freire, 2004, p. 27). In this way, his chronological childhood was experienced as a voyage, within constant trips, including those on the train from Jaboatão to his new school in Recife. These roundtrips were the first of many he would take throughout Brazil.

Later in life, the dictatorship would force his travel outside of the country, but this forced exile was to become incorporated into an incessant style of wandering, a life of wandering. Even upon his return to Brazil, Freire continued to travel. In exile, Freire did not live by traveling, but instead traveled in order to live. He did not seek travels in life, he sought life through traveling. Paraphrasing, but also playing with the famous line of Socrates, Freire believed that a life without travel was a life not worth living.

Throughout his life, Freire highlighted how, since his youth, walking and wandering were irreplaceable elements of his life. For instance, in his epistolary autobiography, *Letters to Cristina*, he writes about the moment in which he returns to Recife and begins to become a more passionate and hardened reader:

> Regarding my development as an educator who thinks about educational practice I would never dismiss my experience of walking through Recife and going from bookstore to bookstore, becoming intimate with the books, or of travelling through Recife's narrow roads and hills conversing with local groups about their problems. (Freire, 1996, p. 80)

Thus, from early on in his life, traveling becomes a form of life for Freire. Traveling by train, but also from bookstore to bookstore, and from there, traveling with the books he read. Traveling in a library or at home with books, from books to the world, and from the world back to books. Traveling with the ideas he encountered in his books, with the characters presented. A vagabond, without any fixed destination, open to the sensations and feelings he encountered in his reading of the world, and in the words found in the books he read. He traveled with thought and words; his life was a voyage taken through the reading he did and the conversations he had with common folk.

What is important to note is not necessarily traveling in itself, but the form in which Freire traveled. Freire the wanderer traveled attentive to his path, always open to changing the route if necessary. An anecdote that Freire himself recounts demonstrates just how open he was to leaving one path for another during his travels. As the story goes, Freire was invited to give a seminar at Kitwe, in the interior of Zambia, on *Pedagogy of the Oppressed*. This was his first trip to Africa. On the way to Kitwe, he had a layover in Lusaka, the capital. Waiting for his connection, he was approached by two youths from the MPLA who were searching for him at the airport in order to invite him to give a talk on the problems of illiteracy in the liberated zones of the country. It turned out to be an irresistible invitation. Freire felt an undeniable commitment to these other people that had searched him out. The youth managed to change Freire's flight and advise those waiting for him that his trip had changed. Freire postponed his original plans so that he could spend an afternoon and night of educational work with whomever was open to conversing with him. It was impossible for Freire to deny those who came to him in a spirit that mirrored his own ideas and life.[3]

Freire the wanderer traveled intensely, with little respite, only enough rest to continue traveling. For instance, between the beginning

---

[3] The same anecdote is commented on in dialogue with Macedo, in which more details of the meeting with the members of the MPLA and how, after being in Zambia, in Tanzania there were also unforeseen and irreplaceable encounters (Freire and Macedo, 1987, p. 67 ff.).

of January 1973 and the middle of February of the same year, he crisscrossed two different states in the United States giving lectures and holding workshops with social workers and teachers on *The Pedagogy of the Oppressed*. At a different moment, this time in the Dominican Republic, Freire lacked the proper documentation to be in the country and was authorized to stay in the country for five days provided that he never leaves the house where his seminars were being given. Many people would feel extremely inconvenienced by such a situation, but Freire felt at home. He took advantage of his extra time on the island to meet with Dominicans from all walks of life. In a sense, because he could not leave his quarters, his encounters with people at his Dominican residence turned out to be richer and more intense. Each of Freire's trips were opportunities for intense exchanges with those who lived the realities of the places Freire visited. And when he was not traveling, he was not thinking of rest, but rather renewing his energy for the next trip.

Marches that Travel

Freire's travels within Brazil found him marching in struggle for an education with, and for, the oppressed, fighting for them militantly, denouncing the unacceptable world they shared together. In this way, and as we have seen, Freire's errant life is definitively marked and integrated with popular social movements, in particular with the marches of the Landless Movement of Brazil (MST), whose marches manifest the "momentum of the loving will to change the world." The marches of the Landless Movement are expressions of their loving errantry. In them, Freire's errantry and love were conjoined. He lovingly traveled with the men and women of the movement. With worn hands and feet, with his heart and with tired eyes, he marched. In his last interview, Freire expressed his desire to see the MST marches expand within Brazil. Many marches were needed, he stated, including:

March of those who have no school, march of those who fail, march of those who want to love and cannot, march of those who refuse a servile obedience, march of those who rebel, march of those who want to be and are forbidden to be . . . I think, after all, that the marches are historical walks around the world. (Freire, 1997)

Here his words greatly resemble a letter written only one month before his death. In this letter, Freire desires for other marches to grow out of the Landless Movement marches. Here he calls for other marches and highlights:

marches of the unemployed, of the disenfranchised, of those who protest against impunity, of the ones who decry violence, lying, and disrespect for public property. Let us not forget as well the marches of the homeless, of the school-less, of the healthless, of the renegades, and the hopeful march of those who know that change is possible. (Freire, 2004, p. 40)

Similar words and desires occur in two separate texts. In both, the emphasis is placed on the dispossessed, those violently uprooted from an education, from a place to live, from health, work, peace, truth, respect, and justice. What all of these people have in common is deprivation, yes, but also an affirmation: the affirmation of hope in the possibility of change; that transformation is possible.

Freire marched with the Landless Movement and dreamed of a multiplication of the marches by all Brazilians who were barred from being who they were, through education, through love, in any place where they might meet. It was necessary then, Freire believed, for people to leave their homes, to walk, travel, wander, as a political act of protest and nonconformity against a world that did not allow them to "be more," that barred them from being who they were, and that remained hostile against all unconsecrated ways of life. The marches would act as a form of contestation as well as the affirmation that another world is possible.

Marches like these are expressions of errantry, a type of traveling that takes one out of their place of comfort and that does not have a fixed end in view. They contain hope that it is possible to change the world. As such, these marches are teachers made up of wanderers of all races, genders, ethnicities, social conditions. By marching, they invite others to leave and abandon the comfort found in the order of things. The marches educate in a double sense. On the one hand, they reveal what is hidden, and, on the other, they entail an experience of inhabiting the world in a way that does not bind us to a state of affairs that only the elite can live in.

The Connective Trips

There is yet another way in which Paulo Freire is a wanderer. In his entry at *Dicionário Paulo Freire* (Streck et al., 2008) C. Brandão highlights how even when he wasn't traveling, Freire demonstrated a "wandering-errant" vocation in his imagination and ideas. Freire composed his thoughts with authors from theoretical backgrounds very different than his own. This demanded that he consistently travel from one context of thought to another. Thought of in this way, Freire traveled not only with his body but also with his ideas. In his work, he moves between very distinct ideas and thoughts written in many different languages. His own writing is often eclectic and unstable, wandering. Perhaps this is best exemplified in *Pedagogy of the Oppressed*, where on the same journey he travels through authors as different as Martin Buber, Mao Zedong, Karl Jaspers, Hegel, Che Guevara, Frantz Fanon, and others. It makes sense then, that Freire, as we will see in the next chapter, referred to himself as a "connective boy." His writing demonstrates a connectivity and an ability to bring together things that at first glance appear very dissimilar.

These journeys of connective thought run throughout much of Freire's work. He was a type of permanent intellectual voyager who sought to connect the most diverse forms of thought with his own. He found and made associations between references from among the most diverse fields and concepts. His thought is in constant movement from one book to the next, and in movement it makes contact and connects with diverse theoretical camps. His was an embodied traveling that searched for connections and conjunctions: the conjunctive means of traveling feeds and enriches the connections made. Without displacing his body, Freire would not have been able to write what he wrote. But it could also be said that he would not have been able to travel the way he traveled had he not journeyed with the books he read.

Fitting for a wanderer and traveler, these movements manifest themselves in the form of Freire's writing, and are found in many of the passages of his more traditionally philosophical early books, as well as in his books composed of his letters and spoken words, many of which are the favorites among his readers and with Freire himself. His writing gained, throughout its journey, a very unique life of its own. It was created both through the movement of his words and through the ways his interlocutors crossed his path, exposing new avenues for thought as they spoke. His books drawn from the spoken word make it possible to come and go in the company of the thoughts of others and, in the process, dislocate those thoughts from their original places. More than this, these books specifically seek to help readers journey and travel attentively with his interlocutors as well as their own memories in a singular way.

Through all of these diverse journeys, Freire the wanderer encountered distinct connections that served as inspiration for his thoughts and renewed his connective educative life. In these journeys he elaborated, formulated, recuperated, cultivated, conceived, proposed, and organized the principal thoughts that would constitute the base of his practice and life. For instance, on his trip to Grenada (between December 1979 and January 1980) he gave form to two of what he considered his most important and complex pedagogical thoughts: (a) always respect the ways in which those being educated understand the world, while also challenging them to think critically about it; and (b) do not separate the content of what is being taught from "precise thinking" ("pensar certo," Freire, 1994, p. 212).

These two principles capture all the complexity of Freire's revolutionary, democratic, political project. The two principles demand a vigilant and consistent thinking and rethinking. They are at once and the same time political principles, as demonstrated by the concepts of respect, intellectual challenge, critical thinking, and the necessity to link content and critique, as well as epistemological principles in their concern with ways of thinking and ways of developing knowledge. They involve a certain knowledge about the world, as well as a certain disposition toward other ways of knowing, and respecting the knowledge of others. In short, the principles can be the foundation, as Freire the wanderer claims: "an entire transformation of school and educational practice" (p. 232).

The reader may wonder: "Okay, but what is the relation between these two principles and the five principles presented in this book?" Are they in tension or conflict? How, for example, might errantry and "correct thinking" be compatible or in tension? Such questions are justified, and I invite the reader to think through these relations. Perhaps the principles operative here, in this book, are those that connect, broaden, and unfold those principles presented by Freire. The principles are intertwined, they complement one another, and are in a dialogue with one another in a way that enriches each one, that reveals the potential of the concepts, but that also manifests certain tensions. They open up and illustrate in another language, and with different words, another collective way to think and live an educative life.

Traveling in Latin America

Paulo Freire's form of traveling with his body and mind can be situated within a rich tradition of Latin American wandering educators like Jose Marti, Andres Bello, Ricardo Rojas, among many others. Within this tradition, Simón Rodríguez, the inventive schoolmaster (Kohan, 2015a), deserves a special place. There is a fine line that connects Rodríguez and Freire (Puiggrós, 2005). Like Rodríguez, Freire was an iconoclastic teacher who contested the established values of his time. Both demonstrated an unconditional hospitality, always attentive to the excluded, to those negated by the dominant system. And both were emancipators, affirming an education that would enlarge freedom of thought and ways of life.

Both Freire and Rodríguez traveled their entire lives. Like the teacher of Bolívar, Simón Rodríguez, who was affectionately called "The Socrates of Caracas" by his student, Freire was an errant teacher in two senses of the verb "to err." *Err* stems from the Latin word *errare*, which means "to stray" or "to wander." Freire wandered through more than a hundred cities on five continents. He journeyed to the most isolated and inhospitable corners of the world. Traveling through the five continents he sought to contribute to the education of the oppressed, but he also looked for, and found, his own education. Wandering for Freire was not just a way of liberating the oppressed, it was also for the teacher an autodidactic and self-liberatory experience.

In another way, Freire, like any other human, lived the second meaning of the verb "to err." He admittedly erred, that is, he made many mistakes throughout various points in his life. Erring, in this second sense, makes up part of the adventure of knowing, of knowing oneself. It reveals the ability of one to reflect on and improve oneself. It is an expression of a spirit that does not accept anything in the world as determined:

> I would be a melancholy and unmotivated being if it could be scientifically proved that the laws of history or nature would take care of surpassing human misencounters without any mark of freedom: as if everything were predetermined, preestablished, as if this were a world without errors or mistakes, without alternatives. Error and mistakes imply the adventure of the spirit. Such adventure does not take place where there is no space for freedom. There is only error when the individual in error is conscious of the world and of himself or herself in the world, with himself or herself and with others; there is only error when whoever errs can know he or she has erred because he or she knows that he or she does *not* know. At last, in this process, error is a temporary form of knowing. (Freire, 2000, p. 89, italics in the original)

As anyone seeking a liberated reconstruction of the world, Freire constantly erred. He erred like someone who knows, through erring, that he knows nothing, as someone who is willing to submit their ideas, reflections, and beliefs to constant revision. His continuous rethinking of his own certainties was a testimony to his learning journey.

We can name a few of Freire's most indisputable and obvious errors: the use of a patriarchal language in his first texts, which Freire himself admitted to, and later adapted, stands out, as does his over-appreciation of the Nicaraguan revolutionary process, as well as unfortunate decisions in the implementation of some of his literacy programs in certain developing countries like Cape Verde and Guinea-Bissau. There are others, but the most interesting aspect of Freire's errors lies not necessarily in the absence or presence of erring, making mistakes or errors. All of us err, in the sense that all of us make mistakes. What stands out about Freire is his relation to his mistakes, and his ability to perceive such mistakes as opportunities to err in the other sense of the word, to wander, remove himself from his place of comfort, to journey.

Pedagogy of Hope may provide the most beautiful example among Freire's books of this dual sense of errantry. It is an exercise of writing that reveals how the errantry of erring provokes an errantry of movement. In a certain way, the book taken as a whole is an example of journeying in the sense that it was originally conceived as an "introduction to" and ends up becoming, during the writing process, a "dislocation from" *Pedagogy of the Oppressed*. As such, the writing in this book testifies to errant movement. In it, there are many examples that demonstrate the transformative force that an error can provoke. Like, for example, in the episode detailed in the book where, speaking at SESI in Recife on a text by Piaget, where the author discusses the ways that parents castigate their children, Freire used an expression completely foreign to the harsh realities he was working in. The supposed man of the people here gives a "lesson on class."

Freire perceives his mistake and makes it an opportunity for learning. The mistake touches him and moves him, provoking him to travel in thought, to distance himself from the academic world, and ask questions like: How can the one that teaches place themselves in the situation of those who are learning? If one thinks they have nothing to learn, how can they possibly be a teacher? This episode also reveals a much more persistent mistake that Freire made during his time as director of the SESI Education and Culture division in Recife. It highlights the inconsistency of implementing a democratic education policy that unilaterally defines the themes to be discussed without considering the interests of the workers who would be having the discussions. The policy sought to take a critical posture, but it did so without listening to the desires and expectations of the people involved: the teachers, mothers, and fathers of the students attending SESI. Freire had to abandon this policy to effectively put in place a more democratic one, one that more coherently interwove the ends desired and the means to achieve them (Freire, 1994).

Another episode worth recalling here from in *Pedagogy of Hope* is a series of letters Freire sent to women who had read *Pedagogy of the Oppressed*. It reveals Freire making two mistakes simultaneously: the first is adopting a patriarchal language, the second is not recognizing his first mistake and instead trying to justify the use of machista language. Over time, Freire leaves behind these errors and changes his writing, not only in new editions of *Pedagogy of the Oppressed* but also in all the books that emerge after this moment of error.

Of course, there were other errors that Freire never perceived and that stayed with him. For example, his insistence on defending the English translation of *Pedagogy of the Oppressed* by Myra Ramos (Freire, 1994), a version of the book which to this day generates interpretative problems in the English-speaking world, as well as in other languages which based their translations off of the English version. This version continues to be considered the only "official" translation because of the impossibility to publish another one, mainly due to the economic interests of the owners to the rights of the book. It is of course necessary to perceive one's errors in to leave them behind, in order to err in the second sense of the word, to move on from them. If one does not perceive one's errors, then how can one leave them behind?

In his capacity to err in the double sense of the word, and to transform one type of erring (making mistakes) into another form of erring (wandering), Freire demonstrated the strength of a life of boldness and courage—a courage that reveals a desire to transform even when things appear to be settled. Freire always chose to act rather than to not act. He knew, for instance, of the difficulties of taking on the position of secretary of education in the city of São Paulo, and yet he took it on because the world he lived in was too excessively unequal to not do anything.

The World Can Be Otherwise

Thus, errantry also constitutes one of the political principles of education. It shows us that the world can be otherwise. The world and the lives that comprise it can be different, and our own lives cannot be indifferent; they cannot legitimize the state of things as they exist now, a state in which some are forced to live without the most basic vital needs and others are discriminated against because of their race, gender, age, or class. It is always possible to do something. We may not know exactly how the world should be; we may not know how our lives should be lived. And we do not want to know, because the proper role of the teacher is to make it possible for a collective and open construction of the world and of life. But we do know that education should put in question, problematize, shake up, and resist this world that is less of a world for so many. Education should transform the way of life that we are living, even if we do not know for sure where the movement of transformation will take us or how it will end.

There are many texts in which Freire specifically affirms a socialist dream of utopia with which we can confront capitalist oppression. I do not wish to ignore these testimonies, but here I would like to privilege others in which the dreams of utopian education appear less formulated and clear in terms of an idea already determined or known. Or, perhaps stated more interestingly, these dreams and utopias I select are open-ended, because they can only be affirmed in their proper becoming and construction, rather than anticipated by the dreams of one educator or another. I dare say this open relationship with utopia is more consistent with some of the elements very dear to Freire's thought and life that I am presenting in this book. In fact, as so many testimonies demonstrate, the principle political enemy is, according to Freire, not capitalism, or any other specific political system, but instead it is fatalism, the conviction that "things cannot be any other way," a determinist understanding of history in which no other possibilities for becoming exist, whether this be the case for poor rural people or for the most sophisticated postmodern intellectual (Freire, 2000, p. 30 ff.).

For this reason, on numerous occasions Freire insisted on the importance of concepts like "untried feasibility," which reveal his belief in a future open to possibilities not yet experimented with. The *inédito viável* signifies that what is to come has yet to be lived, and, at the same time, that what is to come is not a utopia that negates, but rather one that is affirmative, positive, realizable, and achievable. Such an idea of utopia is related to Freire's existentialist conception that there is no specific human essence, and that instead we constitute ourselves through existence. It is through this concept that education gets its meaning:

> Education makes sense because the world is not necessarily this or that, because human beings are as much *projects* themselves as they may have projects, or a vision, for the world. Education makes sense because women and men learn that through learning they can make and remake themselves, because women and men are able to take responsibility for themselves as beings capable of knowing—of knowing that they know and of knowing that they don't. They are able to know what they already know better and to come to know what they do not yet know. Education makes sense because in order to be, women and men must keep on being. If women and men simply were, there would be no reason to speak of education. (Freire, 2004, p. 15, italics in the original)

We can see, then, a clearly expressed anthropology that sustains Freire's conception of education as a common project of bringing another more beautiful, just, and democratic world into being. A world where men and women are always becoming. Where they are incomplete beings made through doing, constituted by how they live, and realized in their way of being. And it is for this reason, particularly in the context in which economic, political, and social relations drastically impede who or what humans are or can be, like we are living through in a neoliberal Latin America, that a philosophical education is so necessary. It is this type of education that permits, through critical comprehension and dialogue, an understanding of how we (students and teachers more and more caught up in a logic of competition and of a "save yourself if you can" ideology) can transform who we are being and who we are becoming (micro-enterprises, individualists, consumers, etc.) in order to become in another way, closer to what we can, and wish, to be, and less shaped by an institutionalized logic that is rarely thought about or questioned.

Thought of in this way, if we already know what the utopia will be, if at the end of the educational path there awaits in some prefigured way an anticipated utopia, then an education constituted by critical praxis and dialogue would lose its meaning. It would consist of a technique of formation or training, rather than education as we have been defining it. Education only has meaning if in fact the future is open, if it allows us to learn in dialogue with other humans and nonhumans in a shared world, to learn about the world we are living in and the world we want to share. If someone already knows how the world should be, and only wants to achieve a project which they have no questions about, then it is best that this person dedicate themselves to something other than teaching. This does not mean, of course, that educators do not have their own projects in and about the world, that they should not share these and defend them with their students. On the contrary, educators should not give up on realizing these projects if they are committed to contributing to a less horrid, less exclusive, less unjust world. But what it does mean is that education only has significance when the political dream is born during or after, and not before, the educational practice.

There are distinct ways in which Freire gave content to what he called political dreams or utopias. In a text written in February of 1992, where he speaks of the education of adults, the dream appears as a foundation of educational practice and reflection, and is described as a world, different than ours, with less negativity, where there is less presence of the characteristics we do not desire:

> This has been a concern that has consumed me always: to give myself over to both an educational practice and to a pedagogical reflection based on the dream of a less evil, less ugly, less authoritarian, more democratic, more human world. (Freire, 2001b, p. 17)

As we can see, the dream involves ridding the world of the capitalist values that devour it: evil, greed, and authoritarianism. It is in this way that the politics of education is a politics that confronts the status quo, and helps us perceive and face all that is horrid and authoritarian.

Ethics, Aesthetics, Politics

There are three dimensions at play in the movement we are discussing: ethical, aesthetic, and political. These are the modes by which we can understand what is good and beautiful, which help to exercise the power needed in any type of pedagogical practice. It is not possible to educate without, in a certain way, denouncing the unacceptable ethics, aesthetics, and politics of this world. Moreover, the form of making such denouncements is artistic.[4] The landscape that an emancipatory

---

[4] According to Camnitzer (2017), it is typical of Latin American educators to resort to aesthetic strategies to face political and educational issues. Referring to both Simón Rodríguez and Freire, the author affirms that, in Latin America, art, education, and politics are closely related to the need to expand access to education and to provide people with tools to create; in this way, in art and in pedagogy, it is a question of passing from a creation for the people to a creation by the people. "Freire's belief that 'reading the world precedes reading the word' could be treated as a paradigm for both conceptual art and new progressive forms of education" (p. 112). In this sense, it can be affirmed that art is present in different ways in Latin American educators: in the search for a style (of

education helps us perceive can be more or less complete, detailed, or precise, but it always has to be composed of a movement which reveals that which is not perceived, and which makes visible a horrid reality, that sophisticated apparatuses present in an opposite way. Education has a revelatory character: it permits us to see what we do not see.

The emphasis of leaving the educational project open-ended is so important to Freire that he decides to dream of and name the things that the world *does not need to have* rather than to list what it needs. He opposed cruelty, horridness, and authoritarianism with broad and vague concepts of democracy, humanism, and his own version of democratic humanism, which was another open-ended concept if we take into consideration the ways in which Freire understands these words. The human, for Freire, is something that is never fully constituted, inconclusive, a project in construction, and democracy is conceived by him as a non-hierarchical form of dialogical relations in social life. It is, as we have seen, a way to exercise power among equals.

In a lecture given in the same year, Freire implores that we need a world that is "more round, less harsh, a more human one" (Freire, 2001b, p. 20). The word used here is *arestoso* (harsh), which has various meanings in Portuguese, including "untidy, rough, conflictive, difficult to deal with." Most certainly, we live in a world that is difficult to deal with, and it is necessary to work toward a more livable, less harsh and conflictive world. "Roundness" can be conceived of as having a more perfect shape or configuration, an aesthetic, an archetypal form that the world appears to be losing. It is a type of beauty that makes us think of the aesthetic dimension that the "wanderer of utopias" helps us remember is so necessary to constitute a new world, one which cannot be fully defined or anticipated.

In one of his spoken books with Ira Shor, Paulo Freire states his position clearly on the necessary political commitment of educators:

writing, teaching, and existence), as a methodological strategy or path, but also as an undeniable dimension of an educating life.

In the liberating perspective, the teacher has the right but also the duty to challenge the status quo, especially in the questions of domination by sex, race, or class. What the dialogical educator does not have is the right to impose on the others his or her position. But the liberating teacher can never stay silent on social questions, can never wash his or her hands of them. (Shor and Freire, 1987, pp. 174–5)

The main commitment that Freire calls for here seems to be this: educators must contest the state of things in which dominance, oppression, and inequality exist. One can never be quiet nor wash one's hands of such issues. Get your hands dirty, Freire tells us repeatedly. Shout against the barbarity of the state of things, but do so without imposing another world in its place. And never lose your tenderness.

The Errantry of Questioning

An epistemological correlate to this ethical, aesthetic, and political posture of Freire is the ever-expanding importance that questioning had in his thinking on education. In his book of conversations with Faundez, he repeatedly highlights the importance of questioning and the need to question our questioning. Here questioning is conceived of not only as an intellectual game but also as a way to inhabit the role of an educator. One must live the question and the investigation it can initiate. The educator should allow the question to affect them and allow it to become part of oneself. Questioning has more than an epistemological force; it also has a political force that opens one to a "radical pedagogy of questioning" in which there is no place for the dichotomy between feeling a fact and learning the reason for it being the way it is. Freire's critique of traditional schooling was not limited to techniques or methodologies or the relations between teachers and students but included critiques of the capitalist system itself (Freire and Faundez, 1989, p. 45).

The weight of questioning in educational practice reveals and unfolds its meaning. Putting the world into question and exposing it for what it is, for Freire, shows how it can be otherwise. This is the primary force of Paulo Freire's educational thought: history is not finished. Seeing the world in this way, as he did, he saw that the world could be radically different. His wandering life contributes to our perception of this political dimension. By putting us in touch with other worlds, we perceive its precise character; the contingency of our world becomes an inspiration so that the world turns itself into other possible worlds.

Childhood[1]

Fifth principle: childhood is not something to be educated; it is something that educates. In a political education, one does not only or above all try to form the child without first being attentive to the child, to listen, to care, to keep alive, to live with. Childhood crosses all of life as a form that gives it curiosity, joy, and vitality. A political education is an education in childhood: in its attention, sensibility, curiosity, inquietude, and presence.

Paulo Freire and Childhood?

I never felt inclined to accept reality as it was, even when it was still impossible for me to understand the roots of my family's difficulties. I never thought that life was predetermined or that the best thing to do was to accept obstacles as they appear. On the contrary, even in my very early years I had begun to think that the world needed to be changed; that something wrong with the world could not and should not continue. (Freire, 1996, p. 13)

Until March of that year we had lived in Recife, in a medium-size house, the house where I was born and that was surrounded by trees.

---

[1] Note from the translators: Kohan uses two terms in Portuguese ("*infância*" and "*meninice*") and neither term refers directly to the English word "childhood." We have chosen to use the term "childhood," however, for negative reasons: the cognate of "*infância*," "infancy," is too developmentally limited and the equivalent of "*meninice*," "boyhood," is limited by its gendered expression. A neologism like "kidness" would only introduce confusion.

Some of those trees were like people to me, such an intimacy had I developed with them. (Freire, 1996, p. 25)

We are aware that childhood was not one of Freire's central preoccupations. On the contrary, even though it is not possible to register his preoccupation with the education of children—in particular children from the lower classes (Peloso and Paula, 2011)— Freire's emphasis is clearly upon popular and cultural education and the education of youth and adults, not children. Nonetheless, these qualifications should not be overdetermined. Freire's preoccupations are not with this or that educative practice. He is interested in any practice, of any age, in any context. For example, in *Pedagogy of Freedom*, when speaking of his vision of ethics in educational practice, he affirms,

> The ethic of which I speak is that which feels itself betrayed and neglected by the hypocritical perversion of an elitist purity, an ethic affronted by racial, sexual, and class discrimination. For the sake of this ethic, which is inseparable from educative practice, we should struggle, whether our work is with children, youth, or adults. (Freire, 1998, pp. 23-4)

This reference is one among many others. Collectively, they help us see that Freire is interested in educational practice as a whole and how educators live this practice much more than in this or that level of education. Aware of this wider sensibility in Freire, the master from Pernambuco, I intend to highlight his contribution to one of his "minor" topics, albeit one present in the background of his preoccupations. Perhaps childhood takes up a special—surprising and unsuspected— role in his corpus after all?

An Invitation to Revisit Childhood

For me to return to my distant childhood is a necessary act of curiosity.

(P. Freire, 1996, p. 13)

Freire speaks of and writes repeatedly about his chronological childhood in books, interviews, and letters. One of the texts in which he speaks most of this childhood is *Letters to Cristina*, written between 1993 and 1994, when Freire was more than seventy years of age. As the title indicates, the book is in the form of letters written to his niece Cristina. His childhood is chronologically distant to him in this book. The epistolary exchange with Cristina begins while Freire lives in Switzerland in the 1970s. In a moment of determination, his niece makes a special petition to her uncle,

> I would like —she said—for you to write me letters about your life, your childhood and, little by little, about the trajectory that led you to become the educator that you are now. (Freire, 1996, p. 11)

Freire does not miss out on his niece's invitation. On the contrary, he takes it as a challenge for autobiographical research, a search and encounter with himself. As we see in the epigraph of the present section, he considers in this research a necessity in the sense that it can allow for a better comprehension of his present. This encounter is of special interest to me not purely out of biographical curiosity about Freire, but because I think it holds great promise for elucidating reasons from the depths of Freire's personal history, and, above all, shows the historical path of someone who loves and lives for education. In other words, this search can offer meaning and sense not only for the private life of Freire, but for that of any educator who feels inspired to think and to live in the singularly childlike relation to one's chronological childhood. Freire's search, his need to look back on his distant childhood, could also prove significant in opening a new idea of childhood in the relationship of educators with their own childhood. This does not mean that an educator's recovery of his or her own childhood guarantees a questioning education. Much less does this mean that Freire's recovery of his childhood is an ideal model to follow. Nonetheless, this recovery of childhood could inspire and give birth to other possible ways of understanding our educational lives. Who knows, perhaps we can also find beginnings—and not only chronological beginnings—of another relationship with childhood? Indeed, we may find that there is a non-chronological childhood for a life of education available to any educator.

The epistolary form of writing that pleases Freire the *Pernambucano* (i.e., the person from Pernambuco) contributes to this mode of expression becoming a kind of public dialogue with himself as he reflects on his early years in Recife and, thereafter, in Jaboatão. For Freire, revolving through his memories, through his chronological childhood, develops into an imperative to understand himself better, to establish an archeology, a historical continuity between his present as an internationally known educator and his past as a child, with all the contrasting yet specific marks of his childhood: the harshness of hunger, but also the intimacy of his relationship with nature; the inability to pay for secondary school, but also the intensity and voracity in which he studied and read, with the encouragement of his mother and father, when the doors of the school opened. In the end, we encounter the diverse fears and joys of living of as a child of his class, in his context, in the historical time in which he lives—in Pernambuco during the crisis of the 1930s. At the end of his life, during his last years on earth, Freire returns to his world of chronological childhood trying to revive, return, and again make present that not so excessively distant past of his first years of life, sitting beneath the shade of mango trees.

A Childlike Reading of Childhood

Today, from my vantage point of my seventy-two years of age, I can look far back into the past and clearly see the extent to which language, and its comprehension have always been of concern to me.

(P. Freire, 1996, p. 49)

Freire's reading of his own childhood in *Letters to Cristina* is the reading of an adult, not a child. It could not be otherwise. This is "Freire the man," with mature ideas and having lived through major adventures, even those never finished, writing and looking for those embryonic marks in "Freire the boy," marks that already arrange him into who he will become. For this reason, the principal aspect of Freire's dialogue with himself is the continuity he perceives between his chronological childhood and his chronological adulthood.

Freire recognizes himself in his chronological childhood in the following way. The first strong impression he recognizes is a disposition toward a political rebellion of sorts, confronting the world in which he lives. This first mark is a species of dissatisfaction with the order of things. Freire registers this in himself from the time when he was a young boy. In this way, Freire can anticipate in his thinking and his life during his childhood what will manifest itself more clearly later in adulthood. This extends from a political formation of a certain kind, beginning with his military father, Joaquim Temístocles Freire, especially his critique of the division between manual and intellectual work, to the testimony born in the words and flesh of his uncle, João Monteiro. They are both central and formative figures for Freire, providing important political lessons in his early years. We might say that they were Freire's first conscientizers. Both of them, along with his general perception of social life in Jaboatão, are the main sources of his critical reading of Northeastern Brazilian reality. In relation to his early political formation, Freire tells what he has learned, for example, both from his father and his uncle: "I had my first lessons in Brazilian reality by conversing with my father and listening to his conversations with my uncle João Monteiro, a government opposition journalist" (Freire, 1996, pp. 42–3). In the same spirit,

> in 1928, I heard my father and my uncle saying that it was not only necessary to change the state of things in which we were, but it was urgent to do so now. The country was being destroyed, stolen, and humiliated. And then the famous phrase: "Brazil is right on the edge of the abyss." (Freire, 1996, p. 44)

In addition to these powerful words that ignite and form his early political consciousness, at a young age Freire experiences the repression and torture that the police force of Pernambuco inflicted upon his uncle, João Monteiro. Freire not only listens to the words calling for urgency, but he also feels the incarnate testimony of the body that suffers the atrocities of dictatorship. In it, he perceives the concrete effects of repression, but moreover he is able to witness the courage and value of resistance, of a non-paralyzing and irreconcilable fight for freedom, of words and life. His uncle's body, in such a terrible state after being repeatedly tortured, soon exhausts itself and dies of tuberculosis in 1935, only a year after the death of his father when Freire is thirteen. Freire's father also has an enormous impact upon him through the testimony of his words along with the economic conditions that force him to offer less to his family than he would like, despite being an active captain of the army who had to retire because of his own health problems.

In these ways, the basis for Freire's political thinking begins in these first years. In these formative testimonies he discovers his conviction that it is necessary and urgent to transform the world. Freire writes, "On the contrary, even in my very early ages, I had begun to think that the world needed to be changed; that something wrong with the world could not and should not continue" (Freire, 1996, p. 13). This was only possible because, as we can observe in other letters, ever since his childhood, Freire was attentive to everything: "my epistemological curiosity was always at work." (Freire, 1996, p. 100).

In this sense, although moving from Recife to Jaboatão is seen negatively by "Freire the boy," "Freire the man" perceives the benefit of this amplification of the world for a life which exits the comfort of the backyard to directly encounter the most naked and raw marks of what Freire calls the "Brazilian authoritarian tradition" and the "memory of slavery" of the country (Freire, 1996, p. 57). This exercise of authoritarian power that Freire confronts is not only wielded by the governing elites but also by the butcher, teachers, neighbors, and more. Authoritarianism, for Freire is seen as a mark that inhabits those that take part and create a dominant culture which exploits and carries peasants into misery, even in contrasting or opposing social classes.

"Freire the boy" already perceives that the dominated internalize and reproduce the values of the dominant in his culture. This entails a fight against this state of things that will necessarily demand a cultural and, more specifically, an educational transformation. In the quotidian life of the countryside in Pernambuco, Freire sees himself perceiving his vocation as an educator since he was a boy, but not alone or by himself. This direct living-out of the raw economic and political reality allows a reading of Brazilian reality in which Freire encounters the most profound reasons for his political and pedagogical thinking.

It is therefore in this first political mark from his past where Freire recognizes an affirmative relationship to childhood through these letters. Freire searches and finds, in his time as a boy, the Freire who he is. His chronological childhood is not an absence but, instead, a profound presence of his present. His time as a boy makes itself intensely present in his mature life. "Freire the boy" and "Freire the man" are not as separable as they may first seem. In a first mark of childhood, we can see the beginnings of an educator sensitive to a state of things who condemns the injustice against those who inhabit a non-human life, as much as the daily lashes of the conditions in which they live as in the backlash they receive when they rebel against it.

A second mark that also supports this reading emerges from how Freire manifests a taste for the world of letters, for reading, for questions of Portuguese syntax and grammar, of linguistics, and the world of study that captivates him from a very young age. His whole self vibrates with affirmation for his beginning steps in reading the word that also presupposes a reading of the world. In these beginnings he discovers the source of his present, his reason for being.

As an educator who is a specialist in literacy, "Freire the man" judges the question of reading as important and necessary to pass through his chronological childhood to comprehend the complexities of the act of reading. And his childhood does not disappoint him. The description of his own alphabetization is extremely beautiful, delicate, and careful, especially when he narrates the moment in which he is taught to read by his mother and father in the backyard of their own house in Recife, under the shade of mango trees. Branches taken from the trees, used sometimes as chalk, draw the words and sentences on dirt that becomes a chalkboard. Freire is not alphabetized through the textbook but with words made of his world and he goes to school already able to read (Freire, 1996, pp. 28–9). His first reading of words is pleasurable and fun, reading a friendly and hospitable world with great intimacy toward trees and nature—a familiar and loveable world, affable and dialogical. In this alphabetization, the reading of the word begins in harmony with the reading of the world: The first words written and read are the words which make the world; there is no rupture or distance between them. This story about Freire's alphabetization, along with the importance of the trees and backyard of his childhood home, is also referred to in other texts, some with more aspects and details then others. For example, in an autobiographical excerpt from *Pedagogy of the Heart* (Freire, 2000),[2] in a section entitled "My first world," the backyard appears here as "my immediate objectivity" and as "my other geographical point of reference"[3] (p. 38). It leaves a mark so profound upon Freire that it is reborn in an unexpectedly strong way in Switzerland, during his "third" exile.

While reading a letter sent from Recife to Geneva, he sees himself again as the boy drawing words and sentences in the dirt under the shade of mango trees (Freire, 2000, p. 38). In this text, the backyard of the house located at 724 Encanamento Road, in the neighborhood of Casa Amarela in Recife represents what is most unique about his identity as an educator. His literary roots are to be found, literally, on the "(informal) floor of the school" in which he alphabetizes himself. He affirms this as a reference to what forms him into a worldly educator. The loving care of his mother and father initially carry him across this floor and are followed by his enrollment in the private school Eunice Vasconcellos. His first formal school is therefore perceived by Freire as

---

[2] Note from the translators: a literary translation from the Portuguese title would be: *Under the Shade of This Mango Tree.*

[3] Note from the translators: literally Freire says: "my first non-geographical I."

kind of enlargement of his backyard beginnings, with words and letters in branches and earth. There is no rupture between the house and the school; on the contrary, there is continuity; or, in other words, his schooling had already begun, humbly, at home. This reading of words and the world will be amplified even more with his move to Jaboatão, which entails a change toward the past, toward poverty, toward misery, toward hunger, toward traditionalism, toward superstition, toward structures of exploitation, and toward the authoritarianism of the time, culture, and political realities of Pernambuco and the Brazilian Northeast that ignite the fiery dreams of freedom, democracy, and justice in the life and thought of Freire. Upon his move from Recife to Jaboatão, his words are amplified because the world is amplified from the loving and care-filled backyard of his family home to the hard and unjust rural reality of the Brazilian Northeast.

This experience of his own alphabetization as a child is also taken up in another text, transcribed from Freire's intervention at the opening of the Brazilian Congress on Reading, in Campinas, November 1981.[4] In this intervention, he reaffirms the importance of recovering his relationship with reading during his chronological childhood (Freire and Macedo, 1987, p. 20). By relating this story, he shows how concrete this beginning was for him. In this version of the story, he reveals the names of his first words read and written in the backyard of his house. From his childhood universe we see names of birds—*sanhaçu, olha-pro-caminho-que-vem, bem-te-vi, sabiá*—wild animals, pet cats; we meet Joli, his father's old dog; we explore geography and natural disasters, real and imaginary; we visit lakes, islands, rivers, wind, clouds, and the colorful transformation of the mangos which taught him the meaning of the verb *amolegar* ("to soften," in Portuguese). All these words from this natural world make up a harmonious, synchronized part of his chronological childhood.

---

4   Freire's intervention is published as *The Importance of the Act of Reading*. In: Freire and Macedo, 1987, pp. 20–4.

To highlight one aspect of this particular retelling of this story in order to recover his beginnings in letters, we should not miss Freire's insistence on the fact that the "reading" of his world was made in a childlike way, in his words: "*reading* my world, always, basic to me, did not make me grow up prematurely, a rationalist in boy's clothing" (Freire. In: Freire and Macedo, 1987, p. 21), and that his father and mother's pedagogy took care that his "boy's curiosity" ("childlike curiosity," I would say) was not distorted by entering the world of letters. The deciphering of the word *naturally* accompanied the reading of one's own world. Even the materials and the scenery helped for that; there was no rupture between the world of life and the world of letters in the classroom in the shade of the mango trees, where the floor was the board and the chalk was made of branches from the trees.

This observation is significant because it helps us understand some of the reasons why Freire maintained a childlike disposition during his entire life. Indeed, his later pedagogic texts, such as *Towards a Pedagogy of the Question*,[5] seem more childlike than *Pedagogy of the Oppressed*, for example. In the former, the form (dialogue), the tone (curiosity), and the content (focused on the educational value of the question) have a more childlike tone than the latter, more assertive, restrictive, and with stronger theoretical and ideological presuppositions.

Another aspect of this testimony to highlight is the childlike language that Freire uses to refer to his chronological childhood. He is at a Congress on reading, an event of educators, adults. Freire fills his story on his chronological childhood with childlike Portuguese expressions ("*gargalhando zombeteiramente*," "*peraltices das almas*," "*passarinhos manhecedores*"). With others, as we have seen, his "childlike curiosity" fills his memories of childhood and reveals the "missing humility" preserved in his childhood. At the same time, this childlikeness reveals a kind of recognition that, even among educators

---

[5] This is a more literal translation from Portuguese. In English, the title is as follows: *Learning to Question: A Pedagogy of Liberation* (Freire and Faundez, 1989).

(who are probably interested in the education of youth and adults), there are certain things that can only be expressed through childlike words. Freire's childlike language appears as an expressive force that exceeds and goes beyond adult academic language. It seems to me, then, that, beyond the chronological age of the speaking subject, childhood has a singular expressive strength for Freire. As we will see in another section, the things we can name with childlike words are precisely not the unimportant things.

Returning to *Letters to Cristina*: one of them, the tenth letter, expresses this same taste for literacy some years later when he tells the story of his travels when he is now a young man, back in Recife, in a better economic condition. His job as teacher allows him to contribute to the house's budget and also to buy specialized books and magazines; bookstores are his preferred outings and also his preferred place to meet friends. He describes his exercise of walking through the bookstores in the capital of the State with other young people as "childish curiosity" (*"curiosidade menina,"* Freire, 1996, p. 79). This visualizes his friends standing ritualistically around the wooden box of books which is about to be opened. "Childlike curiosity" is the anxiety, the surprise, the curiosity for the new books that arrive, awakening the desire to know: the smell of books that is stored in bodily memory, the singularity of the first encounter with text and letter, which will be later recreated in the tranquility of home. Despite having many bookstores to visit, all close to each other, the ritual of waiting to open the box with books is always renewing in Freire's testimony. Inside the box are books on language: grammar, linguistics, and philosophy of language. The Portuguese language, and a strong aesthetic relationship with it, concentrates his attention. In Recife, his previous life in Jaboatão meets a propitious context for more critical and careful reflection (Freire, 1996, pp. 79–80).

Thus, as we have seen, some of Freire's inspirations are born from a long gestation, where they stay close with him for a long time; but we can trust, as he does, that they will never be gone. Among them, we can include Freire's intimacy with nature, his critical analysis of

Brazilian political reality, his dissatisfaction before this reality and his unstoppable desire for change, his love of letters, his fascination for everything that had to do with the Portuguese language: all of that was born at home, in his childhood. Within this childhood—the form, mode, and figure in which he was born—he was born to remain through time.

A Conjunctive and Connective Way of Living Chronological Childhood

For us our geography was, without a doubt, not only a concrete geography, if I may say so, but a geography that had a special sense. In our geography we interpreted the two worlds in which we lived intensely: the world of children (in which we played soccer, swam and flew kites), and the world of premature men (in which we were concerned with our hunger and the hunger of our hunger). . . . In truth, we used to live in radical ambiguity: we were children prematurely forced to become adults. Our childhood was squeezed between the toys and work, between freedom and need.

(Freire, 1996, pp. 18–19)

Born into a middle-class family that suffered the impact of the economic crisis of 1929, we became "connective kids." We participated in the world of those who are well, even though we had very little to eat ourselves, and in the world of those who did not eat, even if we ate more than they did—the world of very poor neighborhoods on the outskirts of town.

(Freire, 1996, p. 21)

I mean, I am used to saying that my brother and I were conjunctive children, I mean, connective, with the function of connecting one clause to the other, etc.

(Freire. In: Blois, 2005, p. 27)

With the deterioration of Freire's family's economic situation, which demands their move from Recife to Jaboatão, where economic difficulties deepen, a partial change in this relationship with nature, when compared to how Freire lived in relation to nature in Recife, is marked. The epigraphs of this section clearly show how this passage from a more properly childlike relationship, marked by playing, intimacy, and the almost gradual fusion with nature is affected by the necessity of looking, in this same place, for sustenance for his life. The move from Recife to Jaboatão was in some sense a move away from a form of childhood.

Freire also begins to have a greater and more intense contact with children from the lower classes after this move. As we see in the last two epigraphs, he defines himself and his brothers as "conjunctive" and "connective" children: the connection or conjunction is in this case between classes in the sense that they serve as a bridge between the children from the class that eats little (a little, but at least something) and the children from the class of those who do not eat. Jason Mafra has studied this image profoundly, showing that the idea of connectivity is a foundational category in the life and work of Freire (Mafra, 2008, p. 22). More specifically, Mafra sees in this figure of the "connective child" an "archetype" that configures "the existential and constructing locus of anthropology as a practice of understanding and freedom" (p. 62). Thus, the idea expressed here is that the "connective child" and childhood cannot be restricted to a chronological stage; instead, they are a condition for the human being to continue living by transforming what seems to be a given into something else.

"Conjunctive and connective child" means a childhood in love with and interested in unions, meetings, connections, in this specific case between two social realities marked by differences, even those not necessarily confronted directly or even consciously, as it would be in the case of oppressors and oppressed. The ideas of the conjunctive and connective mark two different aspects or nuances within the common form of encounter. On the one hand, the *conjunctive* has the role of adding, increasing, expanding, making grow, augmenting;

it is the generative strength that puts together and helps to pass, in this case, from one to two, from one class to the conjunction of the two. On the other hand, the idea of *connection* marks a form of relationship that can only justly be given from the two, which appears not only as the expansion of the one but already a relation between them. The connection marks the relational character of the child. If the conjunction adds, the connection interlaces, ties. Thus, childhood appears with the affirmative complimentary marks of generation and relation, of encounter and connection.

At the same time, we could say that Freire not only provokes conjunction and connection between classes. We could say that he also lives between the chronological stages of his own life. Thus, the autobiography offers a chronological account of the child, Freire, who lives the life of an adult, woven into an adult condition, by living a childhood in which his worries about his own hunger and of those close to him—conjugated and connected friends, yes, but also his mother, father, brothers—making him jump, without intermediary ladders, from play to work, from having fun in rivers, in backyards and their trees and in the hills, to the search for the most basic and necessary provisions for his own body and for those bodies even more dear to him. Here the categories of "Freire the man" and "Freire the boy" are even less stable. It is good to play in nature, but it is also necessary to find, in nature, food that mitigates hunger. In the house, there is not enough money to provide for the family. The merchants deny his mother credit. She suffers not only the pain of being unable to feed her children, but the cruelty and humiliation of the treatment she receives in the butcher's shop when she asks for their solidarity. The child quickly becomes an adult: he needs to find a way to help his family and himself not be given over to the brutality of hunger. The entrance into the adult world includes the entrance into the world of guilt, of morality, and of "good habits" in which his family lives, with an evangelical father and a Catholic mother, when, for example, the necessity of taking fruit or chicken from the neighbor to mitigate hunger forces him to contradict the values which dominate not only his home but also the society at large. However, Freire makes an effort to show that neither of these two dimensions ends or impedes the other: he insists that he lives his childhood with joy when facing this double existence; that his chronological childhood is, at the same time and with equal intensity, an extremely joyful childhood, charged with a joy simultaneously childlike and adult.

It is interesting to also note one more note on childhood in the narratives from *Letters to Cristina* that winds through the story of Freire's life. Focusing on the present perspective of the educator, he offers a narrative of childlike images and sensations, as he says to Cristina in a short response:

> I am happy today to feel and perceive, after so many sent and received letters, of so much that was missing about which I was curious, sometimes even in a childlike way; so much thirst to know your universe, your "comings and goings," how important your participation, your work, and your questions were for my formation as a professional, woman, and citizen, always so well raised and spoken and your beautiful insistence in fighting for your dreams. (Freire, 2015, p. 298)[6]

As has been noted in the earlier discussion of Freire's recollection of his alphabetization in *The Importance of the Act of Reading*, in this story we see a crossing of his desires and childlike curiosities, affections, emotions, and feelings of childhood: sensations of joy and pain, many fears. For example, the move from Recife, takes him away from his birth home in the safe world, from a new and stimulating school with his teacher, Aurea Bahia. He calls this an exile. His new fears abound, including fear of the convicted souls who appeared at night in his new old house in Jaboatão. His affection for the big clock in the wall of the room diminishes his fear of nighttime silence with its sound, but then there is the sadness and growing fear of the day his family has to sell the

---

[6] Our translation. This letter, written by Cristina Freire, is not included in the English edition of *Letters to Cristina*.

clock. There is also the panic, pain, anticipated desire, and the almost infinite emptiness provoked by the death of his father. His relationship with everything is made personal and intimate in relation to nature— trees, plants, animals, rivers, hills, all those things to which he never loses this intimate relationship, even when they begin to be seen each time more as a source of survival. A certain sensation of childlike vulnerability and precarity runs across the narrative he provides in this small rich text.

This story is filled with images and symbols, or least they are perceived as such by "Freire the adult." Images like the piano of aunt Lourdes and the tie of his father, symbols of belonging to a middle class that, even when the resources of the family are scarce and hunger tightens, they cannot be sold because selling them would be to leave their class behind.

However, Freire's chronological adulthood is predominantly a childlike language referring to his chronological childhood as if, through this recollection, he could in a certain way not only revisit it, but relive it—as if he was still a conjunctive and connective child, this time between two times and, as we will shall see, between two forms of inhabiting the world.

Other References, Not Always Chronological, to Chronological Childhood, to His Own and to His Children's

The necessity of beginning from childhood in order to think about the present appears also in his dialogue with Sergio Guimarães. "From Childhood" is the title of the section in that text where Freire answers the invitation to begin with childhood in the affirmative, not through a history of childhood but, instead, by referring to "childhood as schooling" (Freire and Guimarães, 1982). In this contrast between history and schooling, we can read a contrast between two forms of temporality: *chronos* and *kairos*. History develops within *chronos*; it follows mimetically enumerated movements—consecutive, successive, and irreversible—that constitute chronological time. Chronological time is time that, somehow, does not depend on our perception and is qualitatively undifferentiated. It is the movement of the clock, of planning, of chronograms. In a vastly different way, schooling follows the time of *kairos*: it must happen in the opportune moment, in this and not in that moment, only when the conditions are appropriate. The sciences of life establish a *kairos* for schooling and, within it, alphabetization; but the harsh conditions of daily life—at least in Brazil and many other countries of Latin America—only allow a small minority to have this *kairos* sense of time respected. For a popular educator of youth and adults like Freire—that is, for people who are placed in the position of having to chase after the time that was stolen from them—the opportune time, *kairos*, is always now because it is justly an opportunity, a type of possibility for passage between two worlds. In this sense, when Freire refers to childhood as schooling, we can read this as a reference to a state of childhood beyond the chronological. It is for those in school who are not chronological children that Freire is especially interested in alphabetization: children entering school life, even if they are not in the socially acceptable chronological time to enter school anymore.

In this dialogue, then, Freire refers again to his own schooling that, in his particular case, coincides with his chronological childhood, with the socially established *kairos* for it. He emphasizes how the way in which he was alphabetized as a child, with words from his childlike world, remains present in his ideas about literacy in some form or another. The way in which he was alphabetized left such a deep impression upon him, that it remains present in his way of thinking and practicing it as educator in the same way. In this text, his memory is more crisp, precise, and has even more detail. We see his mother, Edeltrudes (Trudinha), sitting on the side of a wicker chair; his father, Joaquim, is swinging on a hammock in the shade between mango trees—free space, unpretentious, informal—in his backyard. As we have seen, Freire enters the world of letters, almost without realizing it, through the activities of a child populating his childlike universe: Giving words to the beings which inhabit his immediate, everyday world.

Another important aspect of this text is the way in which Freire highlights the importance of relationships during this period of chronological childhood, so instrumental in becoming who he becomes. He mentions his relationships with other members of his family, with animals, trees, and words. The way he was introduced to literacy by his parents is especially highlighted and revealed through his emotional context: it was an affective process, dialogical and loving (Freire and Guimarães, 1982, pp. 15–18). Freire makes clear that his father or mother were not school teachers, but he considers them both as educators and he considers one of the most important things his parents gave him was *time*! His mother on her chair and his father in his hammock were both patiently teaching him to read the words of his world.

It is important to stop oneself and pause in this observation. After all, this is Freire who defends the professionalization of the teacher against attempts to disqualify teachers (Freire, 1997). Yet he is made literate by non-professional educators who take care of what is most important for bringing someone into a world of letters with joy and emotion: they ensure that the reading and writing of words follows the reading and writing of the world, living a dialogical climate and environment and offering all the time their son needs to alphabetize himself. They offer a specific time of affections that one cannot measure with a clock. Freire learns to read within this formula in which his father and mother introduce him to the letters through time.

Freire's alphabetization was so deeply impressed upon him that he affirms that his way of acquiring literacy became the same thing he proposed for the education of adults years later. The dialogical way of his first apprenticeship into letters was so marked upon him that he came to see this form as a central axis that traverses all of his pedagogical ideas in his distinct "pedagogies," where he always begins by shifting the axis from the teacher or the student and replaces it with the dialectical relationship *between* them. Thus, Freire, educator of the pedagogical relationship, recreates in his educational conception the relational formula in which he was educated as a child.

Freire, the restless wanderer of utopia, speaks very positively of his relationship to his mother and father who, although a military man, has a loving and affective dialogical manner with his family and with Freire in particular (Freire, 2000, p. 37 ff.; 1996, p. 27 ff.). We do not find as many testimonies of Freire about his five children—Maria Madalena, Maria Cristina, Maria de Fatima, Joaquim Temístocles, and Lutgardes—in his written works, and the majority of them refer to the years in Santiago, where the two youngest, Joaquim Temístocles and Lutgardes, spent most of their chronological childhood. However, the testimonies from his sons and daughters suggest that this affective dimension that Freire lived in his own childhood was relived with his children, while chronological infants, and not only then either.

One of these references is in the context of a more general reflection on his political exile and his relationship to his first wife, Elza (Freire and Betto, 1985, pp. 90–1). After showing how Elza shared the experience of imprisonment and exile with him, accompanying him without being herself in the legal condition of being exiled, as a political act and in a completely solitary way (indeed, it was Elza who decided to go when Freire was reluctant to leave Brazil). Freire recognizes that Elza supported the biggest part of their family life and "was educator to us all" (Freire and Betto, 1985, p. 90). Indeed, Elza was a primary school teacher and was much more occupied than Freire with the daily education of their children. He comments, "In exile, the children arrived, jumping, to say: 'Old, actually the infrastructure of the family is the old'" (Freire and Betto, 1985, p. 90).[7] He follows this passage, translating this sentence as: "does it mean, open your eye, because if the infrastructure falls, we end ourselves" in order to pay a compliment to Elza and her role in providing for the family during the years of his exile, and to express

---

[7] "No exílio, os filhos chegavam, brincando, a dizer: 'Velho, na verdade a infra-estrutura desta família é a velha!'"

his guilt that it was not easy to avoid "in the difficulty of a son—his schooling, the beginning of a son in school, a bigger need of a son—" (Freire and Betto, 1985, pp. 90–1).

Freire also provides examples of how occasionally he was flooded by guilty feelings because of his wife and children's conditions. For example, these feelings emerged strongly once in the raw winter of Santiago, when one of the boys said that he was feeling cold and Freire did not have money to buy winter clothes for him. Freire observes how he suffered with this episode and how the problem was solved through the solidarity of a loving friend who worked in the United Nations and enjoyed credit in a store in Santiago. His friend bought winter clothes for his entire family. Being from the Northeast as he was, he would say: "the cold will arrive soon and you are from the Northeast, as I am too" (Freire and Betto, 1985, p. 91).

Another reference to his children occurs in this dialogue with Ricardo Kotscho, in which Freire shares (Freire and Betto, 1985, p. 62) that, when he was arrested by the military junta in 1964, his three girls visited him in prison without the two youngest boys, following the suggestion of his wife Elza, who was afraid that they would be traumatized by the situation. "I think she was right," Paulo Freire concludes.

We find a happier anecdote in relation to his children in *Letters to Cristina*. There Freire remembers an occasion in which, for the first time in his life, during the first year of his exile in Santiago, he experienced a snowfall. He was more than forty years old when he first felt the snow on his tropical skin. He got to make snowballs and play with his children. He describes the event to Nathercinha (see next section) with a fabulously childlike word in Portuguese:

I shared with her how surprised I was, feeling a childlike joy, when I saw snow for the first time in my life, near the mountains in Santiago, not very far from where we lived. On the streets with my kinds I felt like a child again myself, making snowballs and playing in the white flakes that covered the grass as well as my tropical body. (Freire, 1996, pp. 10–11)

"I felt like a child again myself" is a single word in Portuguese, a pronominal form of a verb invented by Paulo Freire: *meninizar-me* ("childlike me," or "make me more childlike"), the most informal, active, and joyful word with which to say childhood in Portuguese. Once again, Freire relives a playful childhood playing in the snow, this time with his precious children, chronological children, himself at an age not chronologically childlike. And, at an even more mature age—already a septuagenarian, the age at which writes *Letters to Cristina*—even further chronologically from his childhood, he plays with language and invents a Portuguese neologism, a special childlike verb to describe the action of someone that, despite not being a child, becomes a child in order to play in the snow with his children, who make him become more childlike. Thus, Freire is doubly childlike and, with him, we, his readers of all ages, become childlike, too.

Toward the end, another enigmatic reference appears in a paragraph in which, after realizing the importance of the feeling of having been taken care of and loved by his parents in his life, he affirms that

> unfortunately, we are not always able to express, without constraint and with maturity, our necessary love to our sons and daughters, by using various forms and ways, among them giving special attention. Sometimes, for a number of reasons, we do not know how to let our children know how much we love them. (Freire, 1996, p. 27)

Perhaps the testimony to follow will help us better understand this passage. Indeed, this testimony may be the most educative one of all. It is from his youngest son, Lutgardes, who confirms that Freire followed the same path he walked with his parents with his own children, which seems to be more than expected. Lutgardes, a sociologist and professor, comments in a video made by the *Instituto Paulo Freire de São Paulo* that Freire was always occupied when he was in Santiago, in Chile. He worked the entire week and, on the weekends, he wrote *Pedagogy of the Oppressed*. His children, tired of not having time with their father, decided to converse with him in his office, saying, "look Dad, this way is not possible, you are working the entire week and on the weekend you work the entire time, too, how is something like that possible?" Their father replied, "It is right. From now on, every Saturday we will go out together." Lutgardes, already a father at the time of the interview, sitting with his daughter on his lap, smiles and his eyes shine while he completes his story. "And then it was a wonder, we would go out, go around town, or we would go to the movies, eat lunch together, holding hands . . . Paulo Freire was loving, he was a very sweet person, very affectionate, right?" (Instituto Paulo Freire, 2005). This testimony may help to understand the previous ones because it shows two relational phases between Freire and his children: a lifestyle that made him absent because of his dedication to his academic work and, later, for traveling around the world, but at the same time a life intensively present in the loving form of listening to the word and offering a response, attentively affirming the request of his sons and daughters.

The amorous tenderness with which Freire dealt with his sons and daughters, despite being very absent in their lives at times due to his intense work and trips, is very similar to the way in which he describes the importance of his mother and father's listening to his childhood inspirations. To exemplify the posture that he and his wife Elza maintained in relation to his sons and daughters, we read:

> My father played an important role in my permanent search for understanding. Being affectionate, intelligent, and opened, he never refused to listen to us talk about our interests. They exemplified for us what it means to be understood and to understand, never showing any sign of intolerance. Although my mother was Catholic and my father was a spiritualist, they always respected each other's religious opinions. From them I learned early on the value of dialogue. (Freire, 1996, p. 28)

In consequence of this posture of his parents in relation to him, he highlights that "I never felt fearful when asking questions and I do not remember having been punished or even simply adverted for disagreeing" (ibid.). As we have seen, he retains the love and tolerance that he receives from his mother and father's education as a father.

In another text, *Towards a Pedagogy of the Question*, when thinking about the importance of questions and answers in human formation with Antonio Faundez, Freire shows himself to be a father who looks to his own father, who illustrates the connectivity that made questions maintain a link with his sons and daughters:

> One of the disciplines which Elza and I always placed upon ourselves in our relations with our children was never to refuse to answer their questions. Whoever we were with, we would break off our conversation to pay attention to their curiosity. Only after showing our respect for their right to ask questions did we duly draw their attention to the presence of the person or people we were talking with. I believe we begin this authoritarian denial of curiosity at a very early age by making remarks like "My, what a lot of questions from a little boy!," or "Go to sleep, leave those questions till tomorrow." (Freire and Faundez, 1989, pp. 35–6)

In this way, Freire shows how he and Elza care for the curiosity of their sons and daughters: their "right to ask questions" is respected. In this passage, he contrasts an authoritarian posture before the questions, a posture that discourages them, and a respectful posture, the one which responds. It seems clear here that Freire is not considering other options to face the questions of children or, in other words, we could ask: is responding to their questions the most respectful way to face them? What other alternatives do we have when facing the questions of our daughters and sons?

The Letters to Nathercinha

It is a good thing, Natercinha, that we never stop being a child.
(Freire. In: Lacerda, 2016, p. 50)

The letters that Freire wrote during his exile in Santiago, Chile, to Nathercia Lacerda (Lacerda, 2016) have recently been published. Freire mentions them in *Letters to Cristina*. The publication is the result of a very beautiful work by Cristina Laclette Porto and Denise Sampaio Gusmão with Nathercia Lacerda and Madalena Freire, one of the daughters of Freire. It is a carefully composed aesthetic work, with historical pictures, a presentation of Nathercia, six letters by Freire, an actual letter of Nathercia to Freire, one letter from Madalena to Nathercia and other details that, together, express the care and affection in which the project came to be. The six letters of Freire are typed and photographed conforming to the original manuscript.

Nathercinha is Freire's second cousin. Freire is the son of one of the sisters of her grandfather, Lutgardes, and therefore a nephew of the grandfather, that is, a cousin-brother of her mother. Freire was closer to being her uncle than a cousin, due to his age, although he refers to her as "cousin" in the letters. The correspondence was initiated by Nathercinha when she was nine and he was forty-five, in 1967. The letters of Freire to Natercinha (he wrote the nickname of his cousin without the "*h*" after the "*t*," perhaps because the name of his grandmother was Natércia) are dated between the fall of 1967 and the October of 1969. The last letter was sent from Cambridge, Massachusetts, United States, where Freire was living after leaving Chile and before going to Switzerland.

These letters are an anthem to childhood, in form and content. This is the result of careful handwriting, written especially so a child could read it; it has an egalitarian tone, intimate and affective. The writing is filled with poetry, metaphors, childlike images. In what follows, I make reference to the first three letters. When he was forty-five years old he still feels like a little boy, he lives his childhood, keeping it always alive. The other children, those who inhabit a chronological childhood, are equals and friends to Freire, someone who one converses and corresponds with. As Madalena Freire says in a letter to Nathercinha, he proposes "a conversation between friends, placing himself as an equal. Little by little, he differentiates himself as an adult, without losing the egalitarian sense between you." (Lacerda, 2016, p. 82).

To make a dialogue between adults and children possible, the adult needs to put himself at the same level as the child, being a friend and an equal. After all, in the life of a human being, childhood is what keeps us alive, supplying the curiosity to discover the world and to comprehend ourselves better with other human beings. Regarding himself as an equal with a child is like relating to a childlike part of himself.

The first letter has excerpts of "grown-ups," when Freire affirms that the world is the way it is because the human being has forgotten its childhood. The tone of the letter is diaphanous, clear, and emphatic: human beings and the world need childhood. In the second letter, he returns to the snow. It is the end of fall, the mountain peaks are covered by snow and Freire, with Elza and another couple, plays in the snow, making a snow man. He then adds: "Never allow the Natercinha of today to die within you. The girl that you are today should follow the young woman you will be tomorrow and the woman you will be thereafter" (Lacerda, 2016, pp. 54–5). The third letter, by contrast, is perhaps the most "political" of them all, the most explicit in terms of the justly political strength of childhood:

> The city is becoming full of flowers of all colors. The garden of our blue house is green with grass. The rose trees are beginning to open their buds. We look to the rose trees and they look like people laughing. Children laughing with the purity of a childlike laugh. If the old men, as grown-ups could or wanted to laugh as the rose trees, does it not seem to you that the world would be beautiful? But I believe that one day, with the effort of humanity and the world, life will allow grown-ups to laugh as children. Even more so—and this is very important— life will allow that all children can laugh. Because today not all children can laugh. Laughing is not only the opening of the lips to show teeth. It is the expression of the joy of living, the will to do things, to transform the world, of loving the world and humanity; in the only way we can love God. (Lacerda, 2016, pp. 57–8)

Freire affirms that it is precisely that all human persons, of every age, can smile like a child so that the world becomes more beautifully true, or, in other words, more just, more joyful, more filled with life. We can almost feel uncomfortable with the normative tone of these texts and what could be read as an idealization of childhood, but it is notable how Freire allows us to see that the bounty of the child's universe is not accessible to all children, that joy today accompanies only certain privileged lives. Childhood, then, is also this will of transforming the world so that not only certain lives are real lives of joy, of curiosity, of love. The world needs what childhood brings to make the world more worldly and life more alive.

In another text, Freire says that childhood is transformational, revolutionary, and, for this reason, "Conservatism is also incompatible with youth. What is in effect cannot be preserved, what is effective stands on its own" (Freire, 2000, p. 74). Here we have the political strength of the ever-present youth of childhood, its rejection of the maintenance of the injustices and oppressions in the world.

In a text published as a preface to a book of memories of Freire in English (Wilson et al., 2010), Freire's second wife, Ana Maria (Nita) Freire, makes tribute to that intimate relation to childhood that the great teacher of Pernambuco preserved during all of his life. This text, titled *Paulo Freire, the Eternal Child*, rings as a homage of that intensity and intimacy with which Freire lives in a childlike way his entire life. What this means, as Nita Freire shows us well is "to have *announced* a new [world], as only children of pure character, serious, and childlike adults can do" (p. xxv). The exaltation of childhood can sound exaggerated and idealized, but it contains a singular potential: to affirm childhood as a serious force that crosses all ages. In the same way, Nita remembers some of the recognitions and honors such as the title *Bambino permanente* (permanent child) bestowed upon Freire by the Biblioteca Comunale di Ponsaco, in Pisa, Italy, on March 31, 1990. Again, the permanence of childhood shows that it is not attached to chronological age.

In this text and in the biography that she wrote about Freire, Nita remembers a writing that her husband, speaking of his own death, wrote with childlike joy:

Damn, son! Childhood joy continues with life and still entirely childlike. I believe I am going to continue to live and die in Brazil.

After all, when I die: This joy will still be childlike! (Freire cited in: A. M. Freire, 2006, p. 621)

His words were cut short, but the childlike joy of Freire endures among us, among whosoever finds themselves with his thought and childlike life.

The Revolution: Freire's Most Affirmed Childhood

The infant is still lively, still learning to question, still committed to building a pedagogy of questioning. (Freire and Faundez, 1989, p. 140)

For Freire, childhood is an idea that goes much beyond chronology, and this has already been highlighted by various scholars. For example, in a comparison with the Italian Giorgio Agamben, E. Santos Neto and M. L. Alves emphasize that, for Freire, childhood is understood as a condition of human existence, associated with the human person's unfinished quality (Santos Neto and Alves, 2018 [2007], p. 9). In turn, Célia Linhares highlights that in Freire the child is "what yet reserves itself as dream, potency, desire and, therefore, what is still wrapped in mysteries, in possibilities never seen and, as such, does not achieve finding words to express itself clearly" (Linhares, 2007, p. 11). Thus, if this assimilation of childhood to desire confers to it a certain lack or negativity in an anthropological dimension, as a "metaphor of human existence" in its ethical and political dimensions, then childhood contains the most affirming form of freedom as the creation of a collective life carried by possibilities, dreams, and utopias (ibid.).

At the same time, one of the most affirming visions of childhood in the work of Freire appears in the last part of his dialogue with Antonio Faundez. Maybe it is not a coincidence because, as we have just affirmed, this is the most childlike of his various "pedagogies." In it, childhood appears not as a developmental stage, nor as a condition of life or metaphor of existence, but, instead, as a quality of a revolutionary process. Effectively, this is how Freire, from Pernambuco, ends his dialogue with the Chilean Faundez:

> On my first visit to Managua, in November 1979, speaking to a large group of educators at the ministry of education, I said that the Nicaraguan revolution seemed to be a revolution in its infancy—in its infancy, not in the sense that it was newly arrived, but by the evidences it was giving of its curiosity, its restlessness, its delight in questioning, its not being afraid to dream, its desire to grow, to be creative, and to bring about change. I also said on that hot afternoon that it was necessary, essential, for the Nicaraguan people, in their struggle to bring their revolution to maturity, not to let it to grow old by killing the infant in itself, which was part of its being. I was back there recently. The infant is still lively, still learning to question, still committed to building a pedagogy of questioning. (Freire and Faundez, 1989, p. 140)

The image of childhood could not be more affirming and powerful. Freire uses it as a compliment, a way of beautiful speech, a species of praise to a revolution that does not erase its curiosity, its restless, its taste for asking questions, its desire to dream, its desire to grow, create, transform. This is what a childhood without age is for Freire: A desire, a taste, and a sensibility for the forces of life like curiosity, dreams, and transformation.

The inner child of the Nicaraguan revolution has nothing to do with its chronological time of being in the world. It is, yes, a child of young age, but it is not a child because of its young age, because it was born a short chronological time ago. The revolution is not a child because it is "recently arrived." No. It is not a child for what it lacks, for its smallness or shortly lived time. Nor is the revolution a child for what it will be, for its projection into a future time. The (Nicaraguan) revolution, for Freire, is a child for what it is, for its mode of inhabiting the time of the present, for the affirming force it reveals, for its potency, its curious, restless, dreaming, creating, transforming way of being revolution. It is a child for the way in which it affirms a revolutionary life, for its way of revealing revolution to the world, of making itself not only a revolution, but a revolutionary mode of existence.

We are in the end of the 1970s, which is also the end of what Freire considers to be his third exile (he believes himself to have had two exiles before: the first, his arrival to the world, exiled from his mother's womb, and the second his move from Recife to Jaboatão). He returns to Brazil but continues his travels around the world. He finds himself in Nicaragua before a revolution that is also a chronological child; it only has a few years of age and, as such, anticipates diverse possibilities for its growth through time.

There are many possible revolutionary notions to grow from this, and, among them, Freire highlights two ways of relating to childhood which could distinguish themselves if they mature: (a) the first understands maturing as a growing old and, therefore, as an erasure of childhood to overcome or convert it into something else. This is the possibility where people understand childhood as something that needs to be transformed into something else that overcomes it. From this possibility a conception of education unfolds where education is about presenting the most appropriate path toward this exit, a type of transformation of childhood that will convert it into what has been idealized for it and that will also become what it is not; (b) the second, here implicitly defended by Freire, understands childhood as something that maturity would do well to preserve, feed, and care for to the extent that it supplies vitality to life and, for that reason, it never should be abandoned. This way of understanding childhood detaches itself, for education, into another relationship to childhood, another logic of formation that closely attends, cares, and listens to childhood, because if childhood is overcome or erased, life will lose something that would diminish its vitality: without childhood, life would be less alive, for all ages. Following this possibility, education can leave behind it worries about forming childhood—and children—into something which it is not, occupying itself instead in cultivating and attending to it so that childhood always remains alive, being what it is in all ages.

This inner child of the Nicaraguan revolution is the creative and curious potency of life at any age. It is an engaged child, committed, fruitful. It playfully throws itself into building a pedagogy of the question, that which learns and teaches to ask questions. It even ventures to asks itself "what does it mean to ask questions?" (Freire and Faundez, 1989, p. 37), what is its sense, why, and for what? It is a pedagogy that puts itself permanently in a questioning state, that intensively lives the question and the asking of questions.

As we have seen, Freire, who did not dedicate himself particularly to the education of chronological children but instead to the education of a childlike people without age, proposes an affirmation of childhood as childhood: a properly childlike view, so much so that it becomes the greatest compliment given to a revolution, and nothing less than a revolution, something that is the most serious thing in the world, the most important and adult of all among the things of adults and, even for that, childhood does not need to stop at the same time being the most joyful, playful, and demanding of all things. The most adult of all needs, the most childlike thing in the world. Nothing seems more necessary than a revolution of the present state of affairs and the dominating modes of life in Latin America. What Freire is suggesting is this: a childlike revolution is the most educative of all revolutions.

Ever since he was a child, Freire has known the necessity of revolution for life in Latin America. It is one of the things he learned when he was a boy in Jaboatão, which followed him always. With this sense of necessity, he also affirms that a revolution without childhood is a revolution that loses its capacity to create, to ask itself questions, to be restless. In other words, for Freire, childhood is a condition of revolution that is proud of being who and what it is.

This is not the place to judge the judgements that Freire makes of Nicaraguan education, much less the Nicaraguan revolution itself, without evaluating its historical successes or failures. This is not what it is that Freire affirms. Nor does childhood guarantee the success of a revolution; perhaps it is exactly the contrary: the world in which we live may appear more hostile with childhood conceived of in this way. The inner child of revolution affirms a pedagogy of the question, which, in turn, exposes it to the hostilities of the system. Childhood has nothing to do with a tactic of success. What Freire is affirming is that a "more proper" revolution—a revolution that is and wants to be a true revolution, or, in other words, the most revolutionary of the revolutions—cannot forget or erase its childhood. The most revolutionary revolution is the most childlike revolution. And, in being childlike, it educates in childhood: in joy, in curiosity, in asking questions, in what does not have age.

As we have seen in the first sections of this work, Freire does not only consider it essential to maintain childhood beyond chronological childhood, but he also uses his own life as an example of a permanent cultivation of his own childhood. In this way, we can extend this affirmation of the inner child of revolution to any educator. Childhood is a condition in which to live an educational life, sensible to self-questioning and to engagement in a restless and creative pedagogical act.

In the same way, perhaps we can extend the risks of this childlike posture. The more childlike educators are, the more they can be exposed to the hostilities of a system. However, at the same time, the more childlike they are, the more educative this or that person who does not erase their childhood will be and they will keep this childhood alive in a questioning mode, joyful and curious, inhabiting their educative practice.

In other words, according to the educator from Pernambuco, we could say that childhood acquires its ontological statute first in the environment of the human, of what realizes its historicity while being thrown into the problematization and transformation of a present life. In Freire's words, "within the understanding of History as possibility, tomorrow is problematic. In order for it to come, it is necessary that we build it through transforming today. Different tomorrows are possible" (Freire, 2000, p. 55) because "the future is not a given datum, a destiny, a doom" (Freire, 1994, p. 112, translation modified). Thus, childhood realizes the political sense of a properly human existence: its unstoppable vocation for being more, for affirming the future as possible and not as predetermined, its permanent becoming instead of being once and for all. "The fight does not reduce itself to slow what will come or to secure its arrival; it is necessary to reinvent the world" (Freire, 2000, p. 55, translation modified).[8] Childhood, for Freire, is a reinventing force of world.

Childlike Words for Those Who Never Stop Being Children

And so it was that, one rainy afternoon in Recife, under a leaden sky, I went to Jaboatão in quest of my childhood.

(Freire, 1994, p. 36)

As we have just affirmed, this inner child that Freire attributes to the Sandinista revolution in Nicaragua can also be attributed to Freire's own life. When re-reading some of his affirmations of childhood, whether about his own chronological childhood or about the childhood of a revolution, when we perceive the style and manner of his writing, always questioning and loving at the same time, we see Freire's childhood as something that he is constantly feeding and does not want to ever abandon.

Even in the last of his public interventions—interviews, encounters, and ceremonies—we can see his childlike way of being. Until the very end of his life he walks through the world questioning himself and others in a childlike way. To sing these childlike notes in his words: the perennial childhood of Freire expresses itself in his curiosity, his unquietness, his taste for asking questions, for not fearing to dream, for wanting to grow, create, and transform, in his childlike speech, in the originating use of words that first formed his world during his own childhood. He talks as a child talks, with the language and way of a child—even in the most solemn and important occasions—

---

[8]   The English translation ends: "it is necessary to reinvent the future." But the Portuguese says: "é preciso reinventar o mundo."

justly because only the child can handle such an occasion. Freire is born and grows, keeping his childhood alive: curious, attentive, and always engaged in the construction of a childlike pedagogy, a childlike pedagogy of the question. Let us hear it from the great educator from the Northeast of Brazil:

> The main criterion for evaluating age, youth, and old age cannot be that of the calendar. No one is old just because he or she was born a long time ago or young just because he or she was born a short time ago. People are old or young much more as a function of how they think of the world, the availability they have for curiously giving themselves to knowledge. The search for knowledge should never make us tired, and the acquisition of it should never make us immobile and satisfied. People are young or old much more as a function of the energy and the hope that they can readily put into starting over, especially if what they have done continues to embody their dream, an ethically valid and politically necessary dream. We are young or old to the extent that we tend to accept change or not as a sign of life, rather than embrace the standstill as a sign of death. (Freire, 2000, p. 72)

Childhood is a curious life that neither tires nor is satisfied, it is mobilized, lively, hoped for; a life that begins everything anew or is in constant renewal; a life that sees in transformation a sign of life and in the lack of transformation a sign of death.

In this way, childhood is not a matter of age, of having few years, of a fixed quantity of time.[9] In the first letter of the pedagogical letters included in his posthumous *Pedagogy of Indignation*, at an extreme distance from his chronological childhood (only a few months before his death in January 1997), he comments on the dynamism of urban life, the transformation it demands, especially for people who are over seventy years old, like himself, and concludes, "It is as if today we were younger than we were yesterday" (Freire, 2004, p. 4).

---

[9] For an exploration of childhood as a philosophical concept in children, adults, and even beyond human beings, see Kohan and Weber, 2020.

This statement is a declaration of childhood, a precise definition: childhood is a way of experiencing time when it inverts itself. Today we are younger than yesterday; there is childhood without age, of every age, at any age. Childhood is living time in a childlike way, open to the worlds which a question opens; the chronological age one has does not matter. It is a way, continues Freire from Pernambuco, of being "at the level of our time" (ibid.), a level which is not measured in its distance from the ground, but in the disposition to take risks, openness to the unusual, intimacy with the secrets of the world, a disposition to be able to be otherwise and to "comprehend teenagers and youngsters" (ibid.).

We can all be more childlike. We can be children at seventy years of age if we dare. There are children of seventy years who are younger than adults of forty, youngsters of twenty or, even, children of nine. Some years earlier, at the age of more than sixty years old, Freire affirms something similar about himself:

> Sexagenarian, I am seven years old; sexagenarian, I am fifteen years old; sexagenarian, I love the wave of the sea; I adore seeing the snow fall, it seems alien. Some companion of mine from the Left will be already saying: Paulo is irreparably lost. And I would say to my hypothetical companion from the Left, I am found: Precisely because I lose myself looking at the snow fall. Sexagenarian, I am 25 years old. Sexagenarian, I love again and I begin to create a life again. (Freire, 2001a, p. 101)

Loving the wave of the sea, adoring to see the snow fall when one belongs to a region where snow does not exist, losing oneself in what seems small, insignificant, unimportant, in the beauty of a mere detail, aesthetically relating oneself to the world, appreciating its beauty without saving time within it: in the end, for Freire, loving childhood means to risk beginning to live anew every time. Rebirth after death. To love after the death of one's beloved. To be born again in love after this death of the beloved. To begin to love when it seems like love is over, when the love of one's entire life dies and it seems that it has ended love in life, childhood calls us to begin to love anew, as if we had never loved before, as if we began to love only for the first time. Childlike love, love of childhood, a childhood of love.

Thus, childhood is a way to relate to time; to invert it and become younger with its passing and to relate to the future as something always open, as something that does not make us (Freire, 2004, p. 34). We must fight to remake the future and, in this fight, to remake ourselves anew. Childhood is a way of looking to the future with eyes wide open, as if it also disposes itself to us, in the incomplete condition that inhabits us as humans (Santos Neto; Alves; Silva, 2011, p. 53). Finally, before anything else, childhood is a way of inhabiting the present, of being entirely present in the present, as if time were just time, embodying the now, as if we were only children, as if the future was just one other form of the present. In childhood, there is not much past and there is a wide open future, undefined. The time of childhood is the present. Freire, a child of conjunctions and connections, is the one who says, "I think that the best time is the time that you live, it is today" (Freire. In: Blois, 2005, p. 30).

Justly because childhood is this presence and this relation to the present, it is needed that chronological children

> grow in the exercise of this ability to think, to question and question themselves, to doubt, to experiment with hypotheses for action, and to plan, rather than just following plans that, more than proposed, are imposed upon them. Children's right to learn how to decide, which can only be achieved by deciding, must be ensured. If liberties are not constituted on their own, but rather in the ethical observance of certain limits, the ethical observance of these limits cannot be accomplished without putting liberties themselves and the authority or authorities to which they dialectically relate at a measure of risk as well. (Freire, 2004, p. 37)

This may be one of the principal marks of a pedagogy of childhood for Freire: giving to chronological childhood the conditions under which it can love its childhood in a childlike way, which means that it can also live its entrance into the world of letters in a childlike way through a politically sensible education, attentive and hospitable toward childhood, that does not assault it, that does not let it die. In this respect, the educational preoccupations of Freire, as we know, vastly exceed a chronological childhood. In a lecture on "Human Rights and a Liberating Education," offered at the University of São Paulo in June of 1988, he affirms: "The education of which I speak is an education of the now and it is an education of tomorrow. It is an education which must place us into permanently asking ourselves, remaking ourselves, questioning ourselves" (Freire, 2001a, p. 102). Childhood is the form of all education, at any and every age. This is the paradox of the one who dedicated his life for the education of adults: in the way that Freire conceives of education, including the education of youth and adults, it cannot be, among other things, an education for children, because what constitutes childhood is already a condition of this education. Being unquiet, asking, doubting, asking questions, creating: this childlike education, attentive to childhood, invites students, whatever their age may be, to live in childhood; those that inhabit and dwell in it, keep it alive and take care of it; those who forgot it or lose it must recover it or reinvent it.

Perhaps for this reason Freire has taken care of always feeding his childlike condition, his inner child. In this same intervention, he defends an education in the perspective of human rights that is "courageous, curious, awakening and keeper of curiosity; that is an education that, as much as possible, preserves the child that you were, without letting your maturity kill it" (Freire, 2001a, p. 101). In Portuguese, Freire uses the feminine of child, "girl," to call attention to the sexism of language. This is the same language he used to refer to the Nicaraguan revolution a decade earlier. From this perspective, all are any. All education needs to preserve the child we once were; helping to keep it alive throughout an entire life. Following this, Freire completes his declaration of love to childhood:

> I think that one of the best things that I have done in my life, better than the books I have written, was never allowing the child that I was and the child that I couldn't be to die in me. (Freire, 2001a, p. 101) The condition of childhood, the inner child within, is so powerful that it is necessary to not only keep alive the childhood that we were but also the one we couldn't be: childhood lives from possibility, from which everything can be.

It makes a lot of sense for Freire, the conjunctive and connective child, to keep the other childhoods alive that cannot not be connected, reunited, or lived. It should also make sense to any educator sensitive to their encounter with other and different childhoods, to help to care for or restore the childlike condition in others.

Childhood, for Freire, is something that goes beyond his own biography; it includes it, of course, but it does not exhaust itself in it. In this sense, the place that Freire from Pernambuco gives to childhood helps us to see that childhood crosses the *chronos* of our lives—our past, our present, our future—and also crosses other times that we experience according to different logics. In a less anthropomorphizing vision, we can also perceive that there is childhood in others, in otherness, in plants, in animals, in school, in the world. There is a childlike life waiting to be felt, heard, and fed. There is a childhood of school to recover and reinvent. There is much childhood in the world waiting to be awakened, relived, by conjunctive and connective children.

This is my childlike reading of childhood in Freire, of his childhood. Of his childlike passion. Of his life as a child at all ages. Of the revolutionary strength of childhood. There are many childhoods in Freire. There is an extraordinary boy-child strength in his word and in his life.

Who knows, perhaps readers of the present chapter are now just a little more attentive to childhood, to their childhood and to the childhoods of the world. If that is the case, we will play, we will laugh, we will jump in the snow, in the heat, in the Brazil of today, and always and in any part of the world that demands a little childhood to more properly make a world. I continue writing having almost finished in order to begin again anew, to search for new beginnings, for more childhood and more boyhood, in the words and life of Paulo Freire. As a bridge, I find a girl who carries us to love life in a childhood writing:

> When I was twenty-three years old, and newly married, I began to discover, but I was not always able to state explicitly, that the only way we can stay alive, alert, and to truly be philosophers is never to let the

child within us die. Society pressures us to kill this child within, but we must resist because when we kill this child within us, we kill ourselves. We wither and age before our time. Today I am sixty-two years old, but I often feel ten or twenty years old. When I climb five flights of stairs, my body lets me know my age, but what is inside my old body is deeply alive, simply because I preserve the child within me. I also think my body is youthful and as alive as this child who I once was and continue to be, this child who leads me to love life so much. (Freire, 1985, p. 197)

Epilogue

Five Principles or Beginnings

If ever there was a time to reintroduce Freire into the schools, camps, and political resistance groups that have sprung up across the country, that time is now.

(Carnoy and Tarlau, 2018, p. 100)

Paulo Freire continues to be invaluable for thinking about the relations between education and politics. He unveils the fallacy of negating the political dimension of pedagogical work and proposes a specific way of affirming the relation between the two. In this book, I have not focused exclusively on this relation, but, inspired by it and working within the dimension marked by Freire, I have recreated another form in which to think about Freire. The work here departs from certain beginnings. I accept Freire's claim on the impossibility of political neutrality in education. In this text, I have unfolded from this "politicization" of education five principles. These principles or beginnings can also be understood as reasons to read Freire today.[1] Throughout the book I highlighted five: life, equality, love, errantry, and childhood. Having presented the five in-depth above, here, I recuperate some key elements of each to conclude this book.

The first principle, life, is concerned with a conception of philosophy as an exercise of thinking in life which is affirmed within and outside of educational practices. Philosophy conceived of as an exercise opens

---

[1] Recently, Licínio C. Lima offered four reasons to study Freire today: (a) he is a classic of critical educational thinking; (b) his work has a great critical power; (c) it affirms a democratic pedagogy, participation, and active citizenship; (d) it proposes a permanent humanizing education (Lima, 2018, pp. 29–34).

life up to a questioning of the self, ways of living shared with others, with philosophy itself, and new ways of living. The philosophical-educational life embodies the politics of philosophical questioning that makes us more attentive to the meaning of life, and why we live the way we do. It is a questioning way of life lived by the Socrates (of Athens and of Caracas) that opens a singular, disquieting, and perturbing educational space for those who ask, in the company of philosophy, philosophical questions that give a new force to life. Put in other words, when our educating is sensitive to this dimension, education becomes much more than teaching or learning about theories, content, or the history of ideas, and becomes more than anything else an affirmation of a determined way of life that puts life in question, expanding its meanings, turning it into a shared and always open adventure.

The second principle, equality, is tied to a political presupposition on the equal value of all lives in all their forms of manifestation. It is a political rather than epistemological principle because its value lies not in that which can be proven to be scientifically true, but rather it is a presupposition one assumes about what life can be when we enter into educational relations with others. We do not know what a life can or can't be, but if we assume a principle of equality in education, then education can be a space where everyone has unlimited possibilities to expand their lives. We are confident in the educational unfolding and impact of this principal: the way it promotes self-affirmation, its educational value, and also how it encourages horizontality rather than hierarchy in educational experiences.

The third principle is love, which is an equally political force encountered in educational acts that makes lives more livable and education more educational. The love that Freire inspires in us is a type of connective energy between people and the world. It is a force of encounter with others and of struggle for living lives that are more livable than the lives we are living. It is also a vital force through which education, as a mode of relation between those that teach and those that learn, can interrupt spaces without life, and turn them into other spaces of life, or of other ways of living. It is a creative energy of a world that offers more than the world we are living in now. In sum, the love of all forms of life is a component of education, and the ability of an educator to love is an irreplaceable dimension of her work.

Errantry, the fourth principle, affirms the educational values of both erring and making mistakes. It entails both committing errors and erring or journeying without a predetermined path. It is that which has confidence in the political significance of movement, of understanding life as constant change, and education in tune with this understanding of life. Thought of through this double meaning, education as an erring and making errors gives a space for recreation and reconfiguration. To err/error has meaning because another world is always possible, the end of history is not already written, and the erring and making errors of the teacher opens up an exploration of a world history to come. This double erring also points to a displacement, a decentering, an opening to questions from the outside, that comes from the excluded, those tattered and threadbare, and those within the system who have had their lives negated.

Finally, I have dedicated the last principle to a question that usually is put first, and rarely at the end, one which is even less associated with the life of Freire: childhood. Childhood is a principle of beginnings, a beginning of beginnings that comes from other places, another politics of education. It is a principle that does not form, but transforms, reforms, listens, makes hospitable, and takes care of. Childhood, as a principle, is a form of experiencing time, of inhabiting the present in a way that makes the present curious, puts it in doubt, makes us more attentive, disquiets us, and inspires questioning and expectations. It is a principle that involves a dimension of caring found in, or of, the educator. It is within the person and in the world. An infantile education is not an education of childhood, but rather a becoming child of education, another education, a childlike education born with doubt, curiosity, and absence of certainties.

I have read Freire here as a childlike educator inhabiting the strangeness of infancy. A human who, as a foreigner, learned to value childhood. In his own words:

> It was while in exile that I realized I was truly interested in learning. What I learned in exile is what I would recommend to all readers of this book: each day be open to the world, be ready to think; be ready not to accept what is said just because it is said; be predisposed to reread what is read; each day investigate, question, and doubt; I think it is the most necessary to doubt. I feel it is always necessary not to be sure, that is, to be overly sure of "certainties." My exile was a long time of continuous learning. (Freire, 1985, p. 181)

"What is most needed is doubt," says the child who learned to doubt as a foreigner. His is a pedagogy of doubt and learning, understood as a permanent state of an openness to thinking differently, knowing differently, and living differently. Here is a certainty, the single one that involves inconveniencing certainties to give a place to effective learning. Here we find the political and educational value of childhood. An infantile doubt, born abroad is the driving force of all learning.

As we have seen, this doubting child has something to say not only about educational spaces but also about the lives we live and are constructing. In a dialogue that makes up one of his spoken books, one of the most beautiful and childlike, which has the expressive title: *We Make the Road by Walking*, Freire in conversation with the childlike North American educator Myles Horton, clearly defines the place and value of childhood, not only in education but also in life. Two significant passages from the conversation are worth citing in full:

> MYLES: One thing about learning is that you have to enjoy it. You said to me in Los Angeles that you wanted to become as a little child like I was. Picasso says it takes a long time to grow young, and I say it takes even longer to become as a little child. So that's the height we are striving for.
> PAULO: And Myles, the more we become able to become a child again, to keep ourselves childlike, the more we can understand that because we love the world and we are open to understanding, to comprehension, that when we kill the child in us, we are no longer. Because of that, in Los Angeles my daughter Magdalena said about Myles, "He's a baby!"

> (Horton and Freire, 1990, p. 64)

Horton draws inspiration from Picasso to affirm the power of youth, and even more so, of childhood. For Freire, childhood is a source of lovingness and openness to the world. Education must never, therefore, transform the child into something that would deprive the child of their childhood. To do so would be to strip life of life, in the sense that it would remove the lovingness and openness that constitute us as beings in childhood. Thus, childhood appears in the beginning of the horizon of life as something to be cared for and not abandoned, as something that sustains a loving life, one that is always curious, and open to the new and other lives.

More than Ever/Never

We are approaching the horizon of our childlike book. It is the time, therefore, to return to its beginning, its infancy. I feel the need to end this writing returning to the first words we find in the original Portuguese title[2] if literally translated: *Paulo Freire, More than Ever/Never*. "More than ever/never." It is a phrase that needs to be unpacked, because while it is a phrase we might encounter naturally, and most naturally in Portuguese or Spanish, it appears as if it is missing, in its beginning, an adverb that marks time: Today or Now. When is this "more than ever"? On the other hand, if translated as "more than never" the phrase seems literally banal, any time would be more than no time. Yet if we translate it as "more than ever" it seems impossible: how would it be possible to have a time that is larger/more important than all time, ever? However, this is not the principal meaning. "More than ever/never" could be interpreted as "much more now than in any other moment." In English, this is more explicit when we say, "more than ever," which in Portuguese would read, *mais do que sempre*. The *sempre* (ever) would make more sense than *nunca* (never), if we understand that the meaning of ever is

---

2 *Paulo Freire mais do que nunca.*

not a sum of chronological or historical time, but rather an intensity of time that cannot be quantified—a present that stretches far beyond the today, or a now that is not just a momentary instant. It is a present of a presence, crossing and remaining in the passage of time that "today" and "now" intend to demarcate.

Thus, it is neither "today" nor "now" because the time of "today" and "now" mark a chronological time, a numbering of movements, a time that passes. On the contrary, the present time of "more than ever" is a present that does not pass: this is the time of education. The today and the now are too instantaneous to be attributed to Freire. They are too ephemeral for his loving care, his presence, his temporality. As such, our (Portuguese) title appreciates a presence more than it marks an absence. It expresses, in this way, a cry, a desire, a hope in a present that does not pass. It is, in truth, quite untranslatable, because if by "ever" we mean the sum of all moments in time, then it does not capture the meaning it takes on here.

With this in mind, there are at least two meanings of the original Portuguese title that are offered here. The first suggests that, in the actual political and educational Brazilian context, it is more important now than at any other moment to read and think about the ideas and life of Freire. This is not only true for Brazil. Freirean inspiration is in short supply in many places. In the text from which the epigraph for this section is drawn, Martin Carnoy and Rebecca Tarlau argue consistently that in the Trumpian United States, at least, the presence of Freire is also more necessary than ever. We could include the need for Freire in many other contexts, in particular in this gale of conservatism that has recently irrupted in South America. I hope that throughout this book, I have sufficiently justified this claim by thinking through an education of life, equality, love, errantry, and childhood/infancy.

The other meaning of "more than ever," expresses a call to the presence of the Pernambucan educator for the educational times we are living through. It is as if Freire's life invites us to the present of a presence that extrapolates us from chronological time, to the loving present of educational time. This is a presence inspired by love, equality, life, errantry, and childhood. For this reason, the "more" does not signal a quantity, but rather an intensity, quality, and presence in the radical temporality of education.

One could rightly say that this is all very abstract, conceptual, and difficult to put into practice. Admittedly, the present book does not pretend to be a guide on how one should teach, and even less so does it offer readymade recipes for the everyday. At any rate, we offer here an exercise that perhaps makes it easier to perceive the principle meaning of this book, which is little more than this: to disturb and provoke a questioning of what it means to educate.

Let's try a good-natured experiment then. There are five days in the working week, and we have five principles to work with. What if we tried to practice one principle per day? On Monday, we could enter our schools without leaving our lives behind. We could try and perceive whether or not what we did in the classroom was connected to how we live outside of it, and whether or not what we did in the classroom could transform how we live outside of it. On Tuesday, we would enter our schools full of trust and confidence in our student's equal ability to teach and learn, to live dignified lives. We wouldn't be looking for learning outcomes, which could occur for a variety of reasons. Instead, we would see what happens when we don't under or overestimate the capacity of anyone. On Wednesdays we would dedicate ourselves to attending more closely to love, our affective and amorous relationships in the classroom, the webs of affect generated with our students, our colleagues, knowledge, the rooms we are in. Thursdays would be days of errantry. We would prepare ourselves to carefully travel the thread of thoughts wherever they might take us within the collective fabric of the classroom. On this day, we would not seek to guide students to any predetermined place, instead we would open ourselves up to a shared journey. On Friday, to end the week, we would return to childhood/infancy. Fridays we would be a child, a curious, questioning one who does not allow age to determine their childhood. On this day, we would only ask questions.

To return to the beginning when we are so close to the end of this writing is a way to affirm that, in education, but perhaps not only in education, there is always time to begin, especially when it seems that we have reached the end of times, like in today's Brazil. To feel, like Freire, that we are always at the beginning, is a childlike politics for education (Horton and Freire, 1990, p. 56). There is always a place for another world in this world. Here, inspired by Freire, I have let this childlike politics inspire my thoughts on errantry, love, equality, life, and childhood. I hope that these inspired thoughts inspire others, that they lead to other new beginnings.

In the end, I hope I have shown that the attempt to expel or abolish the ideology of Paulo Freire from Brazilian education is extremely disproportionate to the affirmative values that his thinking and life offer to education. This attempt to expel Freire is, of course, impossible, because his way of living education is present in a time not bound by resolutions, laws, or amendments. It is present in another time, the time of encounters between teachers and students in any school, or outside of schools, who come together in the spirit of equality to err with a love and childhood that puts their lives in question, and how they live with others, even as so many different forces try to push them apart, in separate directions.

It is time to end and to return to the beginning. Now. Today. More than ever/never. Always. Thank you, Paulo Freire. Thank you for your infinite childlike strength. Thank you for your extraordinary presence in the present, a presence which is not of yesterday, today, or tomorrow, but that is, justly so, the presence of the time of education. The presence of a question, of a smile, of a hug. Thank you for your indelible presence in a world full of life, equality, errantry, love, and infancy.

After I had finished the book, I found a paragraph by Freire that I couldn't help but include. I initially had my doubts as to where to put it, but in the end I decided that Freire himself, rather than me, should close out the book with his words that sing a song to life, to an intense, loving, passionate, overflowing life, constantly in creation and recreation, like the one Freire lived and inspired us to live. Here, then, are the words that, I hope, move those who have come this far, to move them every time we read them:

I really like to like and feel good about other people. I like to live, to live my life intensely. I'm the type of person who loves his life passionately. Of course some day I will die, but I have the impression that when I die, I will die with great intensity as well. I will die experimenting with myself intensely. For this reason, I'm going to die with an enormous longing for life, since this is the way I have been living. . . . For me, the fundamental thing in life is to work in life to create an existence overflowing from life, a life that is well thought out, a life that is touched and made and remade in this existence. The more I do something, the more I exist. And I exist intensely. (Freire, 1985, p. 195)

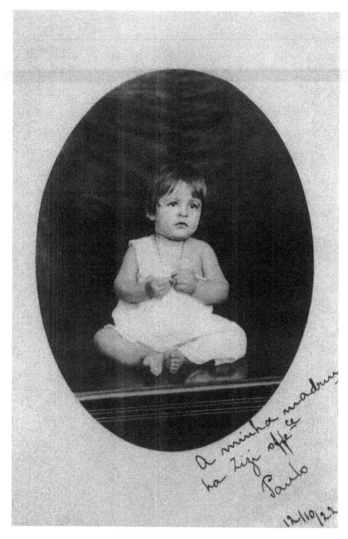

Figure 1 Paulo Freire aged one year.

Figure 2 With workers in a Culture Circle, Angicos, 1963.

Figure 3 Alphabetizing in Sobradinho, Federal District of Brazil, 1963.

Figure 4 Alphabetizing in Sobradinho, Federal District of Brazil, 1963.

Figure 5 Paulo Freire with Clodomir Santos de Morais (on the right) with whom he was imprisoned at Olinda (Pernambuco), 1964.

Figure 6 Paulo and Elza Freire in Guinea Bissau, 1974.

Figure 7 In an alphabetization circle in Fiji, 1976.

Figure 8 Paulo Freire promoting alphabetization in Fiji, 1976.

Figure 9 With the coordinator of the National Program of Alphabetization at Guinea Bissau, 1976.

Figure 10 Paulo Freire with Miguel Darcy de Oliveira (IDAC) and Mário Cabral, Ministry of Education of Guinea-Bissau, in 1978.

Figure 11 The emotion of returning to Brazil after exile, at the airport of Campinas, 1979.

Figure 12 The emotion of returning to Brazil after exile, at the airport of Campinas, 1979.

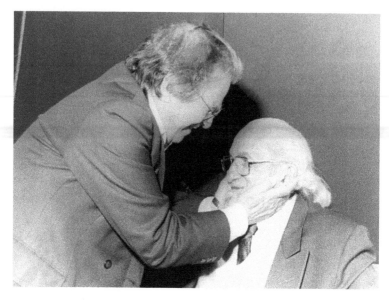

Figure 13 In the hands of the friend and anthropologist Darcy Ribeiro.

Figure 14 Paulo Freire and his second wife Ana Maria Araujo Freire visiting a school at São Paulo, 1989.

Figure 15 Paulo Freire between lights and shadows.

Figure 16 Schools, institutes, libraries, and cultural centers around the world are named after the pedagogue of the oppressed.

Figure 17 Editions of *Pedagogy of the Oppressed* around the world.

Figure 18 Illustration by Claudius Ceccon.

Figure 19 Illustration by Claudius Ceccon.

Figure 20 Nosso patrono é gigante. Our Patron is a Giant. Made on Praça XV (XV Square), Rio de Janeiro, on May 15, 2019 during the event "UFRJ vai à Praça" (UFRJ goes to square) organized by Marta Werneck and Lícius Bolssolan, professors at the Federal University of Rio de Janeiro (UFRJ). Photograph by Wilson Cardoso Junior.

Interview between Walter Omar Kohan and Jason Wozniak

Where and When to Think with Paulo Freire? A Timely Conversation

The following interview took place between the author and the translator of this book at Café Lapa, Rio de Janeiro at the very early days of 2020, just a few days before Covid-19 exploded in Brazil and the United States.

Jason: We are here today, January 17, 2020, with Walter Omar Kohan, author of the new book *Paulo Freire: A Philosophical Life*. The literal translation of the title in Portuguese would be: *Paulo Freire: More Than Never*.

Walter: Never?

Jason: Is that what we are going to say?

Walter: I thought in English it could be *More Than Ever*.

Jason: So, this is the first question . . .

Walter: [Chuckles.]

Jason: Because when we talked at your house, I thought it was *More than Ever*. But you insisted on *More than Never*. the best English translation would be, *Paulo Freire: Now More Than Ever*. In which case, we would add a bit to the title. Do you want to say something about this title choice even though the English title has been changed?

Walter: Yes. I think the original title translated into English is much more interesting than in Portuguese or in Spanish, even though it is not clear enough to be used as the title of the book in English, and that is why we opted for a simpler title. *More than never*, literally, would be the

Portuguese *mais do que nunca*. It is a kind of obvious time. In the sense that any time is more than never because never is no time. So, more than no time is any time. When you say that you could say in English, *now more than never*, it is because it seems that there is something missing if we just say *more than never*. It is not that *more than never* is incorrect, but it could be more natural and obvious if we added a word like in Portuguese we add *hoje* or *agora*.

Jason: Today or now.

Walter: Yes. So *today* or *now more than ever* would be expected. In fact, when I proposed the title *Paulo Freire: Mais do que nunca* to the Brazilian editor, Rejane Dias, she said that a word was missing. She wanted to say, today, *hoje*, more than ever. But I responded that if we include today or now, we would be relating Paulo Freire to a dimension of time that is *chronos*, which is only one dimension of time, and I would say, more superficial in terms of education. It is obvious that *chronos* is very important in educational institutions. They are, in fact, chronological institutions. Differently, when you say just *more than ever* it turns into another time. And if more than never is any time, then more than ever is no time because ever is all time. So, more than all time needs to be understood not quantitatively but relating to another dimension of time that, I would say, is a qualitative, intensive, *aionic* dimension. I think that this is the time of true education, or the time of Paulo Freire.

Jason: *Aionic* time?

Walter: Yes, *aionic* time. This is the time that is important for Paulo Freire. For Paulo Freire this sense of time, *aionic* time, is recorded in the bodies and in the spirit of the Brazilian educated-educators. So, it is not about chronology or quantitative time. If the title was *today more than ever*, or *now more than ever*, it would be saying that it is just at this moment, at this chronological time, that Paulo Freire is important. And, of course this is true in the sense that, today, here and in many other places, to think with someone like Paulo Freire helps us to put into question the present we are living in. It is not untrue that today or now Paulo Freire is important. But the other dimension of time, *aionic*, is even more important or more relevant because it reminds us that, for Freire, education does not merely have to do with chronological time. For him, education has to do with inhabiting the present, a way of experiencing *aion.* Remember that *chronos* has two parts, past and future, but no present other than a limit (now or today). And that *aion* is pure present. The *aionic* sense of time is not easy to experience in schools. Quite the contrary, more and more our societies do not provide the spaces to experience this kind of time, a time that suspends chronological time. So teachers are kinds of artists, magicians, offering *aion* as a way of offering a time that is not given in the institution. In any case, in the English edition, we do not have this complexity because we decided on a more simple and direct title.

Jason: You are suggesting, then, the need for a suspension of *chronos* to open up the possibility of *aion*, and that Freire can help us do that.

Walter: Yes. Of course, this suspension of *chronos* is not something that is literal in the sense that there is nothing we can do to stop *chronos*. *Chronos* happens regardless, but maybe the way we relate to it, the importance we give to it, the way it interferes in the way we live our lives, this is something that we can act upon.

Jason: I wanted to follow up on this question with something we talked about beforehand, which is another Greek word for time, *kairos*. I remember that when we spoke before, if you did say, *now more than ever*, there is a certain sense of urgency. *Kairos* has the meaning of urgency to act, to do something in the moment, now. So, I wanted to hear your thoughts on taking *kairos* into consideration.

Walter: Yes, I think that, in fact, *kairos* is also relevant for education and more specifically for the phrase *more than ever*. In a sense, it is also true that at this particular moment and at this opportunity, let us say, it is precisely important to read Freire. It is an opportunity, a special moment to read Freire because of his potential to help us rethink our *now*, which is really problematic. And probably that is why the book has been received with special attention in Brazil, because of the particular historical moment and how Freire has been so undeservedly vilified.

Jason: By the Brazilian government?

Walter: Yes, as you know. The Brazilian government has adopted as part of its platform a main political goal which is to expulse the ideology of Paulo Freire from Brazilian education, as they say. Each and every week the minister of education says something bad about Paulo Freire. Three or four weeks ago we received the results of the PISA (Program for

International Student Assessment) education worldwide study. The first thing the minister of education said was, "Good morning, we have had horrible results at PISA and this is because of Paulo Freire."

Jason: He is the scapegoat.

Walter: Exactly. Everything that is wrong with Brazilian education has to do with Paulo Freire. So, in a sense, you are right, *kairos* is very meaningful also because of the *now* we are living these days. And *Kairos* was also very meaningful for Paulo Freire. He was trying to recover time for people from whom time has been robbed.

Jason: The oppressed?

Walter: Yes, exactly, Freire's attempt was something like searching for their stolen time, the time that the system took from them by excluding them from educational institutions. In a sense, I think, for Paulo Freire, *kairos* is always now. It is trying to recover, at any moment, some lost past of the lives which have been robbed of time.

Jason: And maybe, I do not know if you would agree, the *now* of action would be the acting in the moment to try and give *aion* or maybe not give, but the opening up of the possibility of *aion* for the people that are constantly forced to live in *chronos* and oppression.

Walter: Exactly, because *aion* is not only the time of education, but *aion* is also the time of art, is also the time of love, is also the time of thinking, of philosophy, and playing. And as you said, *aion* cannot be given, but maybe the role of an educator has to do with creating the conditions so that *aion* could be experienced. Giving time, a lovely double impossibility, as we know from Derrida . . . something impossible and necessary for educators, I would say.

Jason: *Aion* is also the time of childhood, as you mention in many of your works.

Walter: Exactly, it is a time where we can play, and as a chronological child or a non-chronological child we can put into question the world we live in. And we need *aion* for that. We cannot put into question our world looking at the clock or worried about the calendar.

Jason: You brought up love, childhood, and play, and I want to briefly ask you a question about the five principles that you use as a framework for the book, or a way to think about Freire, and as a way to think with Freire. The five principles are life, infancy, errantry, love, and equality.

One thing that struck me in the epilogue is that you suggest you are
not providing readymade recipes or formulas to apply these principles,
but you did have a nice idea that I think is very Freirean where you say,
what if we experimented in the classroom or in any educational setting,
by bringing these principles into play, one for each day of the week. I
thought that this was appropriate also because it brings together theory
and practice, something that Freire was adamant about. I am wondering
if this is something you would care to add to because you only refer to it
at the end of the book.

Walter: First, I want to say something about the word "principle." While I
call these terms principles, I would like these terms to be understood
as principles only in the sense of beginnings, forces of beginning. I
would love to think of them as engines of thinking and of living and
not as something that is fixed or the base for something else. It is more
in the sense of a beginning or inspiring of practices of emancipatory or
liberating education that I understand the word principle.

In the case of Freire, and I think this might make the book different than
others on him, usually you find people trying to interpret what Freire
means in terms of a topic, a problem, a question, even a book, or trying
to apply his ideas. What I am trying to do is have a real dialogue with
Freire about how his life and thinking might inspire our educational
practices, so, in this sense, we can say that I am interested in how we can
begin or re-begin to be educators, by thinking with Freire. In this sense,
these principles work as starting points for education and educators. In
other words, I would love readers of the book to ask questions like: from
this principle (life, errantry, etc.), what new educational life can I begin?
More extensively: "What kind of educational life can I begin practicing
by following these five principles (beginnings)?" This is also related to
the idea of infancy or childhood and how we can be reborn as educators
or re-begin a new life of education. I think that while writing the last
part of the book I was trying to bring together theory and practice,
because on an unconscious level I was probably imagining a reader
saying: "this is very nice and very inspiring. It has made me think a lot
of things, but what has all this to do with practice and how can I put this
into practice?" So, I decided to give a few examples of practice in the
epilogue of the book, not meaning for them to be recipes, or reapplied as

they are, but as a way to focus on the many times we live our lives in our educational practice in ways that are not faithful to equality, love, and errantry, especially when we work with children. I wanted to provoke us to consider whether or not we are embodying the ideas we say we value. In other words, to put into question how we tend to inhabit some fixed spaces even when we do not agree with them or we do not realize that we are doing so. How we forget to err more often than we would think.

Jason: To err, in the sense of . . . ?

Walter: Wander. We usually try to bring students to our knowledge, or at least to a knowledge we think they should know: we want others to move, but we do not move at all. And finally, erring helps us ponder how we educate childhood/infancy. Childhood/infancy is the object of our educational intentions, but we do not listen to childhood/infancy in the same way we expect childhood/infancy to listen to us. More than often, we are not sensitive to the strength of childhood/infancy. Because of all this, I suggest in a very concrete way a practice of these principles so that they might really be practical beginnings and put our own practice into question. This is something Paulo Freire was very sensitive to. He makes it clear elsewhere that questioning should not be a mere intellectual game but the beginning of actual transformation.

Jason: I also thought, because of the way you play with time, one way to translate the word *inícios* in Portuguese, which in English means "beginnings," would be "initiative" or "initiate." We often say that we initiate a project, or adventure, and with this in mind it is compelling that at the end of your book you suggest some ways to initiate some new forms of thinking and practicing education. So really, the end of your book is only the beginning, maybe of erring, and I think that this fits well with the way that you want to rupture *chronos*.

Walter: Yes, and I think this is also why childhood or infancy is the last principle I discuss in the book, because it is a way of realizing that at the end we might also be at the beginning. In a sense, it is a metaphor for what it means to think. I believe that we begin to think when we have a question, which is why I also end the book with questions, because in doing so we might experience the end of the book as a beginning. In a way, there is no real end. We are always beginning (while initiating or finishing), because when we think, we are in *aion's* temporality. In this sense, I would like the reader, when she finishes the book, to experience that she has not finished anything, and that in fact she is beginning or initiating something.

Jason: Which is appropriate if we think back to the Portuguese title where it is not now, and now only that we need Freire, but always.

Walter: Exactly, because, in a sense, if you have to imagine a representation of this kind of time, I would say that *chronos* is a line where there is no way to repeat one moment. Chronos just passes: once you have experienced one moment in *chronos* there is no way to live it again. Differently, *aion* is a circle. You are experiencing a moment or a present that is recurring. It comes again and again. Repetition free and complex, from which difference emerges, as Deleuze would say.

Jason: We have been talking about time and temporality, but I want to ask you a question about place. Or you could say, we have discussed why Freire today, which is a time question. But I also want to ask, especially for English readers or people living in the English-speaking world, a place question of where and why? I think you have pointed to one response to this question, and it is quite clear in the book, why at this current moment in Brazil it is so important to resurrect Freire, to defend him, to let him inspire again. But as we know, unfortunately, Brazil is not the only place where authoritarian tendencies like those exhibited by the Bolsonaro government exist. Part of what you highlight, and it is done beautifully in the book, is Freire as a wanderer, as a journeyer traveling all his life to so many different places. Maybe, you could say something about where and why we might find Freire useful, or helpful, or inspiring today.

Walter: It occurs to me now that something that might be interesting to think about in regards to your question is that there are several Greek words for time. We have named them above: *chronos, aion*, and *kairos*. But there is also more than one word for space. We have the most commonly used *topos*, but we also have, for example, the word *khora*, which is a word that Plato uses in the *Timaeus* when he is describing the birth of the world. It is a kind of intensive space. In a sense, I am thinking now that there is a kind of parallel. *Topos* is a kind of more superficial or extensional way to answer the question of "where Freire?" We could say that the United States, the United Kingdom,

Australia, Brazil, and Latin America in general, are particular places where Paulo Freire is important to dialogue with today because of the public neoliberal policies that dominate, especially in public education. We all suffer from policies that are completely sensitive to big private corporations, and insensitive to the public and the excluded of the system. So wherever the public system is suffering, and wherever teachers are forced to live a more effective, productive, and unthoughtful life, this book has a place. But we could also speculate that, possibly, these principles are not just about a given *topos*. Perhaps they are not related to just this or that space, but instead, they are tied to a more intensive space, like *khora* would suggest: they might be meaningful anywhere, or everywhere, for any teacher desiring a new beginning for her educational life. In this sense, Paulo Freire might be meaningful everywhere an educator wants to deepen her relationship with what she is doing, and how she is living; doing so, she puts into question what it means to be an educator, or to live an educational life, and what kind of practice and relationship between education and the outside world should be cultivated. So, we might say that Freire is everywhere where Freire inspires an intensity of inhabiting the space of being an educator, or living an educational life.

Jason: Then, would you maybe say, and this is just me thinking out loud, that Freire as an educator, or someone who educates with these principles that you mentioned, can open up *khora*, a place to inhabit in a certain nurturing way, *khora*?

Walter: What you are saying is interesting because, thought of this way, *khora* is a condition, but in another sense, it is like a result or a consequence. We might say the same of *aion*, because if we think of ourselves as capable of producing beginnings, we are also capable of producing *aion*. It might be very meaningful to say that *khora* is a kind of condition, but at the same time it might emerge as a new form of inhabiting space if we relate to our practice through these beginnings or principles.

Jason: One of my friends (Derek Ford) in our field, philosophy of education, writes a lot about Henri Lefebvre and space. He taught me something that I think is helpful in this case. For Lefebvre, space is produced and produces. So maybe, in that sense, too, Freirean ideas and way of living, traveling, love are both produced, and produce.

Walter: Precisely. And I think it is also possible to experience education like that. The more you experience an intensive time and intensive space, the more this kind of practice produces new spaces and new relationship to spaces and to time. You might also say new rhythms, in the way we experience time, and maybe new rhythms in the way we experience space also.

Jason: It seems, too, that it is always a process. Again, we go back to it not being linear, but it is always something constantly in motion being produced and producing, and we do not always know what. What is nice about the *khora* idea, too, is that it is hospitable to that which will come . . .

Walter: Exactly.

Jason: . . . which I think you suggest that Freire was very much open to in his travels and his teaching. Whoever and whatever would come, hospitality was granted . . .

Walter: Yes. And something just came to my mind that I do not want to lose, because I think it is nice. Freire speaks about experiencing three exiles. The first one was from his mother's uterus, when she was pregnant of him, and he was exiled to the world. This is literally *khora*, which is powerful. Also, I was thinking about your comment just now, and perhaps it is how I am phrasing it that gives the impression of an either/ or, but it is not.

Jason: Rather than an either/or, we are dealing with a both/and . . .

Walter: Right. You are both produced and producing, rather than an either/ or.

Jason: I want to ask you one more question that leads us, I think, into the book. It has to do with hope and struggle. Freire has a very famous book translated as *Pedagogy of Hope*. He is obviously known for his continuous and never-ending struggle. There is a phrase that you and I have talked about on many occasions from *Pedagogy of the Oppressed* that I cannot exactly translate, but rather rephrase and make plural instead of singular, which is in Portuguese *se temos esperança, precisamos lutar e se lutarmos com esperança, podemos esperar*. In Portuguese there is a nice wordplay with *esperar*, which can mean hope and wait. One way to translate this would be, "If we have hope, then we must fight, and if we fight with hope, then we can wait." I want to ask you about this because I think it is important to keep in mind when considering both Freire and education. We are facing so much, not you and I per se, but the world is in so much danger, and there exists so much oppression, that people become cynical and want to give up. Or, there are people that say, "We can't wait. We need an immediate response." And this makes perfect sense, because there are so many people suffering through injustices that need to end immediately. But it seems to me that Freire is teaching us something different here. He seems to be teaching us that we always have to fight if hope exists, and hope dies last. But also, that we have to commit to the long-term struggle, and understand that we will not change things right away. Emancipation does not come in one second. We have to wait, and we have to cultivate and do education work. I think, too, that that is also very important. Especially with the world that we live in with technology and how we want everything right away. So, I wonder what you think about this, this line.

Walter: Yes, I agree. Your quote makes me remember a quote from another prominent Latin American, Ernesto "Che" Guevara: "the only defeat is not to continue fighting." What both Freire and Guevara seem to be saying is that what is important is not the result, or the achievements of our lives, but the way we commit ourselves in fighting for our ideals, a fairer, beautiful, and joyful world for every human being and not for just a few. And there is no term for this. If we commit ourselves to such solidarity, in such a coherent and inventive way, then we should not be as concerned about the results. We can expect with hope. There is also an expression, another expression close to the one that you mention, where Freire teaches us, inspired by Amilcar Cabral, "to impatiently be patient."

Jason: What would that be in Portuguese?

Walter: It could be *ser pacientemente impacientes*, or *a paciência da impaciência*.

Jason: The impatience of patience. What would that mean in terms of the prior phrase I mentioned?

Walter: I could place patience and *esperar* on the same side, no? We need to be impatient, to not passively accept things as they are, but we also need to be patient if we confront the order of things accordingly.

Jason: Patience and waiting.

Walter: And on the other side, we could place impatience and fighting. In this sense, if you say we need to be patient, or we need to wait, then it might be imagined that we do not need to do anything, and that it is just about expecting another time to arrive through patience or waiting. But, when Freire adds the impatience or the fighting, he is saying, as you said, we should not displace many expectations onto another time, but we can be patient under some conditions. It has to do with not just sitting here to let the time pass. It is more of an active attitude, to intervene and take an active position so that this other time can emerge. And this is related, I think, to many other thinkers in Latin America. So, it is not about expecting something, and it is not about gaining something, but it is about how we relate to the fighting that we need to do. So, it is about how we experience time. Again, I think, it is not about *chronos* and it is not about results, but it is about how we live our lives. In the case of Freire, how we live our educational lives. This for me, as an educator, is very inspiring. The educational reality sometimes looks so desperate, so difficult to transform, so hard to overcome that lack of hope is very close on the road. But it seems to me that the philosophical life of Paulo inspires us to never give up! And maybe today, in such a difficult global situation, this is meaningful here in Brazil, and elsewhere. Finally, I would add someone very different, and from another context. Heraclitus said, "if we do not expect what it should not be expected (what it is impossible to be expected), we are not going to reach it, for it is hard to be sought out and with no path" (fragment 18). The word he uses to say "with no path" is *aporos*, related to aporia.

Jason: Without place.

Walter: Without place, exactly. With no path, no way.

Jason: With no way, yeah.

Walter: No path. And this is very interesting because it seems like a contradiction. He doesn't say, if we don't expect the unexpected. It is not that. He is saying, if we don't expect the unexpectable, what we shouldn't expect, what seems impossible to be expected. This is connected with Freire, because these days people say that politics is the realm of the possible. And I would say that Freire would say that politics is the realm of the impossible, of utopia, no place. So that we expect what should not be expected, and we turn an impossibility into a need.

Jason: Would you say that about education, too?

Walter: Yes, precisely. The educator is not someone who looks for the
possible. The possible is in *chronos*. The transformative educator, the
Freirean educator, is someone who expects the impossible because
this is what we need, at least, in Latin America. The impossible lives in
aion. It is not the possible. It is the impossible. Some people say that
transformation is impossible, or it seems to be impossible, but it is the
only life, an educational life worth living.

Jason: And that is why we have to keep fighting.

Walter: I would say that. Even though it seems that our numbers/forces
are very few and not strong. Even if we feel alone and that the enemy
is so powerful, and it seems impossible. There are so many examples in
education where, let's say, a standard educator would say, no, I cannot do
anything with this child. It's impossible. She is not capable. No way, she
doesn't want to. She cannot learn. And then another more loving, errant,
childlike educator enters with a different attitude, one who says that the
person perceived as not capable, is equally capable, and then everything
changes, a "new" student, the unexpectable emerges. Or something
happens to the standard educator in that she herself changes, her attitude
shifts, and everything changes. This has to do also with the principles.
If you assume that everyone or anyone is capable, then the impossible
tends to be the only thing that is real and that deserves to be fought for.

Jason: Then maybe, if we come back to the principles, and if we fight in
education and in the world to live a life of dignity with equality, with
love, errantry; if we travel, we journey, and we fight in a childlike
manner, in the sense of opening up the world to the impossible, then
maybe that is when education has something to teach us.

Walter: That is my hope. I am sure that some educators will read this book
and say, yeah, yeah, yeah, it would be lovely to put our lives on the line
like this, but we cannot. Or they might say, I would love to consider my
students as equals, but it is obvious that they are not as fully capable as
I am, or that some are more capable than others. Concrete educational
conditions are so bad, and so difficult, that many educators say, "How
can I love being an educator with the conditions that are offered to me
in public education?" Or, some others could say, "how can I wander,
how can I err if I have to arrive to some fixed concepts, curriculum, or
content?" Or, some might question, "how can I experience education as

a child if people demand that I provide answers not questions?" But I would say, when all this seems impossible, then it is more needed than ever, and if we relate to them as beginnings, and with hope, to try to expect what seems to be unexpectable, who knows what can happen? Why shouldn't we try? Why not? Then, a new education and practice might emerge. It might begin. The new always might begin in education. It's just a matter of being sensitive to life, equality, love, errantry, and childhood. Don't you think?

Interview with Lutgardes Costa Freire
At the Instituto Paulo Freire, São Paulo, Brasil

On November 23, 2018, I was joyful and honored to be received by Lutgardes Costa Freire at the Instituto Paulo Freire (IPF) in São Paulo, Brazil. A few months earlier, Inés Fernández Mouján introduced me via email to this son of Paulo Freire who soon accepted my request for an interview. The interview began at 10:30 in the morning, we were visited by Angela Biz Antunes, the director of pedagogy at the IPF. Our conversation with Angela was lively and we suspended the interview for a lunch break for the three of us at a restaurant. The IPF occupies a paradoxical position, in a middle-class neighborhood. After eating, we returned to the IPF and were visited by Moacir Gadotti, with whom we conversed before resuming the interview. Lutgardes was very patient, and we commenced the interview again at 16:00 hours. This transcription was initially taken by Carla Silva.

W. O. K.: Good morning, Lutgardes! Thank you for having me.

L. C. F.: Imagine! For me it is a pleasure and an honor to receive such an erudite person!

W. O. K.: My pleasure! I was saying a few minutes ago that I am interested in philosophy as a way of thinking associated with a life. So, I would like to start more informally by talking about your life, your birth, your childhood, what you remember about your childhood, the first years of your life.

L. C. F.: I was born in 1958, in Recife. A very hot city, in the Northeast of Brazil. I was a very playful child, as we say. I loved to play, because that time was not like today, when the children have to play in specific, preserved, and closed places, I mean, we were free, we used to play on the street. So, I had a very happy childhood, in my first five years. But at the age of five I had to travel to Chile, because there was a coup d'état in Brazil, and my father had been arrested. Thus, we had to take refuge in Chile. But Chile welcomed us so well, very well, you know! The Chileans were caring and had an affection and respect for people that was impressive. A wonderful thing! And I studied in Chile, I learned to read and write in Chile.

W. O. K.: In Spanish?

L. C. F.: Yes, in Spanish. I didn't miss Brazil. I mean, I missed my uncles and aunts, my cousins, my family. But I didn't miss the country, because I had lived there for a short time. All I knew of Brazil was my street and my house, and the sea, where our uncle used to take my brother and I on the weekends. It is important to say that I have one brother and three sisters.

W. O. K.: You are the youngest.

L. C. F.: I am the youngest. The youngest, at sixty years of age. There are two male siblings: Joaquim, Lutgardes.

W. O. K.: And three women.

L. C. F.: Yes. And three women.

W. O. K.: And the men are the youngest.

L. C. F.: Right. The men are the youngest.

W. O. K.: I remember reading, in some part of your father's autobiography, that when he was arrested, your mother, Elza, didn't want to take you to the prison, she only took the women, because you were very small and she was afraid that you might be traumatized. Your father commented on this: "And she did very well, because I think, in fact, it wouldn't been good for them." (Freire and Betto, 1985, p. 62) Do you remember this episode?

L. C. F.: I remember. Between us, the siblings, today there are controversies! [Laughs.] Some think that, perhaps, my mother should have told us. But I personally don't think so. I think she was right.

W. O. K.: To preserve you?

L. C. F.: Yes. Because the child's imagination is a very big imagination, very fertile. You can imagine at that age what it meant to us to be arrested? We thought that the only people that were arrested were people that stole or killed someone. I mean, we were at risk of having a negative image of our father. I think my mother did the right thing to not take us to the prison because it would have shocked us. My sisters, yes, they were older, they took food, *feijoada* to the prisoners and to my father. But I think my mother did the right thing.

W. O. K.: In not exposing you to that situation?

L. C. F.: Yes, in not exposing us to that situation.

W. O. K.: And what are your first memories of your father? The oldest? Do you have memory about that time? Do you have any memory of time with your father? How was family life?

L. C. F.: While he was in jail?

W. O. K.: No, no. It can be even before he was arrested. Before the coup.

L. C. F.: Ah, yes. Before the coup, I remember! I was very small, but I remember. My father had a typical Northeastern way of living. [Laughs.] I mean, he had a certain economic condition, a comfortable one, which allowed the family to have a domestic worker, a nanny for us, Joaquim and I. A "nanny," you understand?

W. O. K.: Yes, yes. A person who took care of you.

L. C. F.: Right. A person who only took care of us.

W. O. K.: And took care of the clothes.

L. C. F.: Right. Washed and ironed our clothes. My father used to work in the morning, would have lunch at home, and then go back to work in the afternoon. My mother also worked, she was an elementary school teacher, and later a principal of an elementary school in Recife. And, if I am not mistaken, she used to work all day and come home at the end of the day. It was an easy-going life, a "*pacata* life." Do you understand "*pacata*"?

W. O. K.: Yes, yes. For kids, it is great. A very peaceful and quiet life.

L. C. F.: Yes, very *tranquila*. Without problems. We had our friends, our neighbors. We were friends with our neighbors. I remember that, during exile, my sisters longed for our neighbors etc. I didn't because I was too young. On weekends, my father used to talk to a friend, he would invite his friend to talk in the living room about politics, and philosophy, amongst other things. I mean, he already had these books (pointing to Paulo Freire's library) here too.

W. O. K.: He was already an intellectual.

L. C. F.: Yes.

W. O. K.: He led an intellectual life.

L. C. F.: That of a professor.

W. O. K.: Right. What about your schooling? Your primary schooling. How old were you when you entered kindergarten?

L. C. F.: I entered when we were in Recife. But when I arrived in Chile I had to go back to the kindergarten because I couldn't speak Spanish. So, at first it was very weird, first of all because no one ever said, "Look, your father is in jail. We have to travel." Arriving in Chile was a bit shocking, because I left the airplane thinking that I was going to land in another city.

W. O. K.: A Brazilian city.

L. C. F.: Yes. And suddenly there I was in another country and I don't understand what people are saying.

W. O. K.: Another climate too. Much colder.

L. C. F.: So, It was a cultural shock. But when you are a child, you can adapt very fast. I remember that I went to kindergarten, then to a more normal school, elementary school, which was very good for me, in Chile. It was a minor seminary, as we called it. It was a school only for boys, children and boys, and it was a school to be a priest.

W. O. K.: A seminary?

L. C. F.: It was a seminary to become a priest. But I had the possibility to choose not to be a priest; I mean . . .

W. O. K.: Secular life?

L. C. F.: Yes. We could decide. I remember one time I asked myself "Do I really want to be a priest?" Then I thought "But priests cannot marry, right? Ah! Then, I don't want to. [Laughter.] I like women." [Laughter.] It was four wonderful years of my life, I have to say, Walter. It was wonderful. The Chileans were fantastic, fantastic! Well, I studied in this school, a minor seminary. It was in 1968. Then my father wrote *Pedagogia do oprimido*, but he was not able to publish it in Chile because, if I am not mistaken (I don't know, I could be wrong) but from what always read he didn't tell me this—he was already being pursued in

Chile, when he wrote this book. In other words, the military and the far right already wanted to take the book. So, he immediately made a typewritten copy and handed over the originals to Jacques Chonchol. I don't know if you know who he is.

W. O. K.: Yes, I read the story in the fifty year commemorative edition of the book. I read that he took the manuscripts and kept them in France.

L. C. F.: Yes, Exactly. Then, my father received the invitation to work in the United States as a visiting professor at Harvard University, and to the World Council of Churches, to work at the Department of Education. So, we left Chile for the United States. And then, it was another cultural shock.

W. O. K.: That's right.

L. C. F.: I hated the United States. I felt so bad. I don't know if it was because of my age, because by that time I was nine to ten years old. There, I couldn't play on the street. We couldn't play on the street. The Americans don't play soccer, they don't like it. They like American Football. I also didn't like basketball, because I was too short. I didn't feel like studying English all the time either. I was a kid.

W. O. K.: You wanted to play.

L. C. F.: I wanted to play. So, I used to go to school, but rarely, I mean, in a very disorganized way. Of course, my father provided a private teacher for Joaquim and me.

W. O. K.: In English.

L. C. F.: In English. For us to learn English. So, we learned at home and learned at school too. It was a short experience, little contact with English, with the United States. We stayed there for a total of eleven months. It was not a long time, not even a full year.

W. O. K.: I imagine you were also wondering why you had left Chile.

L. C. F.: No, our father explained it. My father. I was seven when we arrived in Chile, he explained everything to Joaquim and me. He explained the problem that led to his arrest. I was very angry with the military. But he said: "It's not useful to be angry with the military because this is history, this is history. This is life. It happened this way. I choose this path and I was punished for choosing this path." So, when we went to the United States, we were already aware of the situation, and then my interest for my father academic's life began, interest for my father's books, for what

he said. Because it was very impressive, Walter! Every time my father
started to speak at home, when we had visitors, everyone was silent
and listened to him speak. He had great charisma! His charisma was
impressive. It was something extraordinary. Back then I used to wonder:
"But what does my father have that keeps everyone transfixed like
that?" He taught real classes at home. It was impressive! So, I started to
understand what he did, understand his work, but for a long time, when
I was a kid, I used to ask him: "Dad, what do you do?" And he would
respond: "Son, I am an intellectual." I didn't understand what this meant.

W. O. K.: [Laughs.] "What could this be?"

L. C. F.: It took me a while to understand what he was doing.

[Pause.]

L. C. F.: So, we were talking about United States, right?

W. O. K.: Yes, but before that I remember reading in an interview with you
that your father worked for long periods of the day, and on Saturday
he continued work. One day you stopped and said to him: "Look dad,
that won't do. You work all day and the weekend comes and you keep
working." And he answered: "Ah, that's right. On Saturdays we are
going out, we are going for diner, for a walk." You comment that this
experience had a very good effect on your relationship. I would like you
to talk a little bit more about your relationship with your father. You
were witness to his whole life . . . Did you have time to play with him?
How was the relationship between you two?

L. C. F.: It was a purely intellectual relationship. Because my father didn't
play soccer, didn't play tennis, didn't play ping-pong.

W. O. K.: He wasn't a sportsman.

L. C. F.: He didn't like sports. And when we were children, even in Recife, he
was already like that. He was always an academic, a professor. But what
you said in fact happened. But it only lasted a few week.

W. O. K.: [Laughs.] A very few Saturdays!

L. C. F.: A very few Saturdays. [Laughs.] But Joaquin and I were satisfied,
because we could understand. When he took us out, he used to take us to
the library, to the movies, coffee shops. He used to give us classes about
how to find a book in a library. I mean, over time we came to realize:
"Wow, this man isn't into little games, like playing monopoly. This is a
serious man. A man to talk about serious things with. About philosophy,

about history." So, we came to accept this. We understood him. He was writing something serious. We left him to write his book. Ah, because, Walter, he had talked to so many people about writing this book. My God! He talked to Jacques Chonchol, Ernani Maria Fiori, Fernando Henrique Cardoso, José Serra, Plínio de Arruda Sampaio, Thiago de Melo, Geraldo Vandré, there was an enormous amount of Brazilians who traveled to Chile as exiles at that time. My father would invite these people to come to our home and after lunch time he used to say: "No! Wait a minute and I will read the book!" [Lots of laughter.]

W. O. K.: [Laughs.]

L. C. F.: Sometimes we were listening. I couldn't understand anything, but it was interesting to see people's gestures and reactions. Even though my father was a very reserved person, when he wanted to talk, specifically, to someone, he didn't allow us to interfere. But it was very good. Although in a lot of ways my father was not present, we had, in some way, a lot of history, friendships, many encounters. Of course, once *Pedagogy of the Oppressed* was published in the United States—and from the beginning it was a huge success—from that moment, my father traveled all over the world. And he was even less present. But, on the other hand, it was a festival when he returned from travels. It was such a pleasure. He really enjoyed telling us about how his travels were, what the places he went to were like, whom he talked to, etc.

W. O. K.: And from those trips, do you remember anything that caught your attention, in particular? Something you father had told you and impressed you?

L. C. F.: Not when I was a kid, but as a teenager, while we were in Switzerland, he told me that he had gone to Africa. He said: "My son, I went to Africa." And for us Brazilians, Africa is almost a second Brazil. And he said: "My son, I ate mango!"

W. O. K.: It was a trip to Tanzania?

L. C. F.: Right. "I ate mango, I ate jackfruit!" [Laughs.] He talked about those trips in a very colorful way. We could see where he had been through his descriptions. The Africa full of colors, fruits, foods, which impacted him a lot, our family as well, for sure.

W. O. K.: [Laughs.] In regard to schooling and your studies, for both you and Joaquin, your mother played a major role? For example, when you

had homework, or when there was a problem at school, it was your
mother who handled these things?

L. C. F.: [Sigh.] Ah! That was a problem, Walter, because it was like this: we
didn't have too much homework when we were in Brazil, because we
were too young. But when we arrived in Chile, my mother used to help
Joaquim and I, I believe. I don't remember, but I believe she also helped
Joaquim quite often in the United States.

W. O. K.: She was the private teacher.

L. C. F.: Right.

W. O. K.: And your mother also didn't know English.

L. C. F.: My mother couldn't speak English. Things got more difficult when
we went to Switzerland. My mother didn't speak French, or English, or
Spanish. So, the homework: I couldn't ask my father to help me with
German because he didn't know German, and he didn't understand
anything about modern math. [Laughs.] We had to really manage
homework without our parents. But they also always provided us with
a teacher who could help guide us, to help us in math, for example, in
German, things like that. A private tutor. Because my father. We had a
good life in Switzerland, let's say . . .

W. O. K.: [Smiles.]

L. C. F.: So, as I was saying about the cultural shock in Switzerland: I
remember thinking: "My God! These people have no feelings. They
don't have heart. Are they all machines? Everything automatic?" I said,
"Father, I am not going to school." And he replied "What?!" "No, No.
I am not going. I don't want to be a machine," I told him. He pleaded,
"My son, don't do this to me. I am a foreigner here, I am an exiled here
in Switzerland. I need . . . " And I said, "But you would criticize this
school!" [Laughs.]

W. O. K.: [Laughs.] Thus, he couldn't say anything. [Laughs.]

L. C. F.: No, he didn't have an argument. But he did reply, "Lut, but it is not
the school. It is the system." It took me some time to play that role (note:
he is saying that he had to act or do something he was not convinced), as
an artist who dresses to go to school.

W. O. K.: To disguise yourself?

L. C. F.: Right. Disguise yourself. Everything went in one ear, and out the
other. Geography class, history, there wasn't sociology. But I did observe

the teachers' ideological biases. The ideology behind the content. And in the essays, I used to write about revolution, about social changes.

W. O. K.: How did the teachers react?

L. C. F.: The teachers accepted and corrected me and so on. But I wasn't concerned with their grades. It was a troubling period for me in Switzerland. I remember my father saying: "Well, I will have to tell the government if you don't go to school. I will have to talk to the police to see what I can do, how things will turn out." And I remember people at the school telling him, "Look, it's alright. Your child is experiencing a cultural shock, he is 11 years old, he is not understanding things correctly. He will study with a private tutor for a year. After that, he can go back to school." Because it is not possible for a child not to go to school in Switzerland. At that time, there was a lot of control over children. I mean, it was like this, with the Swiss: "Look, if you see a child walking on the street after 4:00 p.m., you have the right to stop the kid, ask their name, take them to their place and ask why this child."

W. O. K.: Wow!

L. C. F.: Just like that. It was like everyone was a police officer. The whole society. So, today I miss that place, but at that time it was a very strange experience for me.

W. O. K.: Very authoritarian.

L. C. F.: Right, Very authoritarian. So much so that it led me to depression at the age of fifteen. I went to a daylong clinic. This was a place where you enter in the morning, spend the entire day there, and come home at the end of the day. At these clinics there were psychiatrists, nurses, and others who had a variety of problems. For seven months I went to this clinic every day.

W. O. K.: And you didn't go to school.

L. C. F.: No.

W. O. K.: After that year with a tutor you started to go to school again. But you didn't adapt, you didn't like it? It wasn't nice, the school?

L. C. F.: No. I went to a very rigid school, Jesuit, you know? My father, I don't know why he proposed this. First, I studied in France, where I learned French. After that I went to Switzerland, and I started studying there, in high school. But there was a period in Switzerland when I went to a private school. I wasn't able to pass this year. I had some problem, but I don't remember what it was now. I studied at this Jesuit school and I fell into depression. After this passed, I stopped going to that clinic, and I was already close to . . . I started to study music. I studied classical percussion.

W. O. K.: In a conservatory?

L. C. F.: In a conservatory in Geneva. By my fourth year of studying in Geneva, still classical percussion, the politic reopening happened in Brazil. So, we went back.

W. O. K.: You were already twenty years old.

L. C. F.: Right. I was twenty, twenty-one years old.

W. O. K.: Were you alone in France?

L. C. F.: No. I was with Joaquim. It was very close to Geneva. Only 8 km. We used to travel back and forth.

W. O. K.: Only for school.

L. C. F.: Only for school. We were still living in Geneva.

W. O. K.: What was your father's library like?

L. C. F.: My father was gifted many books, and he bought many as well. He didn't place the books in any specific order. Everything was mixed together, there was no order, but nonetheless he was able to locate any book. He knew where everything was.

W. O. K.: We are now resuming after lunch. I would like to ask you to touch on a few things from earlier. I remember that we had talked about homework, about tasks that neither your mother nor your father could take care of, so you had to do it yourselves. And, for instance, I don't know if, in fact, that happened, I don't know if you had. Do you remember talking to him about things that happened at school? Do you have any memories of your father saying something about your school?

L. C. F.: Look, I have memories of my parents going to attend meetings, but I didn't know.

W. O. K.: You were not there.

L. C. F.: No. We couldn't participate. It was only for the parents. I was an average student; I wasn't excellent or terrible. I was pretty average, because, when I was eleven years old, I didn't like Switzerland very much. Today I like it.

W. O. K.: Do you keep traveling (to Switzerland)?

L. C. F.: When I can.

W. O. K.: When you can?

L. C. F.: Yes. When I can. Because it is very expensive. It is a very expensive country. But at that time, I didn't know it. I mean, I ruined the best of my years, of the years of my life, of my youth. Of adolescence. I didn't know how to enjoy it. My mother knew how to do it. She liked the Swiss. She respected the Swiss laws, the authority. For her, it was wonderful.

W. O. K.: Did your mother work?

L. C. F.: My mother worked at home. She took care of us, took care of the house.

W. O. K.: As you father said: "She was the infrastructure."

L. C. F.: Right. Of my father. And my father was her superstructure. And they were a traditional couple; I mean, they fought. Of course, they fought, but not in our presence. They never divorced, but they also didn't have reason for that, because they loved each other. They shared a very deep love story. My mother helped my father a lot. My mother was the first reader of the *Pedagogia do oprimido*. My mother really was the one who encouraged my father to focus on education.

W. O. K.: Tell me more about this. Hearing you talk about this, I thought: you were an average student, and one would think that, in some way, you were surrounded by education at home, your father was so committed to education. Education played such a large role in his life, maybe you had to create some resistance. You didn't want to dedicate too much to education, you didn't like education, you had to find your own place . . .

L. C. F.: No, no. It didn't happen that way. My father had his thing with education, but he didn't. He didn't allow this to change his presence at home. He was a father like any father. He advised us, he would tell us: "Look, do this, don't do this." I was always very loved, even in a life of tensions, travels, displacements, even when, instead of dedicating myself to education, I chose to be a musician and took a route different than what a teacher father might prefer. I told my father, "Father, I want to play drums, I want to be a musician." And his answer was transparent, clear, and precise, "It's all right, my son. You can do what you want. But promise me one thing: that what you're going to do will be done with love." That was his response. It wasn't in his character to say, "No. I don't want you do make music. I want you to follow my path, I want you to continue my work, that you follow in my footsteps." I mean, there was nothing like this.

W. O. K.: How about your brother, Joaquin, and your sisters, they were good students?

L. C. F.: My brother was better. But he dropped out of school for music. He was very young. He was sixteen or seventeen years old when he went to the conservatory.

W. O. K.: So, music was very important in your house.

L. C. F.: Yes! Music. We loved music!

W. O. K.: Were there any musicians in your family? From what source did this love of music spring?

L. C. F.: It was from missing Brazil that this love came. During the whole exile period, we always listened to Brazilian music, American music, and Chilean music. I mean, music was, how would I say . . .

W. O. K.: It was a way to be connected to Brazil.

L. C. F.: Yes. Exactly. And between us. My father also appreciated music a lot. One of the professions he would have love to have had is a guitar player. And the other would have been as a singer, to sing!

W. O. K.: Hmm.

L. C. F.: To sing, to be a singer.

W. O. K.: So, music was already in the family.

L. C. F.: Yes. And my grandpa, if I am not mistaken, also liked music a lot.

W. O. K.: The father of your father.

L. C. F.: My father's father.

W. O. K.: He was a military man.

L. C. F.: He was in the military.

L. C. F.: But, going back to Brazil. Then I came back with my parents, only me. Joaquin stayed in Geneva.

W. O. K.: We resume recording now after talking with professor Moacir Gadotti and professor Angela Antunes. So, Lut!

L. C. F.: I forgot!

W. O. K.: I was asking if the fact of you father being a famous educator would have been the reason you were not too enthusiastic about education, and you said no, that music was a family passion and it was something that connected you to Brazil.

L. C. F.: Right.

W. O. K.: And you five. In fact, you and your brother decide to pursue music, and how about your sisters?

L. C. F.: They decided to pursue education.

W. O. K.: And do you think this may also be related to the fact that your mother was an educator?

L. C. F.: Actually, my father never forced us to be teachers, but we are all teachers. It's interesting, because, for example, I am a language teacher. I learned all those languages, right? Spanish, English, French. Joaquin teaches classical guitar. Fatima is a teacher, educator, and psychologist. And Madalena is a teacher. She is an educator. And Cristina is a Portuguese teacher in Geneva. She was a Portuguese teacher in Geneva.

W. O. K.: Does Cristina still live in Geneva?

L. C. F.: Yes, she still lives in Geneva. She stayed there. She wants to die there, she wants to stay there.

W. O. K.: She started a family over there.

L. C. F.: Yes. She is married. So, you see, it's interesting. By the way, I think this is one of the keys of education, right? You don't want to say to your child, "Look, don't do this!" or "Do that!" Instead of saying that, you say, "How about doing this?" You make your child think "How about that? How about this?" instead of stating, instead of imposing your opinion.

W. O. K.: And like your father said: "Do what you want to, as long as you do it with love."

L. C. F.: Right! That's right.

W. O. K.: Because this is what matters.

L. C. F.: Right: like what you do. So, I studied music in Switzerland, and then with the political reopening in Brazil. I always had a huge passion for Brazil, even without knowing it very well, because I was very small when I left, I was five years old. So, of course, I missed my uncles, my aunts, my cousins, of whom I had a vague memory of as a child. And the return was very emotional, very emotional. First, the climate. Wow! So hot! On our return we went straight to Recife. [Deep sigh.] Walter, I never felt so hot! [Laughs.]

W. O. K.: [Laughs.]

L. C. F.: It was terrible, terrible heat. It took me time to get used to Brazil's weather. I used to write letters to Joaquim and Cristina saying "Look, it is too hot here!" [Laughs.] It is too hot, too hot! And I talked about television. Anyway, I talked about the precariousness of life in Brazil in relation to Switzerland, which cannot be compared. I am not saying that Switzerland is better than Brazil, but it is . . .

W. O. K.: Different, another type of development.

L. C. F.: Different. It's another culture. Another kind of life. And I didn't know what to do, because I had my drums, I brought a xylophone, a percussion instrument made of wood. But I had no desire to continue being a classical musician in Brazil, because the orchestras were very precarious, very. You know? It was very different, very bad, and very precarious. And I said: "I will make my teenage dreams come true: I am going to college." I will go to university. I always wanted to enter university. And there, in Switzerland I couldn't, I couldn't pass the exams, because the Swiss education systems is very strict. It defines you since the elementary school. It directs you to a manual or intellectual area. I would never be able to stay in a class that allowed me to go to university. When I arrived in Brazil I said: "Now I am going to college, here in Brazil." But I had a problem, it was . . .

W. O. K.: The language?

L. C. F.: The language. Written Portuguese. And my accent, I had a Swiss accent. [Laughs.]

W. O. K.: [Laughs.]

L. C. F.: I had a very strong accent. [Laughs.] And I said to my father: "I want to study. I want to go to college." And he replied: "All right, so let's see what you need to do." Then, we went to this building. I remember there was a building of the secretary of education here in São Paulo, and they said: "You have to revalidate your . . ."

W. O. K.: Diploma?

L. C. F.: Right.

W. O. K.: Swiss certificates.

L. C. F.: Right. The Swiss studies. You have to go to the Swiss consulate so they could . . .

W. O. K.: Give you the stamp of approval.

L. C. F.: To stamp an official document, then finish high school as adult . . .

W. O. K.: It's a fast-track high school, very rapid, in a short time.

L. C. F.: Exactly. It's a fast-track high school, dynamic. So, I did that. I went to school in the evening at that time, there were evening studies. During

the day, I studied at Aliança Francesa, because I didn't want to lose
contact with French, right? It was maybe another dream to study French
here in Brazil, to have a French diploma and teach French, live in France.
It was also one of my dreams. But it didn't work. So, I studied at Aliança
Francesa and went to fast-track high school in the evening. Within a
year I passed the exam to study sociology. My father was anxious. He
asked, "So, what did you choose?"

W. O. K.: [Laughs.]

L. C. F.: I said: "Look, I want to be a social scientist, I want to study
Social Sciences. Because I want to know what is power. I want to
know what a coup is, I want to know this whole history. [Laughter.] I
want to know what dictatorship is, I want to study all about it." And
he was very happy. He said, "Well done, go ahead!" So, I studied at
PUC. It was already 1982. I entered in PUC where my father was
teaching. And, as a professor's son, I had the right of free tuition.
And I didn't skip one day, Walter. My only frustration was that I had
one idea about college mainly when I was living in Switzerland, I
thought that when we enter the university, we had a chance to think.
We could say what we think, state our opinion, that we could think,
we had a voice. And we didn't have to be that passive student, quiet,
listening to the professor. You know the whole thing my father talks
about, the banking education. But it was all the same when I entered
the college.

W. O. K.: It was disappointing.

L. C. F.: All students would sit in silence and when I would start talking,
they would say, "No, that's what you do in graduate school." I was a
bit frustrated with this. I thought that in college you could give your
opinion, have dialogue, exchange ideas etc. But, in the end, it wasn't too
bad. They allowed us to talk a little bit, have some opinions. I got my
social sciences degree in 1986.

W. O. K.: You started in 1982.

L. C. F.: Yes. It's a four-year college. But I wasn't sure if I wanted to stay in
the university, because I said to myself, "This is a bubble on the margins
of society. I studied the society here, for four years, but I didn't know
what life was like in Brazil." So, if I had wanted to write a thesis without
knowing the society it would have been something.

W. O. K.: Detached from reality.

L. C. F.: Theoretical.

W. O. K.: Abstract.

L. C. F.: Right. Abstract. So, I said, "I have to work, do something." And I started teaching English at a language school. I gave classes, but I was a very nervous teacher.

W. O. K.: Insecure?

L. C. F.: Insecure, yes, yes! And they had to train us to be a teacher. It was very strict, very strange, you didn't have the opportunity to dialogue with the students. You had to say, "I don't speak Portuguese!" [Laughter.]

W. O. K.: [Laughter.]

L. C. F.: It was horrible. After that, I decided to do something more related to my area. A job I did at the Municipal Volunteers Corps.

W. O. K.: At the city hall.

L. C. F.: At the city hall, under Luiza Erundina's administration. So, when my father left the municipal government, I joined the Corps of Municipal volunteers and started working with children from the periphery. I worked with children aged five, six, seven, ten years old.

W. O. K.: For how long?

L. C. F.: For two years! After that period, I worked in the government office and it was more, let's say, more complicated. I worked at the Youth Welfare Office. This office handles youth who have committed crimes. They were sixteen–seventeen years old who had infractions and were at Febem. At that time.

W. O. K.: Yes, yes, the place of reclusion.

LCH: Yes, a place of reclusion. They used to say, "Look, whoever wants to come to this house," the dwelling house, as we used called it, "can come, but you have to promise to not bring any guns, and you have to obey the house rules." And we would bring together nine, ten, eleven boys and they would work during the day at companies, earning a minimal wage, but they had a home, they had food, they had housing and they had us, who talked to them, and would exchange ideas to see how . . .

W. O. K.: It was working.

L. C. F.: We tried to resocialize them. And I worked there for about two years, I think. Two or three years at the Youth Welfare Office, after that I left. And I was unemployed for a time, until I started teaching language again at one of those schools where you can learn French, English, and Spanish. We were already in the 1990s.

W. O. K.: And you were not married yet.

L. C. F.: I was single. It was in 1992, 1993. I stayed at that school for five years.

W. O. K.: And did you live by yourself?

L. C. F.: I lived by myself. After some time, already in 1996, my father was a little bit weak, he was feeling weak. He had told me so. In 1997, he died. The same year I married Zelia.

W. O. K.: After his death.

L. C. F.: After his death. It was in 1997. And I started working here in 1998. So, I have been working here at the Institute for twenty years. My main task, at the beginning, when I got here, I called Gadotti, I already knew Gadotti from when my father was alive. They both taught in Campinas.

W. O. K.: At UNICAMP?

L. C. F.: At UNICAMP. And I said: "Gadotti, what can I do in the Institute?" He said, "Look, bring me your resume and we will see what we can do." I brought my resume. Gadotti looks it over and says, "It's very good, the resume." [Laughter.]

W. O. K.: [Smiles.]

L. C. F.: "You will do the following: you will put your father's library in order." I was terrified: "Oh my God, how can I put all these books in order? I need more people!" So, I got together with more people and we started to organize the entire library in alphabetical order. Today it is different.

W. O. K.: It is organized thematically now.

L. C. F.: Yes, thematically.

W. O. K.: And it took a long time.

L. C. F.: Took a long time, yes.

W. O. K.: So, for you, being Paulo Freire's son, it seems like it brought some difficulties and it made life easier. I mean, besides the affection, family love, it brought exile. As a consequence, you had an unusual life, for a child who goes to school. You had to leave the country, leave your family, abandon your culture. And, at the same time, it also helped you when you came back, because, for example, you could study at the university where your father was a professor. How do you feel about being Paulo Freire's son?

L. C. F.: That's right. I feel very, very, really very privileged, privileged! Because being a child of a man like my father and a woman like my mother is really not for everyone. I mean, it's very fortunate. It's very good. It's so good! Now, of course there were also drawbacks! My life is made by cuts! Cuts. I mean, not anymore! Friends, for example, I lost friends, the root things, as we say. In other words, I was a *chilenito*! [Laughs.]

W. O. K.: [Laughs.]

L. C. F.: I was a *chilenito*! And suddenly, *vummmm*! We leave there and go to live in the United States. Learn to chew gum like a North American.

W. O. K.: [Laughs.]

L. C. F.: So, you see, these cuts, in fact, made life difficult, let's say, they complicated the normal life of a person who lives in a country, studies and works in a country. But, on the other hand, my life was full of riches, because it's not everyone who can speak three languages, it's not everyone who has the experience that I had with my father, the opening up to the world that it offered me. Because, for example, I have a nephew who lives in Canada and when he says that he is Paulo Freire's grandchild, everyone is amazed, "My God! Wow! What a thing! That is wonderful!" So, Imagine me. If I arrived there and said, "I am Paulo Freire's son!" [Laughs.]

W. O. K.: [Laughs.] Even greater surprise!

L. C. F.: Even more. [Laughs.]

W. O. K.: In which city in Canada does your nephew . . .

L. C. F.: Toronto. So, you know, of course there were these cuts, but I think there was more, more. How would I say . . .

W. O. K.: Positive things?

L. C. F.: More positive than negative things.

W. O. K.: And if you had to pick out one of these positive things, the most important one, the one you think is related to the fact of having your father and your mother, of having been the son of your father, good fortune, a privilege. What would you say?

L. C. F.: Look, I think it was their affection for me. They loved me so much! So much!

W. O. K.: Even more because you were the youngest. You were privileged. [Laughs.]

L. C. F.: That's right. [Laughs.] And my siblings too. I mean, in fact, I was very spoiled. Until today! Until today, I am loved, really! I think the love in our family is very intense, very strong! I mean, we always have struggles, but the love always . . .

W. O. K.: Won!

L. C. F.: Yes, won! Love always conquered.

W. O. K.: And you also feel that with your sisters, your brothers, do you feel that love maintains your connections?

L. C. F.: Ah, yes. Yes. Of course, each one of us now has their own family. So, it becomes more difficult for us to see one another! But there is a loving feeling that our parents left with us, very strong!

W. O. K.: Just out of curiosity: your name, do you know the etymology?

L. C. F.: My name came from, if you read Natercinha's book, you must have realized that Lutgardes was my grandfather's name!

W. O. K.: What does Lutgardes mean?

L. C. F.: It is German. And in German you say: "Lutgardes." [Imitating the German pronunciation.] It means "the one who defends his people with his own spear." [Laughs.]

W. O. K.: [Laughs.] Such responsibility.

L. C. F.: It's a very ancient name, from the German Middle Ages. This is a German Lancelot. There is a French Lancelot and there is a German Lancelot.

W. O. K.: What question would you have liked to ask your father and didn't? One thing you would have liked to ask him, if you had a chance now, what would it be?

L. C. F.: [A long silence, followed by few sighs.] "Father, how can I better educate my daughter?" This is what I would ask him. How can I live better? How can I live while loving others without suffering, and without making others suffer?

W. O. K.: And one thing you would say to you father that you were not able to?

L. C. F.: [A short silence, a few sighs.] "Thank you father. For everything!"

W. O. K.: And one thing you would say to a person who studies your father, or writes about him, or thinks with him?

L. C. F.: I would say to this person something that a revolutionary of Guinea-Bissau, Amilcar Cabral, used to say and my father also liked to say as well (he had much admiration for this revolutionary): "Be patient impatiently." I think, in this moment that we live, we have to "be patient impatiently."

W. O. K.: Even more now.

L. C. F.: Even more.

W. O. K.: It is a vigilant patience!

L. C. F.: Right. To see if there is a gap/opportunity. If there happens to be a gap, we can enter.

W. O. K.: And the main thing you learned from your father, what would that be?

L. C. F.: [Thoughtful, speaking aloud.] The main thing. Wow! I believe that what I was talking about, I think it's the love for life. The love for the birds, love for the sun, love for nature, the love for people. I once asked my father, "Father, how do you deal with your sorrow? Sorrow for women, for example, how do you deal with that?" And he said, "Look, first, I think that sorrow is a virtue. And I think it is a virtue I was able to transmit to you. But I never, ever, let my sorrow take over, over all my being. But sorrow is a virtue!"

W. O. K.: It is a sorrow about what life could have been but wasn't. Or about what life . . .

L. C. F.: No, no! Sorrow, feeling sorrow toward the others, the poor. Sorrow.

W. O. K.: Sadness?

L. C. F.: Yes, sadness.

W. O. K.: So, the disturbance, the discomfort, it must be kept alive in any human being for the world to change.

L. C. F.: Right. Exactly! Exactly! I think we have discomforted human beings. Uncomfortable. Constantly perturbed. I mean, my father always said that the human being has the vocation for "being more." And this "being more" doesn't mean "being more" than others, it means being more human. It means being able to have affection for people, respect for people. Respect for women, respect for minorities. Respect. And I think this is what is missing a lot in the world today. People don't have respect anymore. They think they own the truth, when, in fact, no one owns the truth.

W. O. K.: The truth has no owner.

L. C. F.: Yes. The other day, I was at the bakery and somebody said, "Would you like water, professor?" They called me professor. [Laughs.] I said, "If I have to pay for this water it is not right, because water belongs to everyone. The earth belongs to everybody." They pretended they didn't understand. [Laughs.]

W. O. K.: [Laughs.]

L. C. F.: Of course, it was a provocation. But this is the truth. You see, at the same time that we are dehumanized, we are creating mechanisms that facilitate our humanization, because the technology brings us closer, technology brings us together in an impressive ways! In other words, if we know how to use this instrument in a way that favors us, it would be fantastic, do you understand? It leads us to believe, to observe. Take for example, the relationship of Paulo Freire, my father, with technology. There are many people who think (I don't know, maybe) that Paulo Freire was against technology. On the contrary, he was always in favor of it. He was one of the first educators to utilize a projector to project the image of a native hunting a bird, for the peasants to see that image, I mean, he was the precursor of that. Until the 1990s, when the computer began to appear, he said, "Look, there is only one problem with this technology: that only a third of the world's population has enough money to buy this machine." If over time it becomes cheaper, and we know how to use it for our benefit, it will be fantastic.

W. O. K.: The problem is that technology, by itself, does nothing. The problem is, what is it used for?

L. C. F.: Exactly! Exactly! This is, for example, how Bolsonaro was elected, by utilizing technology. Or they guided him to it.

W. O. K.: To use this strategy.

L. C. F.: To use this strategy. But we didn't know. I think one of the biggest mistakes of the left is that we only talk to ourselves. Because being a left-wing person sometimes means to be against many things that you think are bad. But sometimes those things that you consider bad can also bring good things: having a job, having better living conditions, right? In a higher quantity than we have now, right? Anyway, Dilma used to talk about a middle class in Brazil, "the big middle class." I don't know if this is possible, but I think her idea is right. It is correct in some ways because it is absurd, Walter, that still today there are people starving. I mean, we have people who are sick.

W. O. K.: And the number hasn't diminished. It's a lot of people!

L. C. F.: It's a lot of people! A lot of people! And as I was saying, the world is getting poorer. People are receiving less and less money. The value of work is being devalued.

W. O. K.: And tell me something, if you could imagine your life otherwise, what would be something you would dream of doing in your life?

L. C. F.: As you know, I would try to create a relationship between my life and my father's writings.

W. O. K.: And how would you proceed to make this relationship happen? Can you give me an example?

L. C. F.: It's difficult for me. I don't know. For example, love: he ends the *Pedagogia do oprimido* saying . . .

W. O. K.: "If nothing remains of these pages, something, at the very least, we hope will endure: our trust in the people. Our faith in people to create a world where it is less difficult to love."

L. C. F.: That's it. Where did he get that from? He took this from us! From his children, from his wife, from his life.

W. O. K.: In other words, it would be to connect your father's ideas with life.

L. C. F.: Right, exactly. The ideas with life. Because the ideas don't come, they don't come . . .

W. O. K.: From nothing?

L. C. F.: From nothing. The ideas don't fall from the sky on your head. The ideas, they started from the reality that you, my father, lived with us, and it was through living with us that he was driven to write what he wrote.

W. O. K.: You were nurturing his ideas.

L. C. F.: Yes, feeding him ideas. So much so that when he wrote, he didn't allow anyone to be around. Why? Because he was loaded with the things we said to him. And it was a moment of concentration for him. Writing takes a lot of concentration. You must also know this. So, I think if you can do this, it would be wonderful!

W. O. K.: I will try.

L. C. F.: That's right! [Laughs.]

W. O. K.: [Laughs.]

Appendix III

An Interview With Esther Pillar Grossi

Some Risks of Misreading Freire[1]

Walter Kohan: Esther, first of all, I greatly appreciate the opportunity of this interview, to converse and make dialogue. I feel privileged to have worked together in GEEMPA [Group of Studies on Education, Methodology of Research, and Action] and to have shared not only that work as colleagues, but also our friendship over the last ten or twelve years. I consider you one of the people who did the most in the last decades for the education of Brazil, and more specifically for the literacy of children and the training of literacy teachers. Another Brazilian who did a lot for education in Brazil was Paulo Freire, who is today being attacked by ultra-conservative sectors of the country as the main person responsible for the current state of Brazilian education. Could you tell me what you think about Paulo Freire?

Esther Pillar Grossi: In the first place, I was a great friend of Paulo Freire, and he was an extraordinary figure, raising, precisely at a very necessary moment, the flag in favor of the oppressed. And the relief work in relation to that oppression began in Angicos, Rio Grande do Norte, with adult literacy. From there, he wrote *Pedagogy of the Oppressed*, in which he addresses the relationship of the oppressed masses and their leaders, advocating a great respect for them. I think that there was really a

---

[1] Esther Pilar Grossi (1936–) is a well-known Brazilian educator. She was secretary of education of the City of Porto Alegre while Paulo Freire was secretary of education of São Paulo. She was a member of parliament for the Workers' Party (PT) between 1995 and 2002. She is the founder of GEEMPA (Grupo de Estudos Sobre Educação, Metodologia de Pesquisa e Ação) which since 1970 has been conducting research and staging interventions in the areas of literacy and teacher education in several regions of Brazil and other Latin American countries. This interview took place in November 2017 over WhatsApp.

confusion between what Paulo Freire proposed and its immediate, direct transposition to the school, causing certain confusions to be practiced in the school concerning what the construction of knowledge within it should be.

W. K.: Can you talk a little more about that confusion, Esther? Because Paulo Freire was also, after returning from exile, as you know, municipal secretary of education in São Paulo, and was directly involved with the work in schools.

E. P. G.: It seems to me that Paulo Freire, as secretary of education of São Paulo (at that time I was a secretary in Porto Alegre), really did not do very well with the task, so much so that he left office before the end of the mandate of Luiza Erundina, passing the secretary of education to Sérgio Cortella. And I even remember that he was venting to me about his difficulties with teachers, in particular with the idea of electing principals. It may seem incredible, but Paulo Freire perceived that there was an error in the election of directors, at least in the way it was directed, and I think that, even with his experience in the Ministry of Education, he did not manage to undo the misunderstanding of the left, particularly the PT, when judging that there is a popular knowledge that has to take priority in the school, and that then the teacher has to listen to the students, and, interpreting the phrase that Paulo Freire expresses more than once, return structured what students present in a disorganized way. That idea works precisely for his ideas in the struggle for the liberation of the oppressed, but it is not what happens in school, with the knowledge of literacy. He himself once told me: "Look, Esther, the one who understands literacy is you." He did not create, in fact, any method. In literacy, it is clear that students do not have knowledge. That knowledge needs to be built. I feel, I presume, that Paulo Freire anticipated the idea of the psychogenesis of learning, taking into account the fact that students construct hypotheses about what they urgently need to learn. And those hypotheses are a knowledge of born of ignorance. Sara Paín says that ignorance is not stupidity, but a form of intelligence. So, a student who thinks that he writes with pictures has already evolved in relation to knowing that writing is to transport to a surface something that relates or creates something permanent from what he is thinking or what is happening. And, later on, the other hypotheses that the students make, evolving in sequence, when they find that "it is not written with drawings, but with graphic signs," but still without any link to pronunciation. So, obviously, knowledge is made from an elaboration of the apprentice, and the teacher must take into account what the student is thinking.

W. K.: I found a phrase by Paulo Freire in which he says something that may have to do with what you say that he anticipated. It is from an interview from the 1990s:

Literacy is a creative experience and that means that literacy has to create, he has to change, to use a more technical expression, "the system of graphic signs" . . . that is to say, he has to be, basically, architect of this production or of this creation, obviously he or she helped or helped by the educator.

Can you comment on this?

E. P. G.: I have a very clear concrete example of this construction by the student, which was the expression of Antonio, one of the first students who was in my literacy room and who, when asked about who had taught him to read and write, said " Nobody, I learned by thinking and asking." It is exactly that. The presence of the teacher disappears from the creative authorship of the student. But, obviously, he had a teacher, and I wasn't there at all: I prepared the conditions for Antonio to think.

W. K.: Exactly, Esther; Antonio's testimony is precious! But imagine if, based on his claim, some thought that, since no one taught him, then the teacher does not need to know nor teach anything. My impression is that Paulo Freire would totally agree with what you say, but there is a misleading reading someone could make of Antonio's idea here. And, certainly, the experience of Paulo Freire in the secretary of education of the city of São Paulo shows that ideas, theories, are one thing but another thing is the reality of an educational system as complex as that of São Paulo. You yourself must have experienced enormous difficulties in putting your ideas into practice in Porto Alegre. It is a pity that the Lula government did not give you the opportunity to experience these difficulties in the Ministry of Education, but that is conjecture about the past. It also seems clear that Paulo Freire proposes ideas, more than a method; that is, a way of thinking about education. In addition to this question of popular knowledge, what do you think of his other most significant ideas, for example, the impossibility of the neutrality of the educator, what he calls the "politicality" of education?

E. P. G.: Of course every person, every professional, is framed by their political, religious position, which permeates everything they do. However, really, in my opinion, I, as a literacy educator, by making students literate or presenting good mathematics, am leading my students to what I want: I am ensuring that they think and have criteria to make their choices. So, I think that, really, "politicality" does not mean a direct indoctrination in relation to a political position. It is evident that no teacher should say neutral, because that neutrality does not exist. We all have our ideologies and they exert great force, and today I believe it is a crime to consider that it is "ideology," for example, to deal with problems such as racism or homophobia at school. I, for example, am accused by Bolsonaro's son of inciting students to use drugs because we have an activity notebook about Patrick, who was a child from there in the city of Santa Maria (in the State of Rio Grande do Sul) who had been in school for three years and had not learned to read. To make him literate, we dealt with the problem of drugs because he was involved in that and had learned a lot in it. And we know that if we do not engage what we want to teach with the knowledge that the student acquires in their day to day and that is important to them, we do not teach. Well, specifically at GEEMPA, when we work on the question of death, a profound question on which each one of us has a position, we approach it in such a way that students can have an idea from their culture, having a positive opening on the question of death. And we work with works of literature, we have a series of books, among them the one on the history of a leaf, in which we leave the question open, but, obviously, help students to think and define themselves.

W. K.: So, I think that, regarding non-neutrality, you would agree with Paulo Freire: he does not say that the teacher must make their option prevail, as some suggest. What he says is that the teacher should not hide it and that he simply does not think that it can be neutral, because it would be impossible, as you say, because the way I would be working in favor of the instituted state of affairs, which is certainly not neutral. For example, that criticism that Bolsonaro's son makes of GEEMPA is parallel to the one being done today against Paulo Freire and what they call "gender ideology." What you say (i.e., that you want the students to think with their own criteria) is precisely what is being criticized in those subjects, such as, among others, those from Schools Without Party (SWP), who see this as a threat to the values of family and religion. What they want is precisely to be the priests of the public school with the power to contribute to the formation of thinking people with their own criteria. And Paulo Freire was betting on the same sense of public education, right?

E. P. G.: It may be that today that group on the right is inflicting upon Paulo Freire the responsibility of wanting to indoctrinate people, but unfortunately, that is not the confusion I am referring to from a didactic-pedagogical point of view. Starting from a misinterpretation of Paulo Freire, the idea that the teacher should not even have knowledge about what they are going to teach, because that would already be authoritarianism: the teacher would have to be learning with the students, that they do not bring anything prepared to the classroom, because they are going to listen to what the students are going to deliver, disorganized, for the teacher to return to them structure. That really is a mistake. A teacher has to be literate and from that poor understanding of Paulo Freire, the MOVA was built, a literacy movement in which the literacy teachers were not teachers, they were any layperson already literate. And, in that movement, another fault appears regarding the idea that the teacher does not need to have knowledge of what they are going to teach. For example, I have to teach mathematics, I cannot count on what the students bring as popular knowledge of mathematics. In mathematics, we know very well that, for example, it is possible for a person to build an additive structure in their day to day, as Terezinha Nunes Carreher indicated so well in the book *In life ten and in school zero* (1991). Some knowledge is built with more meaning in life, but that knowledge has a rather restricted upper limit. If it is well-known and proven, in the science of the teaching of mathematics, that the structure of multiplication is impossible to be built without the organized systematization of didactics, then, it is necessary to know the didactics of mathematics in addition to knowing mathematics. That was the conclusion that there was: teachers do not need to have knowledge because they will learn together with their students. That is absurd, but unfortunately, wrongly anchored in Paulo Freire, a lot of it happened, so much so that, in literacy, we have a disaster; we can't even get out of the same figures as forty years ago: fifty million illiterate adults who went through school. Why? Because of that confusion.

W. K.: There are many examples in which Paulo Freire emphasizes the need for the teacher's knowledge, their teaching, etc. The question we have today is really that tragedy that you say: fifty million illiterates.

E. P. G.: As a consequence of that mistake, the faculties of pedagogy themselves deviated from the focus, and the peripheral disciplines took the center . . . Now, in Cachoeira, in Bahia, I went to visit a school, and two teachers were crying when I arrived . . . It was a visit. Absolutely free, I went to see a school in one of the first Brazilian cities, and two teachers were crying and saying: "We have literacy classes, and in the Pedagogy faculties we don't learn anything about literacy. And even in mathematics we do not learn anything in the Pedagogy courses, and then we see ourselves in front of students to carry out that teaching." But, in compensation, they learned a lot about popular education, about ecology, about many other issues that really divert them from their main focus, from their political obligation.

W. K.: That's right, one part of that tragedy of the fifty million illiterates is misguided teacher education. But, if you allow me, Esther, I don't think that teachers have a good political training, but instead they have a deficient "technical training." I wish it was at least that, but I think it's even more serious.

E. P. G.: Unfortunately, teachers absorb the dominant ideology and also believe that poor students cannot learn.

W. K.: Exactly, Esther. There we have a principle of the "politicality" of education, which we have worked at so hard together, inspired by *The Ignorant Schoolmaster*: no one can truly teach if they do not assume that everyone, regardless of their age, class, gender, is equally capable of learning. That political knowledge is essential to teach anything, and, although it may be politicized in other ways, teacher education in Brazil is not very much oriented by this principle.

E. P. G.: Exactly, Walter. For someone to learn that universal, scientific truth that we can all learn, they have to overcome the ideology that the poor will not learn, that we can all learn except the poor, those who are of another class, dominated, and so on.

Sadly, the conversation with Esther stopped here. We agreed to continue at another time. Due to various difficulties, nothing bad, we ended up not taking it up again. Thus, the interview remains open, like thought, the word, and life. And this book, like this interview, also has an open ending.

A Few Critiques of Paulo Freire

For What Kind of Politics Is There Space and Time for in Education?

A pedagogy will be that much more critical and radical the more investigative and less certain of "certainties" it is. The more "unquiet" a pedagogy, the more critical it will become. A pedagogy preoccupied with the uncertainties rooted in the issues we have discussed is, by its nature, a pedagogy that requires investigation. This pedagogy is thus much more a pedagogy of question than a pedagogy of answer.

(Freire and Macedo, 1987, p. 36)

When I affirm the political nature of education, I want to stress that education is a political act. That is why there is no reason to talk about politics as a character or aspect of education, as if it had only a political dimension, but was not a political practice. And there is no school that is good or bad in itself as an institution. But, at the same time, it is not possible to think about school, to think about education, outside power relations; that is to say, I cannot understand education outside the problem of power, which is political. Educators must be warned of this because, to the extent that the educator realizes that education is a political act, he discovers himself as a politician. In fact, the educator is a politician, he is an artist, he is not just a technician, who uses tools and techniques, who uses science.

(Freire, 2018b, p. 40)

How should one relate to an author? I recall my training in philosophy at the University of Buenos Aires. At that time, the most important way to relate to the writing and thought of an author was through "critique," which was understood as an exercise in pointing out the problems and limits of someone's thinking or of a system of thought. The authors we worked with were generally distant, deceased for many years. Little to nothing about their lives was on the table for discussion. This is the habitual way of doing work in the academic world of philosophy. It has its warrant and charm, but it also has its limits. (Am I being too critical here?) I believe that the principal drawback to this approach is that it ends up dominating the space, diminishing the opportunities for more lively and creative thinking to emerge. It isn't that this approach is incompatible with creative thinking, but rather that more often than not critique succeeds in seductively pointing out the limits of another thought without strengthening the potential of affirming one's own thinking. When a way of thinking is removed from life, when it only dialogues with an intellectual history of ideas, critique can become abstract and disembodied. Little by little, I have distanced myself from this approach. It is not that I do not carry a part of it with me (e.g., at least part of what follows below clearly demonstrates how complex our relationship with our own education is, even in those aspects we explicitly put into question), but rather that it was more and more incorporated with a growing disposition that was more affirmative and connective, instead of being a confrontational approach to other ways of thinking (and living). This approach involves the work of directing attention to what allows for thinking and composing together, rather than signaling the outer limits of a thought.

Thus, I have learned to appreciate this approach by reading certain philosophers that practiced it, Deleuze perhaps being one of the most evident examples, but certainly not the only one, and also observing people, philosophers and others, living with this disposition. In this way, the majority of my learning experience did not come through reading books, but rather through years of living, teaching, and learning with the people that exhibited this force in Brazil and other places I traveled to. At the same time, my immersion in the "philosophy for/with children" movement left me feeling the necessity to live philosophy, more than just study it.

This is what I found (or found anew) in Freire, who is almost a symbol of a Brazil filled with its contradictions, challenges, treasures, delicacies, and tensions. And I thought that a re-reading and writing about one of the greatest educators of our time would be an excellent opportunity to deepen this path of learning to think and live education. It would be an opportunity to enlarge this "state of learning" in which I have lived for a long time now, that wasn't natural for me, but in which I learned Freire (not knowing exactly how) among others. I learned something that I do not want to unlearn. What I have tried to do in this book, through reading and thinking of the life of Freire, in particular through asking certain "classic and basic" questions about education like "What does it mean to educate?" "What is the meaning of education?" "What makes one a teacher?" I have attempted to compose with him a way, always in movement, open and provisional, to think through a philosophical-educational problem that affects us.

I have also tried to respond to a continually present question: Can Paulo Freire still help us think about how to live the educational and philosophical life that we want to live today, in the present? If he can, then how? What can he inspire in us? What do we learn through the work and life of Freire that helps us think through the problems of our time? With my limits, defects, and distractions, I stubbornly sought to provoke anything that would lead me to compose, bring together, and think and write with him. I hope that this reinvention with Freire and the philosophical-educational problem that this book proposes will be an inspiration for other reinventions.

Once, at the beginning of my travels around the world, someone asked me, I don't remember where, "Paulo, what can we do to follow you? To follow your ideas? " and I replied, "If you follow me, you will destroy me. The best way for you to follow me is for you to reinvent me, and not try to adapt to me" (Freire, Paulo; Freire, Ana Maria, and Oliveira, 2009, p. 24)

Let us bluntly describe things as they are. Brazil is living in a politically scandalous situation. A political alliance between opposition parties, the media, and judicial sectors decided to do what they couldn't do through the vote: remove the Workers' Party (PT) from government. They did so by fabricating the impeachment of President Dima Rousseff and imprisoning former president Lula, the only PT member who would have been unbeatable in fair elections. One of the most shocking aspects of these maneuvers is the way in which the media assisted in convincing a large portion of the population to support them. Even worse is the fact that to continue the process of removing the PT from power, these same actors helped elect an ex-military official who explicitly and clearly believes in regressive policies against sectors of the population that have been historically marginalized: the landless, Afro-Brazilians, indigenous groups, women, the LGBTQ community. In other words, he has lashed out against the oppressed, threadbare, and tattered of this torn country. It is as if the anti-PT sectors believe that the hunger, exclusion, inequity, and misery of Brazil will be resolved by greater economic liberalism. And it is not just humans who are suffering. The earth, air, animals, and public natural resources are all subjected to the law of the market, of money. Within this political-economic context in place, the country's educational program is diaphanous. It operates according to the rationality of meritocracy and entrepreneurship and aims to "purge the ideology of Paulo Freire." We are all living in a burning house, but most especially the marginalized are at risk.

This is the reality in which we live in Brazil. It is important to see that it is a reality which differs from the 1964 coup that forced Freire into exile. It is legitimatized by a popular vote. This would have certainly amazed Freire. Here, of course, critique is more than welcome. For example, it is evident that the PT is not only a victim, but that it also bears great responsibility for the situation. And it is not only the PT, but all of those self-described "progressives," including those, like me, who are professors in public universities who cannot but put in question the role we have played in this process. The current moment demands that we rigorously critique ourselves. But the question is not whether one is, or is not aligned with the PT, as many would like to believe. The PT practiced a type of politics that it had once critiqued, and that it still critiques today. In the end, the PT changed the content, but not the form, of practicing politics in Brazil. At the end of the day, the question remains whether we can practice a different type of politics.

As such, the current moment is in need of affirmative and creative responses that address the reality we are living through. This book is a response to the infamous attack against the most renowned educator of Latin America. Disputes about the legacy of Freire are often circumscribed by fierce and passionate attacks versus equally fierce and passionate defenses. Here, in a way that differs from the more customary defenses of Freire, I have been seeking something different. I have sought to demonstrate the impropriety of attempting to destroy Freire by bringing into focus his philosophical and educational values, his thought, and his life.

I need to trace the shape of the current debates around Freire, which have taken various forms of expression in Brazil during the last few years, before moving on. One of the key protagonists has been the "Schools Without Party" ("Escola Sem Partido") movement, which, as their name suggests, tries to dissociate school and politics. They do so in a way that prescribes proselytism instead of political parties, which further separates the fundamental link between schooling/education and politics. The movement argues for "neutrality" in schools and among professional educators.

The most evident objective of the SWP movement is the strengthening of institutions like the family and church. Less often openly declared is their desire to weaken the role of public education and public school teachers through claims of objectivity and neutrality by limiting education to the transmission of scientific and technical content. In their view, education and school should be apolitical, and for this reason their main enemies are those, like Freire, who defend the political nature of educational work. Thus, the SWP cannot but manifest certain tensions. In the name of academic freedom, and departing from technocratic conceptions of teaching, they annul or limit the liberty of expression of teachers. They try to make education juridical and they criminalize teaching by, anytime politics or cultural diversity is taught, falsely labeling the practice as ideological indoctrination. Moreover, they promote the persecution of teachers through methods of vigilance and punishment administered by students themselves. Thus, they seek a school in which one cannot discuss themes like sexual diversity, gender, and ethnic and racial prejudice. Generally speaking, a school without politics would lead to a school that does not present different visions of the world and ways of being in it. In this way, it is an elitist school, one that is conservative and patriarchal.

Freire himself is a testimony to these clashes. For instance, in his last written text, *Pedagogy of Freedom* published for the first time in 1996, he affirms:

> A pragmatic reactionary educator would probably say that there is no connection between one thing and the other. That the school is not the Party. That the function of the school is to teach and transfer contents-packages to the students, which, once learned, will operate automatically. (Freire, 1998, p. 37)

After almost twenty years the "pragmatic reactionaries" have taken to the streets. On March 15, 2013, in a protest against Dilma Rousseff in Brasilia, a banner prepared by the twenty-seven-year-old professor of history of the federal district, Eduardo Sallenave, implored: "Do away with the Marxist indoctrination. Enough of Paulo Freire." The declared political enemy was Marxism and communism, and in their line of fire was the person they said was responsible for integrating Marxism into the Brazilian school system: Paulo Freire. It is worth noting that the SWP movement has existed since 2004,[1] but it is as

---

[1] One of the followers of SWP, Thomas Giulliano, a history teacher, published a book, *Deconstructing Paulo Freire* (2017), in which he accuses Freire of "intellectual and pedagogical genocide, who manufactured pampered children," which made the student "A person holding non-negotiable positions." According to Giulliano, Freire's pedagogy proposes "the total control of man over man," and accuses him of believing that "through his pedagogy we would reach the end of history, the formation of the perfect man." The website where the book is promoted (www.historiaexpressa.com.br)

if it has encountered, in the present Brazilian political moment, the conditions to penetrate into three institutional branches of the State. Of course, these actions have encountered resistance that has prevented the SWP from accruing the legal instruments it so obstinately pursues. Many of their actions have either not been approved, or been approved and then reversed.[2]

even has the name of the publisher that published it, which suggests that Giulliano himself is at the same time the author, editor, promoter, seller, and distributor of his work. We take the references from the interview offered by Thomas Giulliano to Diego Casagrande in the program "Opinião livre" on July 25, 2017, in the Boletim da Liberdade (retrieved on September 22, 2017, at <www.boletimdaliberdade.com.br>), and Giulliano's intervention in the public hearing of the Chamber of Deputies on March 21, 2017. The attack on Freire is not only intellectual, political and pedagogical, but also aesthetic and moral. According to Giulliano, the pedagogue of the oppressed "was someone who, in addition to being insufficient in aesthetic and stylistic development for a country like Brazil (?) That has so much culture to be our patron, and from the moral point of view is far below any reference for discussion." Giulliano considers that "having him as employer is a shame" and that he should be "replaced and placed in theoretical limbo where he deserves." Guilliano also accuses Freire of being, indirectly, the cause of the current lack of control and violence in schools, which "indirectly has to do with Freire: he raised the students to a disastrous role." And links the thought of Freire to teachers: "He is responsible for emptying the teaching role." Teachers have lost their role in favor of the protagonism of the student and, according to Giulliano, "they are the main ones responsible" for the lamentable state of Brazilian education. It is an obviously prejudiced, dogmatic, and tendentious attack: it is not based on any analysis, reason, or foundation, other than a profound contempt for the world and for the aesthetic, ethical, and political values that Freire affirms and represents; that is, those of the Northeastern people, popular culture, and the careful and committed writing that expresses that culture.

2 Despite not having legal force, the project expands throughout the country, gaining several followers, but also mobilizing protests and tensions on the part of people who resist the ideas of SWP, from public bodies to a large contingent of teachers and students from all levels of education. Among the first, the Advocacia Geral da União (AGU) stands out, which issued an opinion to the Supreme Federal Court defending the unconstitutionality of the law approved in the state of Alagoas in 2016, revoking it. In addition to that, other instances issued opinions contrary to the idea of SWP, such as the Attorney General's Office; the Federal Public Ministry, through the Federal Promontory dos Direitos do Cidadão; the National Council of Human Rights, which issued a resolution repudiating SWP initiatives; the United Nations High Commissioner for Human Rights, who treated the bills promoted by the movement as a threat to basic human rights; the Brazilian Society for the Progress of Science (SBPC), which affirms that SWP is a serious threat to science, education, the secular state, and freedom of expression in Brazil. And this without counting various associations of teachers of basic and higher education and of rectories of federal universities. Resistance to SWP was also one of the slogans of the student mobilizations of 2016, in which various high school and university students occupied educational institutions in protest against that bill called the "Law of the Muzzle." Still with regard to resistance, the actions of the Teachers

Among the accusations leveled against Freire is this one: that he weakened the role of the teacher. Here it is perhaps helpful to recall Freire himself to reveal the fallacious character of this charge:

> I cannot resist repeating: teaching is not the pure mechanical transfer of the contour of a content from the teacher to passive, docile students. Nor can I resist repeating that starting out with the educands' knowledge does not mean circling around this knowledge ad infinitum. Starting out means setting off down the road, getting going, shifting from one point to another, not sticking, or staying. I have never said, as it is sometimes suggested or said that I have said, that we ought to flutter spellbound around the knowledge of the educands like moths around a lamp bulb. (Freire, 1994, p. 87)

Only someone who has not read Freire could accuse him of weakening the role of the teacher. To affirm that the teacher is more than just a mechanical transmitter of content does not negate her fundamental role, which, for Freire, is to be the principle provocateur of a specific way of learning:

> Teaching someone to learn is only valid—from this view-point, let me repeat—when educands learn to learn in learning the reason-for, the "why," of the object or the content. (Freire, 1994, p. 101)

What is at stake then, is not a difference between a teacher who teaches and a teacher who does not, but rather the difference between a teacher who teaches unreasonable content to students who are perceived to know nothing versus a teacher who, recognizing her pupils' knowledge, teaches them the reason for being and the significance of the content that she teaches.

> What especially moves me to be ethical is to know that, inasmuch as education of its very nature is directive and political, I must, without ever denying my dream or my utopia before the educands, respect

Movement against the Schools Without Party stand out, created by teachers from the education area of the Fluminese Federal University, as well as the National Campaign for the Right to Education, coordinated by Daniel Cara.

them. To defend a thesis, a position, a preference, with earnestness, defend it rigorously, but passionately, as well, and at the same time to stimulate the contrary discourse, and respect the right to utter that discourse, is the best way to teach, first, the right to have our own ideas, even our duty to "quarrel" for them, for our dreams—and not only to learn the syntax of the verb, haver; and second, mutual respect. (Freire, 1994, p. 97)

The critique of neutrality and the affirmation of a direct and political education demands that a teacher respect her students while accepting and promoting a discourse that often contradicts her. If this is to be done in a respectful way, for both the student and the teacher, then it must be done openly and honestly. We again turn to Freire:

Respecting the educands, however, does not mean lying to them about my dreams, telling them in words or deeds or practices that a school occupies a "sacred" space where one only studies, and studying has nothing to do with what goes on in the world outside; to hide my options from them, as if it were a "sin" to have a preference, to make an option, to draw the line, to decide, to dream. Respecting them means, on the one hand, testifying to them of my choice, and defending it; and on the other, it means showing them other options, whenever I teach— no matter what it is that I teach! (Freire, 1994, pp. 97–8)

The lines are from *Pedagogy of Hope*, which has as its subtitle, "A re-encounter with *Pedagogy of the Oppressed*." Twenty years after the publication of the latter, Freire re-reads himself. He maintains that teachers' expressing their own perspectives on matters is a sign of respect for their students, and he problematizes schools that are isolated from the exterior world, and that are conceived of only as places where the transmission of content occurs, noting that schools are situated in social, historical, and cultural contexts. Furthermore, he argues that teachers should not only share their own perspectives, but also defend the perspectives of others. One would have to read Freire blindly, loaded with preconceptions and bad faith, in order to read him as an advocate of indoctrination. We read, yet again, a bit of the so-called indoctrinator:

And let it not be said that, if I am a biology teacher, I must not "go off into other considerations"—that I must only teach biology, as if the phenomenon of life could be understood apart from its historico-social, cultural, and political framework. As if life, just life, could be lived in the same way, in all of its dimensions, in a favela (slum) or cortiço ("beehive"—slum tenement building) as in a prosperous area of São Paulo's "Gardens"! If I am a biology teacher, obviously I must teach biology. But in doing so, I must not cut it off from the framework of the whole. (Freire, 1994, p. 98)

It is clear here that Freire affirms that the teachers of biology should teach biology! Could it be that Freire's accusers have not really read him? Or, if they have, they have only read with very little attention? Or could it be that their reading of his work is biased by certain ideological and discursive positions established by a variety of organizations, intellectuals, journalists, and legal projects which label Freire and others as theoretical enemies of "the Left," "Marxists," and "Communists," and the representatives of these theoretical frameworks, such as Freire (but also others like Augusto Boal, Leornardo Boff, etc.) as serving the Workers' Party, which is ultimately their main target? If this is the case, then who in reality is hiding their ideologies? And what political-ideological interests does it serve to depoliticize education in contemporary Brazil while simultaneously trying to hide an exaggerated reactionary political project?

These questions allow us to perceive a common belief shared by Freire and his enemies, one which possibly explains in part the immense hostility toward him. Both Freire and his enemies possess an evangelical or pastoral educational element. That they fulfill this element in different opposite ways (one theoretical framework proposing salvation via Christian Marxism, which is viewed as the work of the devil by the other camp), does not erase the fact that they share a common aim. The opponents of Freire also want to "save" education, but through other means like technocracy, ideologies of meritocracy, and the God of the market.

In these pages, I have tried to show that the ideas and life of Freire can be reterritorialized in a politicized but secular way with a commitment to certain principles like equality, errantry, an unanticipated transformation of the world, and through a dialogical education that is more than just a faith or an ideological belief in education as a process of critical consciousness raising. Before ending with some final thoughts, I would like to touch on some critiques leveled against Freire, beginning with those made by Latin American academics.

Some Academic Critiques

The school we need so urgently [I said in 1960] is a school in which persons really study and work. When we criticize, on the part of other educators, the intellectualism of our schools, we are not attempt-ing to defend a position with regard to the school in which the study disciplines, and the discipline of studying, would be watered down. We may never in all of our history have had more need of teaching, studying, learning, than we have today.[3]

(Freire, 1994, p. 143)

The connection between the deplorable state of Brazilian education and the figure of Paulo Freire is not exclusively made by the SWP movement. In 2017, we find another example, a book titled *When No One Educates: Questioning Paulo Freire* by R. Rocha from the Federal University of Santa Maria (UFSM). In this book, Rocha makes a connection between what he classifies as "the actual crisis of Brazilian education" and what he postulates as the relevant elements, "democratic populism and a particular reading of Freire," needed to understand the pedagogical and curricular makeup of the country since the 1970s (Rocha, 2017, p. 13). In the introduction of the book, Rocha justifies his interest in the pedagogue of hope, who he

---

[3] Paulo Freire brought this text written by himself in 1960 for the sake of its bearing on the question under discussion in this part of *Pedagogy of Hope*.

admits he never studied systematically, by stating that, to his surprise, he discovered in the principle book of Freire, *Pedagogy of the Oppressed*, certain categories affirmed in the work that make possible not only a historical period but also certain "concepts still in operation" (Rocha, 2017, p. 15). According to Rocha, this is because the book is "no longer read, or better, is read against itself."

Seemingly motivated by an ahistorical and decontextualized reading of Freire's work, Rocha takes it upon himself to tell his readers how to read Freire. Considered a philosopher by profession, his aim to lead the readers of Freire out of the cave and into the light, should not surprise us. This is the classic move of philosophy, which portends to form a type of critical consciousness by shedding light on reality for those of us living in darkness. The light in this case, as we read in the subtitle of the book, "*Questioning Paulo Freire*," emanates from a philosophical approach to questioning Freire's work. Putting aside the agreeable and non-agreeable aspects of philosophy and its role as illuminator, the project appears at first glance to be laudable given the impact that the work of Freire has had, and the context in which it is taken up today. Thus, I read Rocha's book with great interest, expecting to find elements to think with in it.

Lamentably, however, the book has less to say about the famous Brazilian educator than it promises, and more than raising any new questions about Freire's work, it offers an appreciation that does not significantly differ from the critiques of *Pedagogy of Oppressed* that have been in circulation since its release, many of which Freire himself would agree with. Some of the details of this book, however, are worth mentioning here.

The principle discovery made by Rocha is that *Pedagogy of the Oppressed* is in fact not a book about pedagogy because it has very little to say about school. It is instead directed at revolutionizing many intellectuals and political parties of the 1970s (Rocha, 2017, pp. 67–9). If the book can in any way be said to be usefully applied in pedagogical practice, it should only be used with adults learning to read and write, and not, as has often been the case, used in the primary grades (p. 72). Accompanying this "discovery" appears a series of rebukes against Freire (p. 71). According to Rocha, Freire (a) abandons relevant activities in favor of learning: "the act of paying attention and being hospitable to what someone says to us"; (b) "dispenses with the role of memory and of testimony"; (c) understands in a biased way the role of propositional knowledge; and d) offers a "simplified description of human knowledge, made in favor of a cause of an epoch." Rocha supports his conclusions by reading very short excerpts from *Pedagogy of the Oppressed*, passages in which Freire does not disregard or invalidate these activities per se, but instead problematizes them as instances of what he calls a banking education.

It is a shame that Rocha decided to not pay more attention to a specific reader of Freire: Freire himself! There are not many authors outside of Freire who have re-read their own work as carefully as Freire did, especially *Pedagogy of the Oppressed*, in light of the critiques it received. Had he given it a more careful reading, Rocha might have encountered the critiques he levels against the author in Freire himself. For instance, one of the things that Rocha could have found is that Freire concurs in part with his reading of *Pedagogy of the Oppressed*:

> To criticize the arrogance, the authoritarianism of intellectuals of Left or Right, who are both basically reactionary in an identical way— who judge themselves the proprietors of knowledge, the former, of revolutionary knowledge, the latter, of conservative knowledge— to criticize the behavior of university people who claim to be able to "conscientize" rural and urban workers without having to be "conscientized" by them as well; to criticize an undisguisable air of messianism, at bottom naive, on the part of intellectuals who, in the name of the liberation of the working classes, impose or seek to impose the "superiority" of their academic knowledge on the "rude masses"— this I have always done. Of this I speak, and of almost nothing else, in *Pedagogy of the Oppressed*. And of this I speak now, with the same insistence, in *Pedagogy of Hope*. (Freire, 1994, pp. 99–100)

In 1992, Freire affirmed that he had exhaustively done exactly what Rocha clams he did: critique the intellectual leadership of both the revolutionaries and the conservatives of the 1970s. So in a way,

Rocha is correct in saying that Freire wrote *Pedagogy of the Oppressed* thinking not of schooling, but of certain messianic trends of the critical consciousness raising intellectuals of the 1970s. The only problem here is that Freire himself already admitted as much twenty-five years ago. More significantly, Freire argued that it was for this reason that it is important to think about what happens in schools from preschool onward, and for this reason *Pedagogy of the Oppressed* is more than pertinent to schools.

> The teaching of a content by appropriating it, or the apprehension of this content on the part of the educands, requires the creation and exercise of a serious intellectual discipline, to be forged from preschool onward. To attempt or claim a critical insertion of educands in an educational situation—which is a situation of cognition—without that discipline, is a vain hope. (Freire, 1994, p. 102)

There is no opposition between the two camps applying the lessons of *Pedagogy of the Oppressed*. On the contrary, because the book was written against a certain type of intellectual leadership, it is completely pertinent to schooling. But this type of subject formation demands a problematizing education, rather than a banking model, precisely because the intellectual leadership, whether they be from the left or right, under critique is the best expression of what is produced by the latter type of educational approach. What is necessary, therefore, is a different type of schooling from preschool onward, one that creates and inspires the "intellectual discipline" of future educators of educators.

Consider a few passages of *Pedagogy of the Oppressed* that Rocha transcribes and analyzes:

> The problem-posing method[4] does not dichotomize the activity of the teacher-student: she is not "cognitive" at one point and "narrative" at another. She is always "cognitive," whether preparing a project or engaging in dialogue with the students. (Freire, 2005a, p. 80)

---

[4] The word "method" does not exist in the original Portuguese version of the text. It says instead "*A prática problematizadora*," which more literally refers to a problematizing practice.

This small passage precedes the claim made by Rocha that "There is not a clear characterization of an emancipatory education, instead it is presented via a negative framework" (Rocha, 2017, p. 71). It just so happens that this passage corresponds to chapter two of *Pedagogy of the Oppressed* in which it seems more than logical for Freire to present an emancipatory education through a negative framework given that, in this chapter, a banking education is put into a dialectical relationship with an emancipatory one. Let's, however, continue with the "analysis" of Rocha as it progresses on the same page. He writes, "A possible interpretation of this obscure passage is the following: there is no essential distinction between the teacher and the student; no one teaches no one." Such an interpretation, if it is possible, violates what Freire affirms, and which he repeats many times in *Pedagogy of the Oppressed*. For Freire, both the teacher and the student, and not just one or the other, are subjects of knowledge. There is not someone who knows and narrates knowledge to another. An emancipatory education does not exist unless the student and the teacher are considered to possess knowledge. To consider both subjects who possess knowledge does not mean that there is "no essential difference between the two." Furthermore, the phrase "no one educates anyone" seems to be taken out of its context and is interpreted by Rocha to mean that "it is common sense to suggest that it is not up to one adult to educate another." As a matter of fact, such a claim does not seem "commonsensical" within a reductionist reading that ends up inspiring the title of Rocha's book. To note, the complete phrase by Freire, which is well-known, reads:

> Here, no one teaches another, nor is anyone self-taught. People teach each other, mediated by the world, by the cognizable objects which in banking education are "owned" by the teacher. Freire, 2005a, p. 80)

In a problematizing education no one educates anyone according to a banking logic, in which the teacher deposits knowledge into passive subjects. Teachers and students educate each other through dialogue. This does not mean that all knowledge has equal value, or that teachers do not have a specific role in this dialogic practice. At any rate, we must note once again that Freire had already heard and responded to Rocha's critique years earlier:

> One of these ways of criticizing the defense that I have been mounting of the knowledge acquired from living experience, criticisms not infrequently repeated today, to my legitimate astonishment and dismay, is that which suggests or asserts, basically, that I propose that the educator ought to stay spinning in an orbit, along with the educands, around their commonsense knowledge, without any attempt to get beyond that knowledge. And the criticism of this tenor concludes triumphantly by emphasizing the obvious failure of this naive understanding. And it is attributed to me—this defense of a tireless circling around commonsense knowledge.
>
> But I have never actually asserted, or so much as insinuated, "innocence" of such proportions.
>
> What I have said and resaid, untiringly, is that we must not bypass—spurning it as "good for nothing"—that which educands, be they children coming to school for the first time, or young people and adults at centers of popular education, bring with them in the way of an understanding of the world, in the most varied dimensions of their own practice in the social practice of which they are a part. (Freire, 1994, p. 106)

It is more than a bit curious that an author who expresses an interest in how still today the thought of Freire is taken up, did not consult other books by Freire like *Pedagogy of Freedom*, which is especially dedicated to delineating the specific knowledge that teachers should possess, and which contains in its three chapters no less than twenty-seven demands for teaching. One must ask what value exists in questioning Freire, the most internationally renowned Brazilian educator, by over and over again attributing to him something that he never said?

The Pernambucan professor Flavio Brayner (2011) conducts a much more interesting critical reading of *Pedagogy of the Oppressed*. Brayner contends that the most innovative and central contribution that Freire's most well-known book makes has to do with the fact that, in it, for the first time, the problem of education, in this case overcoming oppression, has less to do with an external issue in the world, and more to do with a problem to be worked on within oneself. Thought of this way, oppression lies within everyone, in both the oppressed and the oppressor, and whomever wants to overcome it must work on herself or himself.

However, for Brayner, Freire succumbs to the same problems faced by all modern liberatory or emancipatory pedagogies. First, how oppression is being defined. And second, it is assumed that people in fact want to be liberated from what the pedagogy defines as oppression (Brayner, 2011, p. 42). Brayner considers many of Freire's ideas to be obsolete. For example, the factory is no longer at the center of society, it has been replaced by shopping malls, and the dream of people today is to consume. If before there was an interest in taking the cover off appearances, now the only thing that matters is to live within appearances, and to appear. I consider Brayner's critiques to be very pertinent, and I subscribe to them. There is not much to object to here. In truth, some of the ideas presented in *Pedagogy of the Oppressed* can be considered obsolete within the contemporary context. And critiques like Brayner's can help us evaluate the real value of the book. It is also true that Freire continued to live and produce work after *Pedagogy of the Oppressed*, and many of the ideas that appear after this book are also open to critiques. Here, however, as I have already noted, I have taken another approach to his work, one which has more of a creative rather than a critical composition, even while exploring a critique of Freire's critics.

A critique that to a certain point coincides with the previous one, but from a very different field, comes from the Argentine thinker Rodolfo Kusch. In a book dedicated to thinking through the particularities of popular culture in Latin America (Kusch, 1976), Kusch dedicates a chapter titled "Geoculture and Development" to critically analyze developmental approaches to popular and peasant culture, and in doing so launches a critique of Freire who is placed alongside other thinkers who euphorically embraced developmentalism in the 1950s and 1960s. The text is from the 1970s, and while Kusch recognizes in Freire a favorable and understanding attitude of the peasantry, he accuses him of trying to think of rural life through Western categories, like the opposition between nature and humans, and hence Freire, in Kusch's view, disrespects the "popular ethos" of the people. Kusch also critiques the way that Freire considers education as a general promoter of development or liberation of the oppressed, when in fact it is always local and plays a role in adapting someone to their community and the notion of reality proper to it. Thus, in essence, Freire's emancipatory education is nothing more than a Westernized and Eurocentric denial of Native American views. Hence a Freirean defense of popular culture would be accompanied by a pretense of passing on a true consciousness that this culture would not have on its own. This would make the culture something other than it already is. And the approach is an Enlightenment, modern, and Eurocentric one that effectively does not recognize what is really proper to continentally American cultures.

This critique by Kusch is not easy to confront. Although I disagree with the way Kusch characterizes the adaptive characters of education, and it should be noted that Kusch himself makes use of some of the same European categories that he criticizes Freire for using, his critiques are very pertinent. Kusch is correct in stating that the use of Freire's categories come from Marxist, existentialist, and phenomenological traditions, and hence reproduce a certain Eurocentric logic.

In that same sense, Freire is justly liable to criticism from a "decolonial" (and postcolonial) perspective[5] in the same way that, during his life, he was harshly criticized by certain movements, from feminism[6] and

---

[5]   Among these criticisms, I highlight that of Facundo Giuliano (2018), inspired by authors such as Kusch, Mignolo, and Dussel. Giuliano makes a critique of what he calls "the colonial character (evaluative and moral)" in the thought of Paulo Freire. Interestingly, he gives special emphasis to the last work published in life by the author, *Pedagogy of Freedom*. Giuliano accuses Freire of supporting an "epistemological racism" and of "pedagogical moralization" by the use of modern categories such as "apprehension of reality," "critical evaluation," "good judgment," and of dichotomies such as "naive curiosity" versus "critical" or "epistemological" curiosity. In addition to presenting Kusch's critique of the enlightened character of Freire's vision of the peasant, this inspiration leads Giuliano to also criticize what Freire calls the ontological vocation of the human being, the "being more," to which he opposes a "being being" and a "nothing else being" ("mere being") affirmed by Kusch. This criticism of Giuliano is also subject, to a large extent, to the same criticism he makes of Freire.

[6]   In the early 1990s, Weiler (1991) questions the Freirean assumption that there is an experience of oppression and what he calls its abstract goals of liberation. Weiler's

other positions.[7] On the contrary, however, other authors see Freire as
an inspiration for a Latin American decolonization project.[8]

That said, once again, I must state that it is not this line of thought
that I have chosen to transmit within this book. Having briefly visited it,
I leave this critical approach behind that sanctions what can, and what
cannot, be thought. The attacks against Freire, and also the defenses,
bring one to a field overly traversed, one which is more reactive than
affirmative. In place of this, I insist on thinking, composing, connecting,
and reuniting with Freire's thought. For this reason, I have proposed in
the present book to unravel those elements of Freire's thought that today
can help us think more forcefully about the meaning of an eminently
political education. I have left aside those elements that would not help
in this attempt, and focused instead on the elements that can inspire us
to think. For this reason I include this piece as an appendix and not in
the core of the book.

position is not just critical: she proposes a feminist epistemology that, while criticizing
some ideas of Freire, expands her work. The three principles of this epistemology are: (a)
questioning the teaching role and authority; (b) recognizing the importance of personal
experience as a source of knowledge; and (c) exploring the perspectives of different races,
classes, and cultures. Perhaps this third dimension is, indeed, the least explored by Freire.
The relationships between feminist thinkers, what in the United States is called "critical
pedagogy," and Freire have been very interesting and complex since the publication of
Pedagogy of the Oppressed.

7   Blanca Facundo is one example, who, in 1984, offers a rather interesting critique not
    only of Freire, but also of the uncritical and romantic way in which, in the United
    States, his thought was being incorporated. Facundo is a Puerto Rican who, seduced
    by the reading of *Pedagogy of the Oppressed*, tries to make various experiences based
    on her ideas, particularly among Latino communities, and, upon encountering various
    problems, consolidates a contrasting critical gaze in front of the vast majority of Freirean
    intellectuals in the United States. According to him, progressive educators need to
    go beyond Freire. She analyzes, for example, specific educational problems such as
    evaluation, in which Freire would enter into contradictions, and the literacy campaign in
    Guinea-Bissau, which, with the support of various research documents, he considers an
    unexplained failure, or at least not enough, by Freire. His text (Facundo, 1984) is not only
    a criticism of Freire, but, above all, a warning for a critical, idealized, naive way of relating
    to his work. Some Freireans, such as Robert Mackie (1997 [1988]), reacted aggressively
    to it. Years later, John Ohlier (1995) compiled a fairly extensive thematic list of criticisms
    of Freire.

8   For example, for Streck, Moretti, and Pitano (2018), *Pedagogy of the Oppressed* was based
    on principles such as solidarity and participation, would be the founding reference of a
    "decolonial" perspective for Latin America.

Paulo Freire and Philosophy for Children

when we kill the child in us, we are no longer.
(P. Freire. In: Horton and Freire, 1990, p. 64)

Introduction

I use questions more than I do anything else.
(M. Horton. In: Horton and Freire, 1990, p. 146)

In this appendix, I will attempt to connect Paulo Freire's educational thinking with the "philosophy for children" movement. In the first section of this text, "The Origins: Was There a Close Relationship between Paulo Freire and Matthew Lipman?" we analyze the relationship between the creator of philosophy for children (P4C), Lipman, and Freire. The relationship between them was not as close as many supporters of P4C might claim, especially in Latin America. In this section, we analyze the sole reference one of these authors makes to the other; that is, in a few paragraphs, Lipman refers to a conversation they had in Freire's house during one of his trips to Brazil. In a second section, "Some Efforts to Connect Paulo Freire and Philosophy for Children," we take note of diverse attempts to establish a relationship between these two educators, both by those who have seen similarities and those who have pointed out contradictions. In a third section "Paulo Freire and Philosophy for Children in Our Times" we briefly present the context of Educational Policies in our time and attempt to infuse some Freire in P4C, out of which a "critical P4C" would emerge. In the fourth section, "Freire, Teaching, Learning, and the Political," we justify why Freire's understanding of the politics of education makes it impossible to be Freirean and at the same time be neutral or favor the status quo. In the fifth section, "Lipman: Philosophy and the Political," we present how Lipman understands the relationship between philosophy, education, and democracy and their connection to capitalism. Finally, in "At the End, a New Beginning," we consider ways to begin/originate the political path of philosophizing with children nurtured by Freire's educational thinking.

The Origins: Was There a Close Relationship between Paulo Freire and Matthew Lipman?

It's really impossible to teach how to think more critically
by just making a speech about critical thought.
(P. Freire. In: Horton and Freire, 1990, p. 173)

The relationship between Lipman and Freire was not as closely connected as many participants of the philosophy for children movement, especially Latin Americans like myself, would have desired and expected. I am referring not just to their personal relationship, but to the connections between their educational thinking and practice. The most compelling and nearly unique evidence to support a connection between them emerges from Lipman himself, in the following paragraphs of his autobiography (*A Life Teaching Thinking*, Lipman, 2008):

> While discussing Philosophy for Children within a global context, I'd be remiss if I did not take note of Brazilian educator, Paulo Freire, who had developed a global reputation as a result of his having bent his philosophical acumen to the service of the education of children. In particular, he aimed to utilize the skills of philosophical discussion in such ways that they could improve the most humble, but at the

same time, most powerful of children's skills: reading and writing. Latin American educators where quick to note the similarities that existed between Freire's educational approach and that of the IAPC's philosophy for children and could be found wondering which of the two of us, Paulo Freire or myself, was the primary influence on the other.

In 1988 the Brazilian curriculum developer, Catherine Young Silva, arranged a meeting between myself and Freire, to take place in Freire's home in São Paulo. It was a friendly visit, in which Freire did most of the talking and devoted his remarks to the influence of the history of philosophy on his educational thinking, thereby recognizing that I have done the same, so that our accomplishments ran parallel in many respects.

It was a thoughtful, congenial conversation, and I don't think we discovered any points of sharp glaring difference between us. From Freire's great window, we could see, far off, the skyline of São Paulo, rising above the city and yet focusing our imagination on the road ahead. Freire's last application of his views was to be found in his becoming Brazil's secretary of education, although even in that exalted position, it was doubtful that the Brazilian educational system could be readily turned around. Nevertheless, thanks to Catherine Young Silva and her family, thousands of Brazilian teachers and hundreds of thousands of Brazilian children have been introduced to philosophy (Lipman, 2008, p. 148).

In spite of Lipman's efforts to fulfill our expectations, the quote speaks for itself: Lipman is imprecise about Freire, who was not the Brazilian secretary of education but of the city of São Paulo and, more significantly, even though certainly Freire's worries included children, he in fact concentrated his efforts not so much in the education of children but in adult education (Horton and Freire, 1990, p. 47). More specifically, Freire aimed to empower the humblest through developing their reading capacities. For Freire, reading was not mainly a thinking skill, but an existential form of being. Reading was a path to concientization (*concientização*, in Portuguese), a reading of the world and not only of the words (Horton and Freire, 1990, p. 31).

Lipman affirms that there were no "points of sharp glaring difference" in the conversation, but from this quote, the only evident coincidence is a parallel in their accomplishments based mainly on the influences of the history of philosophy in their educational thinking. Though the aesthetic and poetic reference to the skyline of São Paulo may make us consider similar educational goals between them, the quote doesn't enable us to go much further.

There is another reference from Lipman to this same conversation with Freire in an interview given in 1994 to a Brazilian Newspaper (Carvalho, 1994). The journalist asks Lipman his opinion about "Paulo Freire's method" and Lipman responds as follows:

> We met when I was in Brazil some years ago. He talked to me about the similarities in what we did. His interest in the formation of communities of work in order to arrive to literacy is very close to our interest in forming communities of inquiry to make children arrive to a social solidarity that might improve their education.

The reference to the shared conversation is a bit different here, with Lipman seeing a parallel between communities of inquiry and Freire's reading circles. But again, this addition does not help us to glean much more with regard to the relationship.

Apart from this pleasant conversation, there is no real contact between their two projects. In fact, Freire does not make a single concrete reference to Lipman or philosophy for children in his entire oeuvre, and in Lipman's main books, there is only one reference to *Pedagogy of the Oppressed* in *Philosophy in the Classroom*. But Freire did not appear even in the bibliography of, for example, *Philosophy Goes to School* or *Thinking in Education*. So, in spite of our desires, it seems evident that Lipman had no obvious influence on Freire nor Freire on Lipman. We can only indicate that the authors had some readings in common (like Dewey, Buber, or Merleau-Ponty), which may explain some of the similarities we find in both oeuvres.

Some Efforts to Connect Paulo Freire
and Philosophy for Children

In trying to create something inside of history
we have to begin to have some dreams.
                                    (P. Freire. In: Horton and Freire, 1990, p. 64)

Let's look at some efforts, mainly from Latin American scholars, to show the parallels between Lipman and Freire.[1] Among the most enthusiastic supporters of these connections is Marcos Lorieri, former director of the Brazilian Center of Philosophy for Children and professor at the Catholic University of São Paulo, where Freire taught. Lorieri sees methodological and theoretical affinities, based on the shared idea of dialogue and the common emphasis on the social construction of knowledge.[2] Weimer (1998) wrote a book exploring the relationship between Lipman and Freire. Wonsovicz (1993) and Giacomassi (2009) also see dialogue as the key point of connection between them, being Socratic maieutic, according to the former, a common source of it.

In other Latin American countries, similarities were also found by Accorinti (2002) who sees a common project, basically under the ideas of autonomy, freedom, and multidimensional thinking. In the same line of argument, Parra C. and Medina F. (2007) see the connection in the common aspiration to the formation of citizen values through communities of inquiry (Lipman) inspired by active silence, and the pedagogy of the question (Freire).

In the Anglo-Saxon world two well-known philosophy for children scholars, P. Costello and R. Morehouse (2012), have seen a "close

---

[1] On the most general impact of Lipman's ideas in Latin America, see Henning, 2005 and Kohan, 2000, 2014.

[2] In private correspondence, Lorieri affirmed that the TV of the Catholic University of São Paulo would record another conversation between Lipman and Freire that would take place in the United States in August 1997. Unfortunately, Paulo Freire died some few months before it, on May 2, 1997.

affinity" between Freire's problem-posing education and communities of inquiry and developing philosophical thinking in schools inspired by M. Lipman. Costello and Morehouse advocate for the teaching in schools of a philosophy inspired by a "liberating pedagogy" (2012, p. 7).

But different voices called for a more cautious look at this relationship. Already in 1999, Moacir Gadotti, Freire's most eminent disciple, and the director of the Freire Institute at São Paulo, participated in a debate (with Ann Sharp, David Kennedy, and M. Lorieri) on the Educational Presuppositions of Philosophy for Children at the IX International Conference of Philosophy for Children, hosted at the University of Brasilia. Though Gadotti saw many common points between Freire and Lipman, he also saw differences (Gadotti, 1999): (a) Freire emphasizes much more than Lipman the ideological issue, even when he refers to ethics; (b) Freire does not give, as Lipman does, such importance to a given method; (c) there is at least, in its origin, a narrow vision of rationality in P4C, for example, when Lipman justifies the need of philosophy as a response to the irrationality of the students' demonstrations at universities in different parts of the world in the 1960s (see Lipman, 1992, p. 3; these movements expressed forms of rationality other than those dominant at the time); (d) Freire would not accept the distinction between teachers, and teacher-trainers or specialists: it would imply a functionalist perspective of teaching.

In 2000, in a more general analysis of P4C foundations, I pointed out that the parallels needed to be carefully considered and that the common use of some words or concepts (like democracy, dialogue, critical thinking, curiosity) hid a very unlikely understanding of them (Kohan, 2000). I've also pointed out that Lipman's emphasis on issues like methodology and criteria were far from Freire's emphasis on the politics of education. In the same line, Gomes Sofiste (2010) points out that, even though there is a great convergence between the ideas of community of inquiry (Lipman) and dialogue (Freire), there are two main discrepancies: (a) even though both consider the main goal of education to achieve a democratic society, the understanding of democracy is very different in both cases; (b) Paulo Freire's "concientization" (or critical consciousness) involves scientific rigor and political engagement, but only the former is present in Lipman educational thought. Magalhães (2008) also shows some differences between them and, inspired by both of them, develops philosophical experiences through popular education with street children in the State of Alagoas (2008, p. 104 ff.).

The most critical approach concerning the relationship between Lipman and Freire was offered by R. T. Silveira (2001) in the context of his critique of Lipman's program itself. Based on what in Brazil is known as "Historic and Critical Pedagogy," a Gramscian approach to education, Silveira called them "opposed pedagogies" in terms of their critique of traditional education, their concept of dialogue, curriculum, their understanding of thinking, common sense, political function of their projects, relationship to students, cultural values, the role of the teacher, and pedagogical scenarios (Silveira, 2001, p. 211 ff.). In all these approaches, Silveira identifies opposed perspectives. Let's consider the role of the teacher. In Lipman's program the teacher does not participate in the formulation of the program which is already given with its text, main ideas, discussion plans, and exercises. This would be unacceptable to Freire, who believed that the teacher should actively participate in all the domains of their task. Lipman would reduce the task of the teacher to a more practical one. Whereas, according to Freire's notion of *praxis*, theory and practice are impossible to separate. The division of labor between the philosopher who thinks and conceives the program and the teacher who applies it is a symptom of an oppressive conception. This same position is taken by Oliveira, who called the role of the teacher the Achilles' heel of Lipman's program given the reproductive and alienated nature of their task in it (Oliveira, 2009, p. 168).

A recent work by Funston (2017) takes a different approach. Presented as an attempt to integrate philosophy for children (P4C) and critical pedagogy, it considers the communities of inquiry capable of working with questions of agency and freedom that are essential to critical pedagogy and specifically to the work of Freire. Funston perceives the common critique of traditional or banking education as the shared agreement between P4C and Freire, though he also acknowledges differences between the community of inquiry and the cultural circles and their concepts of critical thinking. Funston suggests that a teacher in a community of inquiry has a higher epistemic authority than the coordinator of the cultural circles. While P4C considers critical thinking as a set of reasoning skills, critical pedagogy goes beyond this, meaning that critical thinking puts into question the unfairness of the status quo; that is, to think politically (2017, pp. 10–11). As a result, Funston proposes a synthesis of philosophy for children and Freire called "critical P4C" a kind of more politically committed version of P4C.

Paulo Freire and Philosophy for Children in Our Times

I have nothing against teaching. But I have many things
against teaching in an authoritarian way.
(P. Freire. In: Horton and Freire, 1990, p. 193)

Building mainly on *Pedagogy of the Oppressed*, Funston suggests that P4C educators inspired by Freire could enable their students to become more liberated while being "more vigilant to the ways that they might be inadvertently reinforcing dominance and oppression" (Funston, 2017, p. 14). In the following, I would like to unpack this suggestion.

We live in difficult and complex educational times. At the last XVIII ICPIC Conference, in Madrid, June 30, 2017, Gert Biesta described very clearly the educational present in terms of instrumentalism and measurement (Biesta, 2017, p. 415) and the domain of what he calls *learnification*. Biesta has been working largely with this critique of neoliberal education (2006; 2013; 2015), criticizing the process by which education is reduced and centered in the learner and the language of education has been replaced by the language of learning (Biesta, 2006, p. 13): the school has been redefined as a learning environment, and teaching nothing else than the facilitation of learning; national and international policy documents have also made learning their favorite concept; education of adults is now "lifelong learning." According to Biesta, there are certainly positive aspects to these shifts, which certainly are a response to authoritarian and one-sided forms of education that affirmed teaching as an act of control (2017, p. 422). But there are also less positive aspects, mainly the fact that the language of learning facilitates a description of the educational process as an economical transaction in which the learner is the consumer and the teacher the provider (Biesta, 2006, p. 14). From this perspective, the individual learner might be highlighted as an entrepreneur, and values like competition, merit, and talent might be prized, while others like cooperation, equality, and solidarity are relegated. Due to learnification, educational discourse has given up the discussion of essential educational issues about content, purposes, and relationships; that is, how to facilitate learning that has overlooked the fact that we learn something for a reason and from someone. According to Biesta, "the language of learning has taken attention away from these crucial educational concerns." (Biesta, 2017, p. 422).

From this point of view, some doubts may emerge concerning the critical potential of P4C and Freire's educational ideas. After all, isn't Freire's problem-posing education a claim for the importance of learning against teaching? Don't many supporters of P4C also understand teachers to be facilitators of students thinking and learning? In this case, could both Freirean teachers and practitioners of P4C be unwillingly favoring learnification while avoiding the position of transmitters of knowledge? Could they be, in Fuston's terms, "inadvertently reinforcing dominance and oppression"?

Education is always a risk and here lies one of its beauties (Biesta, 2014). But the risks of a Freirean educator reinforcing the actual neoliberal values are not significant, as we'll argue in the next paragraphs. On the contrary, it is not so rare that a philosophy for children teacher could be unwillingly favoring learnification and its underlying values. Why? Basically, because if the terms by which Freire conceives of education as political make it impossible for a teacher to be in the service of the actual status quo and still be considered Freirean, the political dimension of P4C, which like Freire speaks in the name of democracy, is less clearly expressed in its actual pedagogy. In the following we'll justify and unfold these considerations.

Freire, Teaching, Learning, and the Political

An educator should never become an expert.
                    (M. Horton. In: Horton and Freire, 1990, p. 128)

For Freire, teaching and learning are political acts and they cannot be grasped merely with a technical or pedagogical definition. Education cannot be apolitical, politically neutral, or aseptic. At this point, he agrees with another great twentieth-century educator, Myles Horton, with whom he shared a wonderful book (Horton and Freire, 1990) spoken at Highlander, the idyllic hilltop where Horton developed his educational adventure. Horton voices what he shares with Freire: "Neutrality is just following the crowd. Neutrality is just being what the system asks us to be. Neutrality, in other words, was an immoral act" (Horton and Freire, 1990, p. 102). Not recognizing this politicism of education would be taking one political position, the one that contributes to the maintenance of the status quo. This is true both of the early Freire of the *Pedagogy of the Oppressed* and of the late Freire of *Pedagogy of Hope* and *Pedagogy of Freedom*, though the emphasis changes.

Freire's philosophical and theological sources have been widely studied (Dale and Hyslop-Margison, 2010; Kirylo and Boyd, 2017). As Freire points out (1997), the inspiration of *Pedagogy of the Oppressed* is clearly and explicitly Marxist and Christian. The book is in fact a social and political critique of Brazilian geopolitics and also of the role of intellectuals in the liberation of people. Educational terms like school, student, and curriculum appear relatively few times. Education is understood more as a social liberating force than as a specific institution or system. In that respect, there are two forms of education contraposed: banking and problem-posing (Freire, 1987). The former serves the perpetuation of oppression. The latter gives the oppressed (and, eventually, the oppressors) not only the consciousness of their condition but also the desire to transform it.[3] The banking model can be present even in revolutionary programs, under the most noble ideals.

The politics of education is expressed in dialectical terms: on one side/ extreme, what is dominant: oppression, dehumanization, positivism, authoritarianism. On the other side, liberation, humanization, true scientific knowledge, and dialogue. The pedagogical and political pathway has two directions. First, the oppressed reveal their condition and become conscious of it through the perception of the "untested feasibility," which they previously didn't even consider. In the second moment, they search for a way to put it into practice (Freire, 1987, p. 110).[4] Once the oppressive reality is transformed, the contradiction educator-educated is overcome in a dialogical relationship, and the pedagogy of the oppressed turns into a liberating pedagogy for every human being, oppressed and also oppressors (Freire, 2005a, p. 54). The principles, the means, and the end of a Freirean education are political: (a) the end, a non-oppressive society, with no oppressed and oppressors; (b) the path, true dialogue as a "radically necessary to every authentic revolution" (Freire, 2005a, p. 128); and (c) the principle (which is not explicitly mentioned but underlines the whole *Pedagogy of the Oppressed*), "any human being can learn to read (words but mainly the world) if provided with the appropriate conditions to do so."

How does education work as a force in the search for liberation? "Here, no one teaches another, nor is anyone self-taught. People teach

---

[3] A. Cruz shows the complexity of the concept of *concientização* and distinguishes several different levels of it, according to Freire: (magical) semi-intransitive; naive transitive; and critical transitive (2013, p. 173).

[4] Unless originally published in English, I am reading Freire's works in the original Portuguese with my translation.

each other, mediated by the world" (2005a, p. 80). This emblematic phrase of *Pedagogy of the Oppressed* is extraordinary and complex. It denies that education comes from another subject (the teacher) or from oneself (the student). Where does it come from then? From the dialogical relationship established between educators and students, based on a shared reading of the world that this dialogue offers and which a democratic and non-hierarchical relationship makes possible. It cannot be implied from this, however, that teaching disappears. Quite the contrary: in this kind of education, the role of teaching and of the teacher remains fundamental, even though it is no more a fixed subject but a relative position in the educational relationship. The one who teaches does not provide knowledge that the learner lacks. This educational tension between the teacher and the student is resolved in such a way that both teacher and student know and ignore, both teach and learn. The teacher, who knows how to dialogue, also occupies the place of learner and arrives at *concientização* without being just the provider of such conscience. In a problem-posing education, the knowledge that matters is neither that of the teacher nor that of the student, but that which is recreated between one and the other through a dialogical and dialectical engagement of all the subjects in their reading of the world.

These ideas that Freire expressed in the *Pedagogy of the Oppressed* were constantly put into question throughout Freire's pilgrimage around different educational realities during his sixteen years of exile (from 1964 to 1980; see Gadotti, 2001) as well as in his return back to Brazil where, among other things, he was secretary of education of the city of São Paulo for more than two years and had a very concrete opportunity to put into practice his ideas on a large scale (see Torres, 1994). As a result of the self-questioning process, in 1992 Freire published *Pedagogy of Hope* with the subtitle "A reencounter"[5] with the *Pedagogy of the Oppressed* (1994) and, in 1996, *Pedagogy of Freedom* (1998), the last book published before his death in 1997.

---

[5] Translated into English as *Reliving Pedagogy of the Oppressed*.

In both books, Freire is much more moderate but still politically clear. Changes appear in the means: revolution has given its place to a less radical but still unconditioned commitment to the transformation of the status quo through educational praxis: "change is difficult, but possible" (Freire, 1998, p. 76). He describes his perspective no more as revolutionary but as "progressive postmodern" (Freire, 1994, p. 166). Nevertheless, the principle and the ends are still there and education is reaffirmed as political elsewhere.

With regards to the meaning of teaching and learning, Freire reaffirms that, if from a grammatical perspective, to teach is a transitive verb, which asks for a direct and indirect object ("to teach something to someone"), from the democratic and radical perspective in which his work and life are situated it's different: teaching does not exist without learning. More, to teach is: "to create possibilities for the construction and production of knowledge rather than to be engaged simply in a game of transferring knowledge" (Freire, 1998, p. 30).

Once again, "the person in charge of education is being formed or re-formed as he/she teaches, and the person who is being taught forms him/herself in this process" (Freire, 1998, p. 31). In these later works, though, transmission of knowledge is less stigmatized and there is some positive space for it: a teacher must now know what they teach (see also Horton and Freire, 1990, p. 108), but what constitutes her more properly as a teacher is placing her knowledge at the disposal of learning, of the learning of the others but also of her own learning. A teacher does not relate to those who learn as those who do not know but as those with whom, while teaching, it is possible and necessary to learn. According to Freire, learning precedes teaching, not only because historically it was socially learned that it was possible to teach, but because learning gives legitimacy and meaning, both pedagogical and political, to teaching if learning allows the learners to recreate or redo what has been taught, it gives. As in *Pedagogy of the Oppressed*, the teacher does not disappear but is re-signified and finds political legitimacy in a dialogical form of praxis.

In other words, what gives epistemological and political meaning to teaching is the way in which it cultivates the epistemological curiosity of the learner, their critical capacity, creative force, taste for rebellion, and epistemological vocation to "being more than just being" (Freire, 1998, p. 25)—as well as within themselves. A teaching that fosters no creation and rebellion but conformism and submission is politically undesirable and questionable. Thus, teaching means, according to Freire, helping to learn to read the political game being played by what is learned.

Although, Freire reaffirmed the predominance of learning over teaching he is far from fostering learnification. His concept of learning shows that Biesta's critique might be in some sense unspecific: it is not just about giving more importance to teaching or learning but about how both terms are understood. A recovery of teaching could also serve neoliberal policies and, as we see in the case of Freire, the priority of learning can also be critical to neoliberalism. There is even a passage of *The Pedagogy of Hope* where Paulo Freire advises against the priority of learning in very close words to Biesta's. He says:

> Teaching—again, from the postmodern progressive viewpoint of which I speak here—is not reducible merely to teaching students to learn through an operation in which the object of knowledge is the very act of learning. Teaching someone to learn is only valid—from this view-point, let me repeat—when educands learn to learn in learning the reason-for, the "why," of the object or the content. It is by teaching biology, or any other discipline, that the professor teaches the students to learn. (Freire, 1994, p. 101)

Learning cannot be reduced to a technical or instrumental activity, like learning thinking skills or using cognitive tools. Learning means understanding the *raison d'être* of what is learned; that is, its social and political function, the ethical and aesthetical ideals it aims in the actual social world.

Let's express this idea in other terms. Education is political by the way in which the teacher teaches what they teach. In this sense, the distinction content/form needs to be re-examined: while the content of what is taught is important (it would be naïve to underestimate the importance of content), how it is taught is equally, perhaps even more important. Thus, exposure to transmitters of knowledge, who assume the role of the all-important giver, not only transfers/communicates knowledge to students but also transmits, as an unseen content, a way of seeing themselves, specifically as receivers of charity from their superiors. This charity could be traditional knowledge but also thinking skills. This process, unwittingly, nurtures a paradigm of how humans see one another; that is, as those who know and those who need others to know others: a student not only learns knowledge (or thinking skills) but also learns a relationship to knowing (or thinking) and to themselves as someone who needs someone else (the knower, the expert in thinking) in order to know (or think). Freire denounced this process as oppressive and called teachers to be aware that how they interact with their students is as, or more, important than the content they transmit. This is where dialogical teaching plays an important role. When the learner learns through a dialogical process, the teacher also learns from them and they also teach the teacher. They learn to relate to themselves, their teacher, and to their companions as equals, they learn the importance of learning between equals and not as an inferior learning from a superior: they experience education as an egalitarian, cooperative, and democratic form of social life, far from the dominant actual forms/systems of living in our times. In Freire's terms, they experience an educational practice that strengthens through a dialogical process the epistemological vocation of every human being "to be more."

To conclude, for Freire, education always carries a political force; one that can be empowering or debilitating. What is important in education, then, is not the transmission of knowledge or the lack of it, nor the means of communication. Ultimately, what really matters is the kind of interaction that transpires between the teacher and the learner.

Lipman: Philosophy and the Political

No matter where this kind of educator works, the great difficulty
—or the great adventure!—is how to make education

something which, in being serious, rigorous, methodical,
and having a process, also creates happiness and joy.
(P. Freire. In: Horton and Freire, 1990, p. 170)

While writing my PhD dissertation, mentored by Lipman, I invented a dialogue with Dewey on the relationship between education, philosophy, and democracy. I took direct quotes from different texts of Dewey and connected them through a series of questions. I showed this dialogue to Lipman, and his reaction was both enthusiastic and surprised (he didn't recognize some quotes as Deweyan). I asked Lipman if we could have a conversation on the topics of the dialogue.[6] Because of the relevance of his responses to the topic of this paper, I will transcribe some parts of its last part and then comment them:

W. O. K.: How do you see Dewey's connection between philosophy, education, and democracy?

M. L.: Between philosophy, education, and democracy, I see inquiry as a common element. I insist in education as inquiry because students should be questioning, should be dealing with what is problematic in the world, attempting to reconstruct the situations and how to deal with them. Philosophy helps them to identify problems. Democracy has to employ inquiry in order to proceed just in an impartial fashion. If it only used political methods, like majority ruling, then it would probably not deal with issues that could deal through inquiry. I am not convinced that democracy is just a political notion.

W. O. K.: Can you explain in what way democracy is a form of inquiry?

M. L.: When I talk about democracy as inquiry, I am talking about an ideal of democracy. We've got it already in a spotty way. For example, jurisprudence and law introduce rationality into the social process. I am not saying that they are rational institutions because the whole method

---

[6] Both conversations are included in English as appendix to my PhD dissertation ("*Pensando la filosofía en la educación de los niños*" Iberoamericana University, 1996) and are both published in Portuguese Kohan, W. and Wuensch, A. M. (eds.) *Filosofia para crianças. A tentativa pioneira de Matthew Lipman*. Petrópolis: Vozes, 1999, pp. 135–79) and in Spanish (Kohan, W. and Waksman, V.). *¿Qué es filosofía para niños?* Buenos Aires: *Oficina de Publicaciones del CBC*, 1997).

of advocacy is based on confrontation and persuasion. Nevertheless, there is an effort there to achieve rationality.

W. O. K.: How far are actual democracies from the ideal of democracy as inquiry?

M. L.: There is little inquiry going on. And that's not what we are doing in this country. We are not looking to discover the abuses of our democracy. We are looking to conceal them all most of the time. [Laughs.]

W. O. K.: Why is that?

M. L.: Because in this country we are very confused. We respect the notion and the ideal of democracy but we are afraid to see it in its confrontation to capitalism. There we just shrug and turn away, we don't want to talk about the fact that democracy and capitalism may be incompatible. Because we don't know at this point what other kind of economy we could have, we only have the big corporations. There is such a concentration of military and economic power . . .

W. O. K.: Do you see democracy and capitalism as incompatible?

M. L.: I would say that theoretically there is no compatibility. Capitalism is destroying the environment and it is making human beings dispensable. Capitalism in its blind and powerful way just passes over and destroys, and it has very frightening aspects, but maybe some good things come out of it. Similarly, with democracy, maybe some bad things come out of it. Democracy may be good in some respects and not in others. Capitalism at certain times may have some justification.

W. O. K.: Like which ones?

M. L.: Well, there are facts of experience that you don't want to deny. It is a fact that philosophy for children survives, that people learn about it. When I introduced P4C to the American Philosophical Association in 1973 they asked me: "What do you think will happen with this?" And I said in the meeting of perhaps two hundred philosophers: "They will kill us." It hasn't happened, because democracy today is not a monolithic stone tower. It has all sort of cracks and caves and crevasses where people have a certain amount of freedom and protection. Thus, is not fair, because some people have more than others, and some are very vulnerable, exposed to the brutalities of the system, and some are protected as I am. So, there are many good things that have to be identified, acknowledged, and built upon so that we don't throw the baby out with the bath water when we have finished washing. But I really don't know.

W. O. K.: Let me ask you the last question. What's the role of education in a democracy conceived as inquiry?

M. L.: Education is the institution in society that prepares us to be viable, not just to endure or to live but to live well, that's what eudaimonia means, to live well. Without education, we cannot live well. So, it is a very important institution and that's why there is so much fighting around it, everyone wants control on it. In an ideal society, it would be a very powerful institution, much more powerful than economic institutions.

In the first part of the conversation, Lipman emphasizes democracy, education, and philosophy as forms of inquiry. Philosophy explores, in its educational dimension, the problematic dimension of experience. Democracy employs inquiry to proceed in "an impartial fashion." At the same time, when asked to unfold his conception of democracy as inquiry, Lipman introduces jurisprudence and law as efforts to introduce rationality in the social process. Even though he is not explicit here, it seems that what jurisprudence or law does or rather should do is what in other places Lipman calls reasonableness; that is, reason tempered by judgment. What concept of reason is underlying Lipman's analysis? Is the logic (formal and informal) underlying his program its main goal? When questioned about actual democracy, Lipman affirms a theoretical incompatibility between democracy and capitalism. He exposes a very clear vision of the destructive forces of capitalism, of its unfairness and brutalities. He does not consider it irrational: the incompatibility between democracy and capitalism seems to be ethical and political, not logical. Capitalism is logically coherent. It is just ethically and politically not acceptable. Lipman affirms that people do not see it just because they are "confused" and "afraid" (of other economic alternatives). Will the rationality that is at the basis of capitalism be able to put it into question? Should we be impartial in a capitalist system? Impartiality is a very fussy concept. If understood as "not being part," "not taking sides" it seems very problematic in such a biased order of things. It is certainly awkward if we understand capitalistic society in terms of oppression, as Freire does.

We have arrived to the point where huge doubts emerge whether Lipman's attempt to bring philosophical inquiry to the education of children might be politically innocuous in our time. His entire methodology is based on a rationality that is too consistent with the system's in order to put into question its unfairness and brutalities. Again, it is not about just learning and teaching. It is about living well, to say it in Lipman terms. "Without education, we cannot live well." We cannot agree more. Freire would certainly also agree. However, he would probably have severe doubts that P4C as a vehicle/form of a neutral and impartial rationality can help children to learn the *raison d'être* of the never-ending brutalities and unfairness of the system we live in.

At the End, a New Beginning

I always am in the beginning, as you.

(P. Freire. In: Horton and Freire, 1990, p. 56)

In conclusion, I feel it is essential to find a new beginning if we truly believe in the educational possibilities of philosophical inquiry. We do not need to "throw the baby out with the bath water" as Lipman advises. Then again, if we really believe that educational philosophy can contribute to good life, it cannot be impartial or insensitive to the destructive forces of capitalism. We need to reconsider the way our philosophical practices affirm education as political. Freire might be an inspiration for it, as Funston (2017) suggests. In this paper, we have tried to offer other arguments and inspirations to the ones he has already proposed. We need to inhabit a different rationality, one committed to equality and difference, and to justice and freedom. We also need to rethink the politics in education (and philosophy). What approach can we take? There are a number of roads to consider.

At this point we can just mention some of the alternative paths that could be taken. One is to follow the decolonial turn, opening, for example, a "mestiza" (Anzaldúa, 1999) rationality, one of the sensual body, "full of feelings, of emotions, of tastes" (Horton and Freire, 1990, p. 23). It needs to be a rationality sensible to different forms of the minor, class "oppressed" to use Freirean terms, but also others like LGBT, Indian, Black, and women and children as well: a rationality sensitive to contradiction and ambiguity. For example, Elicor has already proposed to integrate indigenous forms of knowledge in Philosophy for/with Children theory and practice (2019) and mapped what he calls "identity prejudice" and "epistemic injustice" in Philosophy for/with Children (Elicor, 2020). Another possibility involves an undoing of identity: a queering of a number of dualisms like teaching/learning, child/adult, mind/body for which feminist post-humanists might be inspiring (Murris, 2016). One more option would be interrupting the capitalist fluxes that inhabit the educational system by affirming a different form of school, inspired in the Greek notion of *schole* (see Masschelein and Simons, 2013) or in the Latin American popular education tradition (like Simón Rodríguez, see Kohan, 2015a and Durán and Kohan, 2018). Another alternative would be to trouble the already troubled, cloudy and chronological experience of time cultivated by learnification in our educational institutions and promote the conditions to disturb and diffract (Barad, forthcoming) time and decolonize childhood (Rollo, 2016). In other words, to interrupt the chronological time of colonization and capitalism that has captured our experience of schooling and childhood, and create the conditions to experience other times, which means other forms of social life.

Of course, all these paths are not exhaustive nor, to some extent, irreconcilable. The paths and the forms to find and walk them are open: we make the road by walking (Horton and Freire, 1990). Philosophy and politics are inspirations to walk the road of education as Freire and

Lipman also are. To think about those inspirations has been the aim of this paper. There is always time, a non-chronological time, to begin to walk differently. It's about moving as if we were beginning to walk, sensitive to childlike walking; to the questioning of a common world of equality, justice, and freedom for every being.

References

Abdi, Ali (2001), "Identities in the Philosophies of Dewey and Freire: Select Analysis," *The Journal of Educational Thought*, 35 (2): 181–200.

Accorinti, Stella (2002), "Matthew Lipman y Paulo Freire: conceptos para la libertad," *Utopía y Praxis Latinoamericana*, 7 (18): 35–56. Available online: https://www.redalyc.org/pdf/279/27901803.pdf (accessed December 25, 2020).

Albuquerque, Susana Lopes de (2019), "Filosofia panecástica de Jacotot nos periódicos brasileiros oitocentista (1847–1848)," in Susana Lopes de Albuquerque, Edgleide de Oliveira Clemente da Silva and Ivanildo Gomes dos Santos (Orgs.), *A história da educação em manuscritos, periódicos e compêndios do XIX e XX*, 78–96. Rio de Janeiro: EdUERJ

Andreola, Bauduino Antonio (2001), "Pedagogia do oprimido: um projeto coletivo," in Ana M. A. Freire (Org.), *A pedagogia da libertação em Paulo Freire*, 43–46. São Paulo: Unesp.

Anzaldúa, Gloria (1999), *Borderlands: la frontera*. São Francisco: Aunt Lute Books.

Aronowitz, Stanley (1993), "Paulo Freire's Radical Democratic Humanism," in Peter Leonard and Peter McLaren (Eds.), *Paulo Freire: A Critical Encounter*, 8–23. New York: Routledge.

Badiou, Alain and Truong, Nicolas (2012), *In Praise of Love*. New York: The New Press.

Barad, Karen (2018), "Troubling Time/s and Ecologies of Nothingness: On the Im/Possibilities of Living and Dying in the Void," in Matthias Fritsch, Lynes, Philippe and David Wood (Eds.), *Eco-Deconstruction: Derrida and Environmental Philosophy*, 160–86. New York: Fordham University Press.

Barrientos, José (2013), *Filosofía para niños y capacitación democrática freiriana*. Madrid: Liber Factory.

Berino, Aristóteles de Paula. "A herança de Paulo Freire – um leitor (marxista) de Foucault escreve a Paulo Freire: carta a respeito de uma estética da existência," in Gabriela Rizo, Lílian Ramos (Orgs.), *Um encontro com Paulo Freire*, 33–45. Rio de Janeiro: Arco-Íris; EDUR, 2008.

Biesta, Gert (2006), *Beyond Learning: Democratic Education for a Human Future*. Boulder, CO: Paradigm Publishers.

Biesta, Gert (2013), "Receiving the Gift of Teaching: From 'Learning from' to 'being taught by'," *Studies in Philosophy and Education*, 32 (5): 449–61.

Biesta, Gert (2014), *The Beautiful Risk of Education*. Boulder, CO: Paradigm Publishers.

Biesta, Gert (2015). "Freeing Teaching from Learning: Opening Up Existential Possibilities in Educational Relationships," *Studies in Philosophy and Education*, 34 (3): 229–43.

Biesta, Gert (2017), "Touching the Soul? Exploring an Alternative Outlook for Philosophical Work with Children and Young People," *Childhood & Philosophy*, 13 (28): 415–52. Available online: https://www.e-publicacoes. uerj.br/index.php/childhood/article/view/30424 (accessed December 25, 2020).

Blois, Marlene Montezi (2005), *Reencontros com Paulo Freire e seus amigos*. Niterói: Fundação Euclides da Cunha.

Bolsonaro, Jair (2018), O caminho da prosperidade. Proposta de Plano de Governo. Available online: https://flaviobolsonaro.com/PLANO_DE_GOV ERNO_JAIR_BOLSONARO_2018.pdf (accessed Feburary 12, 2019).

Brandão, Carlos Rodrigues (2015), "Paulo Freire – a educação, a cultura e a universidade: memória de uma história de cinquenta anos atrás," *Revista Festim, Natal*, 1 (2): 157–72.

Brayner, Flávio (2011), *Nós que amávamos tanto a libertação*. Brasília: Liber Livro.

Brugaletta, Federico (2020), "El papel de las editoriales en la circulación de la pedagogía de Paulo Freire," in M. E. Aguirre Lora (Comp.), *Desplazamientos. Educación, historia, cultura*. México: ISSUE, in press.

Camnitzer, Luis (2017), *Conceptualism in Latin American Art: Didactics of Liberation*. Austin: University of Texas Press.

Carnoy, Martin and Tarlau, Rebecca (2018), "Paulo Freire continua relevante para a educação nos EUA," in Moacir Gadotti and Martin Carnoy (Orgs.), *Reinventando Paulo Freire: A práxis do Instituto Paulo Freire*, 87–100. São Paulo: Instituto Paulo Freire; Stanford: Lamann Center; Stanford Graduate School of Education.

Carvalho, Bernardo (1994), "Jogos cotidianos e lições metafísicas. Matthew Lipman fala sobre seu método de ensino." *Folha de São Paulo*, 1 (5): 1994.

Casali, Alípio Márcio Dias (2001), "A Pedagogia do oprimido: clandestina e universal," in Freire, Ana Maria Araújo (Org.), *A pedagogia da libertação em Paulo Freire*, 17–22. São Paulo: Paz e Terra.

Chetty, Daren (2017), "Philosophy for Children, Learnification, Intelligent Adaptive systems and racism – A Response to Gert Biesta," *Childhood & Philosophy*, 13 (28): 471–80. Available online https://www.e-public acoes.uerj.br/index.php/childhood/article/view/30014/21382 (accessed December 25, 2020).

Chetty, Daren (2018), "Racism as "Reasonableness": Philosophy for Children and the Gated Community of Inquiry," *Ethics and Education*, 13 (1): 39–54.

Cintra, Benedito Eliseu Leite (1998), *Paulo Freire entre o grego e o semita*. Educação: filosofia e comunhão; Porto Alegre: EdiPUCRS.

Cortella, Mário Sergio (2018), "Paulo Freire: utopias e esperanças," in Moacir Gadotti and Martin Carnoy (Orgs.), *Reinventando Paulo Freire: a práxis do Instituto Paulo Freire*, 21–8. São Paulo: Instituto Paulo Freire; Lamann Center; Stanford Graduate School of Education.

Costello, Patrick and Morehouse, Richard (2012), "Liberation Philosophy and the Development of Communities of Inquiry: A Critical Evaluation," *Analytic Teaching and Philosophical Praxis*, 33 (2): 1–7. Available online: https://journal.viterbo.edu/index.php/atpp/article/view/1090 (accessed December 25, 2020).

Cruz, Ana Luisa (2013), "Paulo Freire's Concept of Conscientização," in R. Lake and T. Kress (Eds.), *Paulo Freire's intellectual roots: Toward historicity in praxis*, 169–182. London: Bloomsbury.

Dale, John and Hyslop-Margison, Emery (2010), *Paulo Freire: Teaching for Freedom and Transformation: The Philosophical Influences on the Work of Paulo Freire*. New York: Springer.

Darder, Antonia (2002), *Reinventing Paulo Freire: A Pedagogy of Love*. Boulder, CO: Westview Press.

Durán, Maximiliano and Kohan, Walter Omar (2018), *Manifesto por uma escola filosófica popular*. Rio de Janeiro: NEFI edições. Available online: http://filoeduc.org/nefiedicoes/colecoes.php?#livros (accessed December 25, 2020).

Elias, John (1994), *Paulo Freire: Pedagogue of Liberation*. Malabar, FL: Krieger Publishing Company.

Elicor, Peter Paul (2019), "Philosophical Inquiry with Indigenous Children: An Attempt to Integrate Indigenous Knowledge in Philosophy for/with Children," *Childhood & Philosophy*, 15: 1–22. Available online: https://www.e-publicacoes.uerj.br/index.php/childhood/article/view/42659 (accessed December 25, 2020).

Elicor, Peter Paul (2020), "Mapping Identity Prejudice: Locations of Epistemic Injustice in Philosophy for/with Children," *Childhood & Philosophy*, 16: 1–24. Available online: https://www.e-publicacoes.uerj.br/index.php/childhood/article/view/47899 (accessed December 25, 2020).

Escobar Guerrero, Miguel (2012), *La pedagogía erótica. Paulo Freire y el EZLN*. México: Miguel Escobar Editor.

Facundo, Blanca (1984), *Freire-inspired Programs in the United States and Puerto Rico: A Critical Evaluation*. Reston, VA: Latino Institute. https://www.bmartin.cc/dissent/documents/Facundo/Facundo.html (accessed February 19, 2019).

Feinberg, Walter and Torres, Carlos Alberto (2002), "Democracy and Education: John Dewey and Paulo Freire," in Joseph Zajda (Ed.), *Education & Society*, 59–70. Melbourne: James Nicholas Publishers.

Fernández Mouján, Inés (2016), *Elogio de Paulo Freire: sus dimensiones ética, política y cultural*. Buenos Aires: Noveduc.

Ferraro, Giuseppe (2010), *La scuola dei sentimenti*. Napoli: Filema. (Portuguese translation available online: http://filoeduc.org/nefiedicoes/colecoes.php?#livros)(accessed December 25, 2020).

Fischman, Gustavo Enrique, Sales, Sandra Regina and Pretti, Esther do Lago e (2018). "Para além das métricas simplistas na pesquisa educativa. As lições da contínua relevância e impacto freiriano," *EccoS Revista Científica* (47): 23–40. Available online: https://periodicos.uninove.br/eccos/article/view/10752/0 (accessed December 25, 2020).

Foucault, Michel (1996), "Truth and Juridical Forms," *Social Identities*, 2 (3): 327–42. DOI: 10.1080/13504639652213

Foucault, Michel (2011), *The Courage of the Truth (The Government of Self and Others II) Lectures at the Collège de France 1983–1984*, ed. Frédéric Gros, New York: Palgrave Macmillan.

Freire, Ana Maria Araújo, Org. (2001), *A pedagogia da libertação em Paulo Freire*. São Paulo: UNESP.

Freire, Ana Maria Araújo (2006), *Paulo Freire: uma história de vida*. Indaiatuba: Villa das Letras.

Freire, Paulo (1973), *Education for Critical Consciousness*. New York : Seabury Press.

Freire, Paulo (1974), *Pedagogia do Oprimido*. Rio de Janeiro: Paz e Terra.

Freire, Paulo (1976a), *Ação cultural para a liberdade*. Rio de Janeiro: Paz e Terra.

Freire, Paulo (1976b), *Educação como prática da liberdade*, 6th edn, Rio de Janeiro: Paz e Terra.

Freire, Paulo (1985), *The Politics of Education: Culture, Power, and Liberation*. Hadley, MA: Bergin & Garvey.

Freire, Paulo (1994), *Pedagogy of Hope: Reliving Pedagogy of the Oppressed*, trans. Robert R. Barr, New York: Continuum.

Freire, Paulo (1996), *Letters to Cristina: Reflections on My Life and Work*, trans. Donaldo Macedo, New York: Routledge.

Freire, Paulo (1997), Última entrevista (Last Interview). PUC São Paulo, São Paulo. Available online: https://www.youtube.com/watch?v=Ul90heSRYfE (accessed May 31, 2019).

Freire, Paulo (1998), *Pedagogy of Freedom: Ethics, Democracy, and Civic Courage*, trans. Patrick Clarke. Lanham, MD: Rowman and Littlefield.

Freire, Paulo (2000), *Pedagogy of the Heart*. New York: Continuum.

Freire, Paulo (2001a), *Pedagogia dos sonhos possíveis*. São Paulo: UNESP.

Freire, Paulo (2001b), *Política e educação*. São Paulo: Cortez.

Freire, Paulo (2004), *Pedagogy of Indignation*. Boulder, CO: Paradigm.

Freire, Paulo (2005a), *Pedagogy of the Oppressed*. 30th Anniversary edn, trans. Myra Bergman Ramos. New York: Continuum.

Freire, Paulo (2005b), *Teachers as Cultural Thinkers: Letters to Those Who Dare Teach*. Boulder, CO: Westview Press.

Freire, Paulo (2015), *Cartas a Cristina: reflexões sobre minha vida e minha práxis*, 2nd edn, São Paulo: Paz e Terra.

Freire, Paulo (2016), *Pedagogy in Progress. The letters to Guinea Bissau*. London: Bloomsbury.

Freire, Paulo (2018a), *Pedagogia do oprimido: o manuscrito. Projeto editorial, organização, revisão e textos introdutórios de Jason Ferreira Mafra, José Eustáquio Romão, Moacir Gadotti*. São Paulo: Instituto Paulo Freire; Uninove; BT Acadêmica.

Freire, Paulo (2018b), *Pedagogia da tolerância*, 6th edn, São Paulo: Paz e Terra.

Freire, Paulo and Betto, Frei (1985), *Essa escola chamada vida: depoimentos ao repórter Ricardo Kotscho*. São Paulo: Ática.

Freire, Paulo and Faundez, Antonio (1989), *Learning to Question: A Pedagogy of Liberation*, trans. Tony Coates, New York: Continuum.

Freire, Paulo, Freire, Ana Maria Araújo and Oliveira, Walter Oliveira de (2009), *Pedagogia da solidariedade*. Indaiatuba: Villa das Letras.

Freire, Paulo and Guimarães, Sérgio (1982), *Sobre educação: diálogos*. Rio de Janeiro: Paz e Terra.

Freire, Paulo and Guimarães, Sérgio (2010), *Aprendendo com a própria história*, 3rd edn, rev. e ampl. São Paulo: Paz e Terra.

Freire, Paulo and Macedo, Donaldo (1987), *Literacy: Reading the Word and the World*. London: Routledge.

Fromm, Erich (1963), *The Art of Loving*. New York: Bantam Books.

Funston, James (2017), "Toward a Critical Philosophy for Children," *PSU McNair Scholars Online Journal*, 11 (1): 1–17. Available online: https://pd xscholar.library.pdx.edu/cgi/viewcontent.cgi?article=1189&context=mcna ir (accessed December 25, 2020)

Gadotti, Moacir (1999), "A filosofia para crianças e jovens e as perspectivas atuais da educação," in Walter Kohan and Bernardina Leal (Eds.), *Filosofia para crianças em debate*. Petrópolis: Vozes.

Gadotti, Moacir (2001), *Paulo Freire: uma biobibliografia*. São Paulo: Cortez.

Gadotti, Moacir and Carnoy, Martin, Orgs. (2018), Reinventando Paulo Freire: a práxis do Instituto Paulo Freire. São Paulo: Instituto Paulo Freire; Stanford: Lamann Center; Stanford Graduate School of Education.

Gajardo, Marcela (2019), *Paulo Freire. Crónica de sus años en Chile*. Santiago: Flacso.

Giacomassi, Rejane (2009), "Diálogo e investigação filosófica com crianças," in *Congresso Nacional de Educação (EDUCERE), 9, 2009, Curitiba*. Anais. Curitiba: PUC-Paraná.

Giuliano, Facundo (2018), "Situar a Paulo Freire: entre el racismo epistémico y la razón evaluadora. Una lectura crítica desde la filosofía de la educación," *Pensando. Revista de Filosofia*, 9 (17): 191–225. Available online: https://revistas.ufpi.br/index.php/pensando/article/view/6424 (accessed December 25, 2020)

Giulliano, Thomas, Org. (2017), *Desconstruindo Paulo Freire*. São Paulo: História Expressa.

Green, E. (w.d.). What are the most-cited publications in the social sciences (according to Google Scholar)? https://blogs.lse.ac.uk/impactofsocialsc iences/2016/05/12/what-are-the-most-citedpublications-in-the-social-sc iences-according-to-googlescholar/ (accessed November 2, 2017).

Greene, Maxine (2001), "Reflexões sobre a Pedagogia do Oprimido de Paulo Freire," in Ana Maria Araújo Freire (Org.), *A pedagogia da libertação em Paulo Freire*, 155–6. São Paulo: UNESP.

Guilherme, Maria Manuela Duarte (2017), "Visões de futuro em Freire e Dewey: perspectivas interculturais das matrizes (pós)coloniais das Américas," *EccoS Revista Científica* (44): 205–23. Available online: https://pe riodicos.uninove.br/eccos/article/view/7708 (accessed December 25, 2020).

Henning, Leoni Maria Padilha (2005), "O pragmatismo em Lipman e sua influência na América Latina," *Childhood & Philosophy*, 1 (2): 445–71. Available online: https://www.e-publicacoes.uerj.br/index.php/childhood/ article/view/20465 (accessed December 25, 2020)

Holst, John D. (2006), "Paulo Freire in Chile: 1964–1969. *Pedagogy of the Oppressed* in It's Sociopolitical Economic Context," *Harvard Educational Review*, 76 (2): 243–70.

Horton, Myles and Freire, Paulo (1990), *We Made the Road by Walking*. Philadelphia, PA: Temple University Press.

Instituto Paulo Freire (2005), Paulo Freire. Educar para Transformar. Vídeo. http://www.acervo.pauloFreire.org:8080/jspui/handle/7891/1551 (accessed May 31, 2019).

Irwin, Jones (2012), *Paulo Freire's Philosophy of Education: Origins, Developments, Impacts and Legacies*. London: Continuum.

Juarroz, Roberto (1991), *Poesía Vertical*. Madrid: Visor.

Kirylo, James D. and Boyd, Drick (2017), *Paulo Freire: His Faith, Spirituality, and Theology*. Rotterdam: Sense.

Kohan, Walter Omar (1999), "Fundamentos para compreender e pensar a tentative de Matthew Lipman," in Walter Omar Kohan, Ana Míriam Wuensch (Orgs.), *Filosofia para crianças: a tentativa pioneira de Matthew Lipman*, Vol. 1, 84–134. Petrópolis: Vozes.

Kohan, Walter Omar (2000), *Filosofia para crianças*. Rio de Janeiro: Lamparina.

Kohan, Walter Omar and Kennedy, David (2008), "Aión, Kairós and Chrónos: Fragments of an Endless Conversation on Childhood, Philosophy and Education," *Childhood & Philosophy*, 4 (8): 5–22. Available online: https ://www.e-publicacoes.uerj.br/index.php/childhood/article/view/20524 (accessed December 25, 2020).

Kohan, Walter Omar (2014), *Philosophy and Childhood*. New York: Palgrave MacMillan.

Kohan, Walter Omar (2015a), *The Inventive Schoolmaster*. Rotterdam: Sense.

Kohan, Walter Omar (2015b), *Childhood, Education and Philosophy. New Ideas for an Old Relationship*. New York: Routledge.

Kohan, Walter Omar (2016), Time, Thinking, and the Experience of Philosophy in School. *PES Yearbook*, 513–21. Available online: https://ed ucationjournal.web.illinois.edu/archive/index.php/pes/article/view/5298 .pdf (accessed December 25, 2020).

Kohan, Walter Omar and Weber, Barbara (2020), *Thinking, Childhood and Time. Contemporary Perspectives on the Politics of Education*. London: Lexington.

Kusch, Rodolfo (1976), "Geocultura y desarrollismo," in Kusch, Rodolfo. *Geocultura del hombre americano*, 76–90. Buenos Aires: Fernando García Cambeiro.

Lacerda, Nathercia (2016), *A casa e o mundo lá fora: cartas de Paulo Freire para Nathercinha*, 1st edn, Rio de Janeiro: Zit.

Lima, Licínio C. (2018), "Três razões para estudar Freire hoje, para além da mais óbvia," in Moacir Gadotti and Martin Carnoy (Orgs.), *Reinventando Paulo Freire: a práxis do Instituto Paulo Freire*. São Paulo: Instituto Paulo Freire; Stanford: Lamann Center; Stanford Graduate School of Education.

Linhares, Célia (2007), "O legado Freireano e a educação da infância," *ALEPH*, 10: 8–12.

Lipman, Matthew, Sharp, Ann Margaret and Oscanyan, Frederick (1980), *Philosophy in the Classroom*, 2nd edn, Philadelphia, PA: Temple University Press.

Lipman, Matthew (1988), *Philosophy Goes to School*. Philadelphia, PA: Temple University Press.

Lipman, Matthew (1992), "On Writing a Philosophical Novel," in Sharp, Ann Margaret and Reed, Ronald (Eds.), Studies in Philosophy for Children. *Harry Stottlemeier's Discovery*, 3–7. Philadelphia: Temple University Press.

Lipman, Matthew (2001), *Thinking in Education*, 2nd edn, Cambridge: University Press.

Lipman, Matthew (2008), *A Life Teaching Thinking: An Autobiography*. Montclair: IAPC.

Maciel, Kelvin Custódio (2017), *Michel Foucault e Paulo Freire: um contraponto acerca da educação – sujeição e autonomia*. Riga, Letônia: Novas Edições Acadêmicas.

Mackie, Robert (1997 [1988]), Confusion and Despair. Blanca Facundo on Paulo Freire. Australia: University of Newcastle. https://www.bmartin.cc/dissent/documents/Facundo/Mackie.html (accessed February 19, 2019).

Mafra, Jason Ferreira (2017), *Paulo Freire, um menino conectivo: conhecimento, valores e práxis do educador*. São Paulo: Universidade Nove de Julho - UNINOVE.

Mafra, Jason Ferreira (2008), "A conectividade do presente com a história em Freire e Foucault," *Revista Múltiplas Leituras*, 1 (2): 36–46.

Magalhães, Daniel Alves (2008), *A filosofia pragmatista na educação popular*. João Pessoa: UFPB [Tese (Doutorado em Educação) – Programa de Pós-Graduação em Educação, Centro de Educação, Universidade Federal da Paraíba, João Pessoa, 2008].

Maia, Marcelo de Oliveira (2008), *Sócrates e Paulo Freire: aproximações e distanciamentos. Uma aproximação ao pensamento educacional*. Recife: UFPE [Dissertação (Mestrado em Educação) – Programa de Pós-Graduação em Educação, Centro de Educação, Universidade Federal de Pernambuco, Recife, 2008].

Marx, Karl and Engels, Friedrich (1970), *The German Ideology*. New York: International Publishers.

Masschelein, Jan and Simons, Maarten (2013), *In Defense of School*. Leuven: Education, Culture & Society Publishers. Available online: https://ppw.kul euven.be/english/research/ecs/les/in-defence-of-the-school/jan-massche lein-maarten-simons-in-defence-of-the.pdf (accessed December 25, 2020)

Mayo, Peter (1999), *Gramsci, Freire and Adult Education: Possibilities for Transformative Action*. London: Zed Books.

Mayo, Peter (2004), *Liberating Praxis: Paulo Freire's Legacy for Radical Education and Politics*. Rotterdam: Sense.

Mello, Thiago de (1979), *A canção do amor armado*, 4th edn, Rio de Janeiro: Civilização Brasileira.

Morrow, Raymond. A. and Torres, Carlos A. (2002), *Reading Freire and Habermas: Critical Pedagogy and Transformative Social Change*. New York: Teachers College Press.

Murris, Karin (2016), *The Posthuman Child: Educational Transformation through Philosophy with Picturebooks*. London: Routledge.

Murris, Karin and Haynes, Joanna (2018), *Literacies, Literature and Learning*. London: Routledge.

Nóvoa, António (1998), "Paulo Freire (1921–1997): A "inteireza" de um pedagogo utópico," in Michael W. Apple and António Nóvoa (Orgs.), *Paulo Freire: política e pedagogia*, 167–86. Porto: Porto.

Ohliger, John (1995), "Critical views on Paulo Freire's work," in https://www.bmartin.cc/dissent/documents/Facundo/Ohliger1.html (accessed January 11, 2021).

Oliveira, Avelino da Rosa and Ghiggi, Gomercindo (2004), "Filosofia e educação em Paulo Freire: pensando com práticas de formação de professores," *Aprender. Caderno de Filosofia e Psicologia da Educação*, 2 (3): 9–18.

Oliveira, Marines Barbosa de (2009), *Professores de Filosofia para crianças: quem são eles? Uma análise crítico-diagnóstica da construção da identidade profissional dos professores que trabalham com o Programa Filosofia para Crianças de Matthew Lipman*. Campinas: UNICAMP [Dissertação (Mestrado em Educação) – Programa de Pós-Graduação em Educação, Faculdade de Educação, Universidade Estadual de Campinas, Campinas, 2009].

Oliveira, Rosangela Labre de (2017), *Um diálogo com Freire e Foucault sobre poder e saber*. Goiânia: PUC Goiás [Dissertação (Mestrado em Educação) – Programa de Pós-Graduação Stricto Sensu em Educação, Escola de Formação de Professores e Humanidade, Pontifícia Universidade Católica de Goiás, Goiânia, 2017].

Parra, Reyber Contreras, Medina, Jesús Fuenmayor (2007), "La comunidad de investigación y la formación de ciudadanos: consideraciones a partir del pensamiento de Matthew Lipman y Paulo Freire," *Telos*, 9 (1): 80–9,

Passetti, Edson (1997), "Paulo Freire. Os sentidos da educação," *Margem* (6): 9–14.

Peloso, Franciele Clara and Paula, Ercília Maria Angeli Teixeira de (2011), "A educação da infância das classes populares: uma releitura das obras de Paulo Freire," *Educação em Revista*, 27 (3): 251–80.

Plato (1989), *The Dialogues of Plato*, trans. B. Jowett, New York: Oxford University Press.

Puiggrós, Adriana (2005), *De Simón Rodríguez a Paulo Freire: educación para la integración Iberoamericana*. Buenos Aires: Colihue.

Rancière, Jacques (1991), *The Ignorant Schoolmaster. Five Lessens in Intelectual Emancipation*. Stanford: Stanford University Press.

Rocha, Ronai (2017), *Quando ninguém educa: questionando Paulo Freire*. São Paulo: Contexto.

Rodríguez, Lidia M., Marin, Carlos, Moreno, Silvia M. and Rubano, María del C. (2007), "Paulo Freire: una pedagogía desde América Latina," *Ciencia, Docencia y Tecnología*, 18 (34): 129–71.

Rodríguez, Lidia (2015), *Paulo Freire. Una biografía intelectual: surgimiento y maduración de la pedagogía del oprimido*. Buenos Aires: Colihue.

Rodríguez, Simón (2001), *Obras Completas*, Vol. I e II, edited by CLACSO. Caracas: República Bolivariana de Venezuela. Available online: http://bib lioteca.clacso.edu.ar/clacso/se/20190926042843/Simon_Rodriguez_Obras _Completas.pdf (accessed December 25, 2020)

Rodríguez, Simón (2016), *Inventamos ou erramos. Apresentação, tradução e notas de M. Durán e W. Kohan*. Belo Horizonte: Autêntica.

Rollo, Toby (2016), "Feral Children: Settler Colonialism, Progress, and the Figure of the Child," *Settler Colonial Studies*, 8 (1): 60–79 .

Rowe, C. J. (1998), *Plato. Symposium*. Warminster: Aris & Philips Ltd.

Rowe, C. J. (2000), *Plato. Phaedrus*. Warminster: Aris & Phillips.

Santos Neto, Elydio dos, Silva, Marta Regina Paulo da (2007), Infância e inacabamento: um encontro entre Paulo Freire e Giorgio Agamben. http://www.egov.ufsc.br/portal/conteudo/inf%C3%A2ncia-e-inacabame nto-um-encontro-entre-paulo-Freire-e-giorgio-agamben (accessed June 13, 2018).

Santos Neto, Elydio dos, Alves, Maria Leila and Silva, Maria Regina Paulo da (2011), "Por uma pedagogia da infância oprimida: as crianças e a infância na obra de Paulo Freire," *EccoS. Revista Científica* (26): 37–58. Available online: https://periodicos.uninove.br/eccos/article/viewFile/3214/2231 (accessed December 25, 2020)

Saul, Ana Maria (2016), "Paulo Freire na atualidade: legado e reinvenção," *Revista e-Curriculum*, 14 (1): 9–34. Available online: https://revistas.pucsp.br /index.php/curriculum/article/view/27365 (accessed December 25, 2020)

Saviani, Dermeval (1987), *Escola e democracia*. São Paulo: Cortez e Autores Associados.

Sciencia – Revista Synthetica dos Conhecimentos Humanos, Rio de Janeiro, 1 (3) September 1847, p. 57. Available online: http://memoria.bn.br/ docreader/730076/59 (accessed August 27, 2019).

Sciencia – Revista Synthetica dos Conhecimentos Humanos, Rio de Janeiro, 1 (5) September 1847, p. 82. Available online: http://memoria.bn.br/ docreader/730076/84 (accessed August 27, 2019).

Sciencia – Revista Synthetica dos Conhecimentos Humanos, Rio de Janeiro, 2 (16) September 1848, p. 195. Available online: http://memoria.bn.br/docr eader/730076/197 (accessed August 27, 2019).

Sciencia – Revista Synthetica dos Conhecimentos Humanos, Rio de Janeiro, 2 (18) September 1848, p. 209. Available online: http://memoria.bn.br/docr eader/730076/211 (accessed August 27, 2019).

Shor, Ira and Freire, Paulo (1987), *A Pedagogy for Liberation: Dialogues on Transforming Education*. Granby, MA: Bergin & Garvey.

Silveira, René José Trentin (2001), *A filosofia vai à escola? Estudo do Programa de Filosofia para Crianças de Mattew Lipman*. Campinas: Autores Associados.

Simões Jorge, J. (1975), *A ideologia de Paulo Freire*. São Paulo: Loyola.

Sofiste, Juarez Gomes (2010), "Freire e Lipman: possibilidades e limites de uma aproximação," *Revista Ética e Filosofia Política*, 12 (1): 71–87. Available online: https://www.ufjf.br/eticaefilosofia/files/2010/04/12_1_ juarez.pdf (accessed December 25, 2020)

Streck, Danilo Romeu, Moretti, Cheron Zanini and Pitano, Sandro de Castro (2018), "Paulo Freire na América Latina. Tarefas daqueles/as que se deslocam por que devem," in Gadotti, Moacir and Carnoy, Martin (Orgs.), *Reinventando Paulo Freire: a práxis do Instituto Paulo Freire*, 37–46. São Paulo: Instituto Paulo Freire; Stanford: Lamann Center; Stanford Graduate School of Education.

Streck, Danilo Romeu, Redin, Euclides, Zitkoski, Jaime J., Orgs. (2008), *Dicionário Paulo Freire*. Belo Horizonte: Autêntica.

Torres, Carlos Alberto (1990), "Twenty Years after Pedagogy of the Oppressed: Paulo Freire in Conversation with Carlos Alberto Torres," *Aurora* 13 (3), 12–14.

Torres, Carlos (1994), "Paulo Freire as secretary of education in the municipality of São Paulo," *Comparative Education Review* 38: 181–214.

Torres, Rosa M. (1999), "Os múltiplos Paulo Freire," in Freire, Ana Maria Araújo (Org.), *A pedagogia da libertação em Paulo Freire*, 231–42. São Paulo: UNESP.

Vermeren, Patrice (2017), "Nada está en nada. O todo el mundo sabe la lógica. El método de enseñanza universal de Joseph Jacotot y la emancipación intelectual en las clases pobres," *Hermenéutica Intercultural* (28): 211–27. Available online: http://ediciones.ucsh.cl/ojs/index.php/hirf/article/view/1064 (accessed December 25, 2020)

Vermeren, Patrice, Cornu, Laurence and Benvenuto, Andrea (2003), "Atualidade de O mestre ignorante," *Educação & Sociedade*, 24 (82): 185–202. Available online: https://www.scielo.br/pdf/es/v24n82/a09v24n82.pdf (accessed December 25, 2020)

Vittoria, Paolo (2008), *Narrando Paulo Freire: per una pedagogia del dialogo.* Sassari: Carlo Delfino.

Weiler, Kathleen (1991), "Freire and a Feminist Pedagogy of Difference," *Harvard Educational Review*, 61 (4): 449–75.

Weiler, Kathleen (2001), "Rereading Paulo Freire," in Kathleen Weiler (Ed.), *Feminist Engagements. Reading, Resisting, and Revisioning Male Theorists in Education*, 67–88. New York: Routledge.

Weimer, Mabel Strobel Moreira (1998), *Uma interlocução entre Paulo Freire e Matthew Lipman na educação pública: educando para o pensar.* Cuiabá: UFMT [Dissertação (Mestrado em Educação) – Faculdade de Educação, Universidade Federal de Mato Grosso, Cuiabá, 1998].

West, Cornel (1993), "Preface," in Peter Leonard and Peter McLaren (Eds.), *Paulo Freire: A Critical Encounter.* New York: Routledge.

Wilson, Tom, Park, Peter, Colón-Muñiz, Anaida, Eds. (2010), *Memories of Paulo.* Rotterdam: Sense.

Wonsovicz, Silvio (1993), "A comunidade de investigação e diálogo. Uma incursão em Paulo Freire e na essência do Programa de Filosofia para Crianças," *Philos*, 1 (1): 23–29.

Zanella, Jose Luiz (2007), "Considerações sobre a filosofia da educação de Paulo Freire e o marxismo." *Quaestio – Revista de Estudos de Educação*, 9 (1): 101–22.

Index

adult   37, 42, 116, 123, 126–8, 136, 142, 201, 215, 228, 232, 255. *See also* childlike; National Literacy Plan
  adult education   3, 19, 59, 123, 210, 231, 238, 244
affection/ve   63, 70, 127, 130–1, 136, 157, 189, 204–5, 207
Africa   1, 94–5, 97, 194
Agamben, G.   139
aion. *See* time
American Philosophical Association (APA)   252
anthropology/ical   3, 37, 107, 125, 139
Apollo   32, 38, 69
art   67, 78, 84–5, 109 n.4, 178. *See also* love
ascetics   34–5
authority   54, 147, 198, 235 n.5, 243
autobiography   77, 96, 126, 189, 237

Badiou, A.   85–6, 91
beginning(s)   1, 9, 12, 14, 27, 29, 34, 36, 38, 42, 49, 69, 72, 81, 86, 97, 115, 117, 119, 121–2, 128, 132, 137, 146, 149, 151, 153, 155, 158, 179–82, 187, 194, 204, 219, 227, 237, 254, 256
Biesta, G.   7, 243–4
Bolivia   3–4, 57
Bolsonaro, J.   5, 181, 208
Brandão, C. R.   44, 94
Brayner, F.   232–3
Buber, M.   20, 100, 239

Cabral, A.   41 n.10, 73 n.5, 184, 206
capacity   7, 43, 45–6, 48–9, 51–5, 61, 63–5, 87, 106, 142, 157, 249

capitalism   49, 69, 74, 94, 107, 237, 252, 255
Carnoy, M.   45, 61, 151, 156
Casali, A.   45–6
child   56, 113, 116, 121, 126, 129–37, 139–45, 148–50, 154–5, 157, 186–7, 189, 191, 196, 200, 204, 213, 236, 255. *See also* philosophy (for); revolution
  becoming   151
  chronological   129, 133, 141–2, 147, 178
  connective (and conjunctive)   125–6, 129, 147, 149
  inner   140–4, 148
  permanent   138
childhood   14–15, 42, 87–9, 113, 179–80, 182, 187–9. *See also* education; philosophy; school
  affirmation of   139, 142, 144
  as Aion   178
  chronological   87, 96, 115–31
  conceptualization of   138, 140–1, 145–6, 148–9, 153–5
  experience of   146, 255
  pedagogy of   147
  political strength of   137, 143–4, 149, 154
childlike   11, 115–16, 122, 127–8, 132–3, 136–9, 142, 148–9, 154, 186, 256. *See also* education; life; time
  adults   156
  chronologically   133
  curiosity   122–3, 127
  educator   143, 153–4, 186
  language   122–3, 128, 130, 133, 144, 155
  love   146–7

pedagogy 139, 145, 148
people 142
politics 158
revolution 142–3
world 129–30
Chile 3–4, 57, 73, 81, 95, 133,
135–6, 189, 191–2, 194–5
Chonchol, J. 192, 194
Christ 34, 37–9
Christian 38–9, 245
anarchist 19
ascetics 34–5
Brazil 39
ethic 39
faith 21, 37
humanist 26
ideals 38–9
Marxist 40, 226
Christianity 34–5, 39–40
Chronos. See time
collective 7, 35, 40, 63, 68 nn.1–2,
85, 87, 102, 106, 139, 157
commitment 4–5, 35, 46, 59, 73, 81,
84, 97, 110–11, 226, 248
community of inquiry 241, 243
confidence 52–4, 153, 157
conscientization 23, 23 n.4, 59, 61
consciousness 38, 61, 117, 227–8,
230, 234, 242, 246
Cortella, M. S. 35, 211
Cristina 115, 127, 127 n.6
Letters to 96, 115–16, 123, 127,
127 n.6, 132–3, 136
critique 20, 22, 25–6, 37, 102, 111,
117, 218, 220, 225, 229–34,
234 nn.5–6, 235 n.7, 242–3,
245, 249
culture(s)/cultural 3, 13, 19, 23, 37,
44, 46, 49, 81, 95, 105, 114,
118–19, 121, 191–2, 195–6,
201, 204, 213, 222, 223 n.1,
225–6, 233–4, 235 n.6,
242–3
popular 223 n.1, 233–4

decolonial 234, 235 n.8, 255
Deleuze, G. 181, 218
Derrida, J. 178
Dewey, J. 20, 225, 237
dialectic/al 9, 19–20, 23, 38, 40,
130, 147, 221, 246–7
dialogue(s) 10–12, 14–15, 20,
21 n.3, 27–8, 33, 35, 41 n.10,
47–8, 64, 69–71, 73, 73 n.5, 87,
97 n.3, 102, 108, 116–17, 122,
128–9, 132, 134, 136, 139–40,
154, 179, 182, 202–3, 210, 218,
230–1, 240–2, 246–7, 251. See
also education
dictatorship 4, 57, 81, 83, 96, 118, 202
difference 48, 58, 64, 72, 85, 95,
181, 224, 231, 238–9, 254

education 1–5, 7–8, 10–11, 14–15,
17, 22–5, 32–3, 35, 39–42,
44–7, 50–6, 56 n.3, 60, 63–5,
68, 74–81, 84, 88–91, 93, 95,
98–9, 103, 105–9, 109 n.4,
110–11, 113, 115–16, 123, 131,
134, 141–2, 147–8, 151–8,
176–80, 182–7, 192, 198–202,
210–2, 217–22, 223 n.2, 224–7,
231–2, 234, 238–9, 241–4,
246–8, 250. *See* adult; politics;
teacher/teaching; time
banking 45, 202, 229, 231, 242,
246
Brazilian 1, 5, 7, 9, 44, 67, 84,
158, 177–8, 210, 223 n.1, 227,
238
childlike 148, 154
conception of 107, 141, 148,
234, 244–6
democratic 49–50, 65, 105, 251,
253
dialogical 40, 227
emancipatory/liberating 35,
44–6, 48–9, 52, 55, 58–9, 64,
109–10, 179, 231, 234

erring 153
of feelings 79–80
humanizing 151 n.1
infantile 154
as inquiry 251, 253
language of 243
literacy 59
neoliberal 243
philosophical 11, 17, 23, 33, 72,
    79–80, 84, 108, 251
philosophy of 2–3, 18, 18 n.2,
    182
political/politicality of 7–9, 12,
    14–15, 17, 40–1, 43, 48–51,
    58, 93, 106, 109, 113, 148, 151,
    153–4, 158, 213, 217, 225–6,
    235, 237, 241, 244–6, 249–50,
    254–5
popular 5, 215, 232, 242, 255
public 84, 182, 186, 214, 221
purpose of 35, 46
questioning/problematizing 23,
    115, 229, 231, 241, 244, 246–7
radical 78
revolutionary/utopian 38, 106
role of 24–5, 35, 39, 65, 74, 106,
    148, 155, 253
Secretary/Ministry of 4–5, 24,
    106, 140, 201, 210 n.1, 211–2,
    238, 247
temporality of 148, 155, 157–8,
    176–8
true 176
universal/worldly 51–3, 56,
    56 n.3, 95
utopian 106
educational 7, 18 n.2, 19, 31–2, 50,
    62, 77 n.9, 108, 131, 152, 186,
    226, 230, 244, 247, 253. *See*
    philosophy
adventure 245
approach 230, 238
context 89, 156
conversation 9

crisis 24
discourse 244–5
experience 89, 152
goals 239
ideas 244
inequalities 44
institution 7, 53, 176, 178,
    223 n.2, 255
intentions 180
issues 109 n.4, 244
life 12–14, 31–4, 38, 115, 143,
    152, 179, 182, 185–6, 219
mission 32, 36
policy/politics 14, 84, 236
possibilities 254
practice/praxis 12–13, 13 n.5,
    24, 49–50, 56, 59, 65, 79, 85,
    89, 96, 102, 108–9, 111, 114,
    151–2, 179–80, 248, 250
preoccupations 147, 244
presuppositions 241
problem 219, 235 n.7
program 5, 220
project 110
reality 42, 84, 185, 247
relation/relationship 76, 152,
    247
sciences 13
setting/situation 179, 230
space 7, 14, 43, 152, 154
system 51, 212, 238, 255
task 9
temporality/time 87, 156, 243
theory 68
thinking/thought 112, 151 n.1,
    236–8, 242
transformation 119
value 7, 30–1, 122, 152–4, 221
work 97, 221
world 2
equality 14, 43–55, 57, 59, 61–5,
    81, 85, 151–2, 156, 158, 178,
    180, 186–7, 227, 244, 254,
    256

eros   21, 68, 68 n.2, 69–72. *See also*
   love
errantry   10, 14–15, 96, 98–9, 102,
   104, 106, 111, 151, 153, 156–8,
   178–80, 186–7, 227. See also
   education; love
Europe   1, 27, 95
exile(s)   4, 9, 40 n.9, 56–8, 81, 85–7,
   94–6, 120, 127, 131–2, 135,
   141, 154, 183, 190, 194, 199,
   204, 211, 220, 247
experience   25 n.5, 54, 56–8, 62, 79,
   88–9, 96, 100, 103, 121, 131,
   149, 177, 180–1, 183, 185–6,
   192–3, 196, 205, 211–2, 218,
   232, 234–5 n.6, 250, 252–3,
   255. See also childhood;
   educational; philosophical;
   philosophy; time

faith   21, 37, 39–40, 52, 73–4, 209,
   225, 227
Fanon, F.   21 n.3, 23 n.4, 40 n.9,
   100
feminist   235 n.6, 255
Ferraro, G.   77–80
Foucault, M.   25–9, 31, 33–4, 37
freedom   7, 13, 17, 19, 21 n.3, 38,
   52–4, 60–1, 72–3, 73 n.4, 82,
   103, 118, 121, 124–5, 139,
   221–2, 223 n.2, 232, 234 n.5,
   240, 242, 252, 254, 256. *See
   also Pedagogy of Freedom*
Freire, A. M. A.   8, 138
Freire, E.   88–90, 131–2, 134–5,
   137, 189
Freire, J. (son)   131, 189–90, 192,
   195, 197, 200
Freire, J. T. (father)   117, 129
Freire, L. C.   15, 90–1, 131, 133–4,
   136, 188–209
Freire, M.   131, 136, 154, 200
friend(s)   15, 36, 38–9, 55, 64,
   68 n.1, 90, 123, 126, 132, 136,
   182, 190, 205, 210

friendly   90, 120, 238
friendship(s)   194, 210
Froom, E.   19–20, 21 n.3, 67

Gadotti, M.   4 n.3, 45, 61, 68 n.1,
   188, 199, 204, 241
GEEMPA (Group of Studies on
   Education, Methodology of
   Research, and Action)   210,
   210 n.1, 213
gender   106, 214–5, 222
Guevara, C.   21, 22 n.3, 73, 100,
   184
Guinea-Bissau   3, 21 n.3, 104, 206,
   235 n.7

Heidegger, M.   20, 21 n.3
Heraclitus   185
hierarchy   49, 52, 64, 152
Horton, M.   154–5, 158, 245
humility   39, 43–4, 74–5, 122

ideology/ideological   5–6, 24,
   84, 108, 122, 158, 177, 196,
   213, 215, 220, 222, 226–7,
   241
ignorance   6, 53, 71, 211
indigenous   220, 255
indoctrination   5, 213, 222, 225
Industrial Social Service (SESI)   62,
   104–5
infant   131, 139–40
infantile   153–4. *See* childlike;
   education

Jaboatão dos Guararapes   86, 96,
   116–18, 121, 123, 125, 127,
   141–2, 144
Jacotot, J.   45, 47, 51–60, 62–4
Jaspers, K.   19–20, 21 n.3,
   100
jouney   3, 38, 41, 100–1, 104, 157,
   186
justice   6, 9–10, 44, 99, 121, 254,
   256

knowledge   8, 13–14, 17–18, 24,
    29, 33, 35–6, 46, 51, 55, 57–9,
    61–4, 67, 70–1, 74, 77, 79–80,
    88, 102, 145, 157, 180, 211,
    215, 224, 229, 231–2, 235, 240,
    244–50, 255
Kusch, R.   233–4, 234 n.5

Lacerda, N. *See* Nathercia /
    Nathercinha
Landless Movement of Brazil
    (MST)   87, 98
Latin America(n)   1–3, 51, 94–5,
    102, 108–9, 109 n.4, 129, 142,
    182, 184–6, 210 n.1, 221, 227,
    233, 235 n.8, 235–6, 238, 240,
    240 n.1, 255
learning   6, 13, 52–3, 55, 59, 75–6,
    84, 87, 89, 104–5, 107, 111,
    152, 154, 157, 211, 214–5,
    218–9, 224, 227, 229, 237,
    243–5, 248–50, 254–5
  language of   243–4
  lifelong   244
  love of   75
  priority of   249
  to question   139–40
letter(s)   3, 10, 25, 25 n.5, 42, 53,
    54 n.1, 74, 88–9, 99, 101, 105,
    115, 118–24, 127, 127 n.6,
    129–30, 135–7, 145, 147, 200.
    See also Cristina (Letters to)
life   1–2, 17–41, 43–4, 46, 49, 56,
    60, 63–5, 67–74, 82, 84, 89–91,
    99, 101, 106–7, 113, 129, 134,
    137–59, 178–9, 182, 186–8,
    190–1, 193, 195, 199, 201–5,
    207, 209, 214, 216, 218, 226,
    234, 248, 254. *See* educational
  childlike   138–9, 146, 149
  collective   139
  (ethical and) heroic   39–41
  institutional   78
  intellectual   63, 191
  life's knowledge   63

militant   41
non-human   119
oppressed   23
of Paulo Freire   3–15, 68, 72,
    79–80, 85–91, 96–8, 103–7,
    110, 112, 115–19, 121–3, 125–7,
    131–3, 138, 144, 148–9, 153,
    156–9, 179, 181, 219, 221, 226
philosophical   12, 25–34; 36–41,
    70–2, 84, 185, 219
revolutionary   140
rural   233
social   110, 117, 250, 255
lifeforce   67
lifestyle   134
Lipman, M.   236–42, 250–1,
    253–8
literacy   5, 59, 64 n.6, 119, 123,
    129–30, 210–5, 239. *See also*
    education
  campaigns   3, 5, 36, 94, 104,
    235 n.7
  method of   58–9
  National Literacy Plan   4, 86
Lorieri, M.   240–1
love   5, 14, 43–4, 67–91, 99, 124–5,
    133–4, 137–8, 146–58, 178–80,
    182, 186–8, 198–200, 204,
    206–7, 209. *See* childlike; eros;
    learning; philosophy; teacher;
    teaching; time
  art of   67–8
  errant   87, 98
  pedagogical   75
  philosophical   84
  political   67, 80–5
Lula   5, 212, 220

Macedo, D.   3, 41, 41 n.10, 68 n.1,
    97 n.3, 121 n.4, 121–2, 217
Marx   21 n.3, 22, 24–6, 29, 38, 39
  Marxism   19, 21, 35, 39–40, 222,
    226
  Marxist   5, 19–20, 23–6, 37–8,
    40, 222, 234, 245

Mello, T. de   73, 81, 83, 87
method   1, 5, 22, 35, 52–3, 55–6,
    58–9, 62, 109 n.4, 211–2, 222,
    230 n.4, 239–41, 254.
    See also literacy
Movimento Brasil Livre (MBL)   5
MST *See* Landless Movement of
    Brazil
music/al/ian   14, 73, 79, 84, 87, 90,
    197–201

narrative   127–8, 230
Nathercia/ Nathercinha   132, 135–7
National Literacy Plan. *See* literacy
neoliberal   21, 74 n.6, 108,
    168, 229–30, 249. *See also*
    education
neutrality   151, 213, 221, 225, 245
Nicaragua(n)   3, 104, 140–2, 144, 148
Northeast/ern (Brazilian)   38, 117,
    121, 132, 189–90, 223 n.1

oppression   20, 23, 37, 53, 72–3,
    85, 106, 111, 178, 184, 210,
    232–3, 234 n.6, 243–4, 246,
    254. *See also Pedagogy of the
    Oppressed*
otherness   149

panecastic   51, 53–4
Passetti, E.   19
passion   68, 70–1, 74, 76, 78, 94,
    149, 199–200
patience/t   184–5, 188, 206–7
pedagogy/pedagogical   3, 10, 13–14,
    17, 18 n.2, 20, 34, 38, 40, 42,
    44, 46, 49–51, 55–6, 58–62,
    64, 68, 68 n.2, 70, 72, 74–7,
    88, 101, 109, 109 n.4, 119,
    122, 130–1, 142–3, 147, 151,
    151 n.1, 154, 188, 214–5, 217,
    222 n.1, 223 n.1, 227–8, 233,
    234 n.5, 235 n.6, 241–3, 245–6,
    248. *See also* childhood;
    childlike; love; power

Pedagogy of Freedom   13, 222,
    232, 234 n.5, 245, 247
Pedagogy of Hope   58 n.4, 104–5,
    183, 225, 227 n.3, 229, 245,
    247, 249
*Pedagogy of the Oppressed/
    Pedagogia do Oprimido*   2,
    8, 17 n.1, 39 n.8, 45–6, 53, 57,
    58 n.4, 72–4, 93–4, 97–8, 100,
    104–5, 122, 133, 183, 191, 194,
    198, 209–10, 225, 229–34,
    235 n.6–8, 239, 243, 245–8
philosophical   71, 77
of the question   36, 111, 122,
    135, 139–40, 142, 145, 217,
    240
people   7, 17, 38, 43–7, 49, 51–5,
    59, 64, 67, 70, 73–4, 78–83,
    85, 87, 90–1, 94, 97–9, 104–5,
    107, 109 n.4, 114, 123, 129,
    135, 137, 140–2, 145, 152,
    159, 178–9, 181, 184–7,
    189–91, 194–6, 204, 206–10,
    214, 218, 223 n.1–2, 229,
    231–4, 235–6, 252–3.
    See also childlike
Pernambuco   6, 8, 19, 22, 26, 35–6,
    38, 94, 114, 116–17, 119–21,
    138, 140, 143, 146, 149
philosophical   12–13, 18 n.2, 19, 22,
    28, 30–2, 72, 85, 145 n.9, 228,
    241. *See also* education; life;
    love; pedagogy; questioning;
    school; time
acumen   237
bet   56
experimentation   76 n.2, 242
gestures   12
heroes   26
influence   20–1
inquiry   254
pastor   40
practices   254
presuppositions   18
problem   26, 29, 34, 41, 219

science   2–3, 13, 20, 39–40, 78,
    129, 202, 214, 217, 223 n.2, 247
sources   18–21, 245
thinking   9, 12, 231
traditions   23, 80
value   7, 15, 41, 221
work   77, 101
philosophy   2, 17–42, 56, 71, 77,
    79–80, 151–2, 190, 193, 228,
    250–1, 255. *See also* education;
    Socrates
    academic   18, 217–8
    for children (P4C)   4, 15, 218–9,
        236–44, 252, 255
    Cynic   29–31
    educational   8, 33, 71, 74, 79,
        250–1, 254
    exercise/experience of   32, 79,
        151
    as a form of life   27–9, 33, 188,
        219
    history of   26–7, 238–9
    as inquiry   253
    as intellectual activity   24–9, 33
    loving   83
    militant   52
    panecastic   51
    Paulo Freire's   18–20, 22–4, 42
    teaching of   77 n.9, 80
    time of   78, 178
    western philosophy   18, 29
    word   77
Plato   27–8, 30, 32–3, 71, 181
play   9, 78, 126, 133, 149, 178, 180,
    189, 192–3, 195, 198
poem/t   73, 73 n.4, 81–3, 86–7
politics   6–7, 22, 28, 33, 39–40,
    80–1, 185, 190, 221, 245.
    See childhood; childlike;
    education; educational; love;
    power
    and education   7–8, 14, 32, 41,
        48–50, 59, 63, 109, 151–2,
        158, 217, 221–2, 237, 241, 246,
        254–5

poor   36–8, 56, 62, 107, 124, 207,
    214–6
post-humanist   255
power   7, 14, 37, 40, 56, 59, 64,
    83–4, 109–10, 118, 151 n.1,
    155, 202, 214, 217, 220, 252
    exercise of   6–7, 33, 40, 89
    pedagogical   40, 64, 109
    political   50, 68 n.2
    revolutionary   27, 62
    transformative   24–5
principle(s)   9–10, 12, 14–15, 17,
    34–5, 43–9, 51–2, 54–7, 61–5,
    67, 69–70, 75, 77 n.9, 79, 93,
    95, 101–2, 105–8, 111, 113,
    119, 127, 134–5, 140, 142–4,
    148, 151–3, 157, 178–80, 182,
    186–7, 215, 219, 224, 226–8,
    234 n.6, 235 n.8, 236, 242, 246,
    248, 251
public   17, 30, 32–3, 50, 75, 99,
    116, 144, 200, 220, 223 n.1–2.
    See education; school

question(s)   8, 11–14, 17–18, 20,
    26 n.6, 28, 32–3, 37, 41, 43–5,
    58, 61, 65, 77, 80, 83–5, 87–8,
    106, 108–9, 111, 119, 122,
    139–40, 142, 145–7, 152–4,
    158, 175–83, 186, 206, 212–3,
    215, 218, 221, 226 n.3, 240,
    243, 247, 249, 253–4. *See also*
    pedagogy of the question
questioning   14, 32, 37, 84, 111, 115,
    139–40, 142–4, 148, 152–3,
    157, 180, 228, 232, 235 n.6,
    247, 251, 256. *See also* learning
    philosophical   152

race(s)/racial/racism   100, 106, 111,
    114, 213, 222, 234 n.5, 235 n.6
Rancière, J.   45, 51–2, 58–60
reading(s)   4, 8–11, 15, 18–19, 23,
    25 n.5, 26, 26 n.6, 38, 39 n.7,
    40 n.9, 41–2, 45, 52–3, 55 n.2,

58, 86–8, 97, 109 n.4, 116–17, 119–22, 127, 130, 144, 49, 189, 193, 212, 218–9, 226–7, 229, 231–2, 235 n.7, 238–9, 246 n.4, 247

rebellion   45, 73, 117, 249

Recife   38, 57, 62, 86–7, 90, 96, 104–5, 113, 116, 118–21, 123, 125, 127, 141, 144, 189–91, 193, 200

refusal   31, 44, 53, 74 n.6

repression   83–4, 191–2

resist/resistance   20, 83–4, 87, 106, 118, 150–1, 198, 223, 223 n.2, 224

Revoltados Online (RO)   5

revolution(s)   73, 83, 139–44, 148, 196, 246, 248

   childlike revolution   140–4

revolutionary   19, 27, 38, 56, 59, 62, 73 n.5, 101, 104, 138–41, 143, 149, 206, 229, 246, 248. *See also* education; life; power

Rio de Janeiro   75, 76 n.7, 175

Rocha, R.   227–32

Rodríguez, L.   4 n.3, 45

Rodríguez, Silvio   84

Rodríguez, Simón   50–1, 85, 102–3, 109 n.4, 255

Rousseff, D.   6, 220, 222

São Paulo   5, 24, 58, 106, 133, 148, 188, 201, 210 n.1, 211–2, 238 n.1, 238–40 n.2, 241, 247

   Universities of   5

school(s)   1, 5, 12, 17, 29–30, 41–2, 49–50, 53, 56, 75–6, 76 n.7, 77 n.9, 78–80, 84, 88, 90, 96, 99, 102, 116, 120–1, 127, 129, 131–2, 149, 151, 157–8, 177, 190–2, 195–7, 199, 201–4, 211, 213, 215, 217, 221–2, 223 n.1–2, 225, 227–8, 230, 232, 241, 243, 245, 255

   childhood of   149

   make   2, 7, 94

philosophical   29, 79

public   50–1, 56 n.3, 214, 221

schooling   42, 111, 121, 128–9, 132, 191, 194, 221, 230, 255

SESI. *See* Industrial Social Service

Shor, I.   10–11, 24, 60, 79, 110

Silveira, R. T.   242

Socrates   27–38, 41, 69–72, 77, 85, 96, 103, 152

solidarity   39, 73, 90, 126, 132, 184, 235 n.8, 239, 244

struggle   38, 44, 68 n.1, 81, 83–4, 87, 90, 98, 114, 140, 152, 183–4, 211

student(s)   4, 7, 17, 43, 46–53, 55, 57–8, 60–1, 63–4, 67–8, 76–7, 84, 90, 103, 105, 108, 111, 130, 148, 157–8, 178, 180, 186, 197–9, 202–3, 211, 215, 222, 222 n.1, 223 n.1–2, 224–5, 240–1, 241–5, 247, 249–51

study   9–10, 24, 35, 58 n.4, 61, 68, 68 n.2, 119, 151 n.1, 178, 196–7, 201–2, 204, 219, 227

suspension   50, 177

Switzerland   3–4, 57, 115, 120, 136, 194–7, 200–2

Tanzania   3, 97 n.3, 194

teacher(s)   12, 17, 35, 43, 46–7, 49–55, 57, 63–4, 67–8, 74–6, 76 n.7, 77, 88, 88 n.11, 90, 93–4, 98, 100, 102–3, 105–6, 108, 111, 118, 123, 127, 130–1, 138, 153, 158, 177, 182, 190, 192, 195–6, 198, 200, 203, 210–5, 219, 221–2, 222 n.1, 223 n.1–2, 224–6, 230–2, 238, 241–5, 247–50. *See* educator

   education / training   14, 210 n.1, 215, 241

   loving   75–6

   role of the   57, 61, 71, 106, 111, 178, 223 n.1, 224, 231, 235 n.6, 242, 247, 250

teaching(s)   5–7, 13, 15, 17, 36,
     46, 58, 71, 75–6, 78, 83, 88,
     108, 110 n.4, 130, 152,
     183–4, 202–3, 214–5, 218,
     221–2, 223 n.1, 224, 227,
     230, 232, 235 n.6, 237, 241,
     243–5, 247–50, 254–5. *See also*
     philosophical
  art of   89
  love of   67, 75–6
  universal   51–3, 55–6, 56 n.3
technology   17, 184, 208
thinking   17–18, 25, 34, 37, 48, 58,
     70, 84–5, 98, 101–2, 111,
     117–19, 129–35, 151, 151 n.1,
     154, 156, 158, 178–83, 188,
     212, 214, 218–9, 230, 233,
     236–44, 249–50. *See also*
     educational; philosophical
time   3, 12, 14, 21, 26–7, 34, 41, 55,
     62, 69, 71, 78–84, 87, 89, 91,
     94, 96, 98, 102, 105, 117, 119,
     121, 123–4, 128–30, 132–4,
     140–1, 145–7, 150–1, 154–6,
     158, 176–8, 180–1, 185, 189,
     191–3, 195, 217, 219, 232,
     236, 241, 254–5. *See also*
     child; childhood; childlike;
     education; educational;
     philosophical
  aion / aionic   78, 176–8, 181–3,
     186
  chronos / chronological   78–9,
     129, 138–40, 146, 149, 156,
     176–8, 180–1, 185–6, 255–6
  conceptions of   78–9, 147,
     155–6, 176–8, 185
  diffract   255
  of education   156–8, 176, 178
  experience of   10, 146, 153, 183,
     185, 255
  of feelings   78, 130
  giving   178

historical   116, 156
  inner   78
  institutional   78–9
  kairos   78, 129, 178
  lived/living   140, 146
  loving   78, 87, 89, 91
  play   180, 189, 193
  present   8, 88, 91, 140, 147, 156,
     158, 178
  stolen   178
  thinking/ philosophical   178
Torres, C. A.   68 n.1
Torres, R. M.   8
transformation   22–5, 34–5, 40, 58,
     60, 87, 99, 102, 106, 119, 121,
     140–1, 143, 145, 180, 186, 227,
     248
travel/ing   59, 95–104, 134, 157,
     181–22, 186, 189, 191, 197

unequal   44, 46–51, 55, 64, 106
United States (USA)   1, 3–4, 20,
     53, 57, 95, 98, 136, 156, 175,
     181, 192–5, 205, 235 n.6–7,
     240 n.2
utopia/n   10, 20, 40, 83, 93–4,
     106–8, 131, 171, 210

Vasconcellos, E.   88, 120
voice/s   10, 77, 79–80, 83, 89, 202,
     241, 245

wander/er/ring   94–7, 99, 100–4,
     106, 110, 112, 131, 180–1, 186
West, C.   3, 22
Workers' Party (PT)   5–6
World Council of Churches   3,
     39 n.8, 95, 192
writing   8, 10–11, 14–15, 31, 43, 58,
     62, 89, 100–1, 104–5, 110, 116,
     130, 136, 138, 144, 149, 155,
     157, 194, 199, 209, 211, 218–9,
     223 n.1, 238, 251